## COLLECTION MANAGEMENT

| 9/09 4 | -11/09 | |
|---|---|---|
| 5-12 | 10-1 | 11-22-11 |
| | | |
| | | |
| | | |
| | | |
| | | |

# Conifers for Gardens

# Conifers
## for Gardens

### AN ILLUSTRATED ENCYCLOPEDIA

RICHARD L. BITNER

TIMBER PRESS

Published in 2007 by
Timber Press, Inc.
The Haseltine Building
133 S.W. Second Avenue, Suite 450
Portland, Oregon 97204-3527, U.S.A.
www.timberpress.com

For contact information regarding editorial, marketing, sales, and distribution in the United Kingdom, see www.timberpress.co.uk.


Printed in China

Library of Congress Cataloging-in-Publication Data

Bitner, Richard L.
  Conifers for gardens : an illustrated encyclopedia / Richard L. Bitner.
      p. cm.
  Includes bibliographical references and index.
  ISBN-13: 978-0-88192-830-3
  1. Conifers—Varieties—Pictorial works.  2. Plants, Ornamental—Pictorial works.  I. Title.
  SB428.B55 2007
  635.9'35—dc22
                                                    2006024592

A catalog record for this book is also available from the British Library.

635.935

To Jean Byrne,
that indomitable lady who has given
so many gardeners the courage to write,
and to my good friend,
frequent traveling companion,
and vigilant note-taker,
Elliot L. Heffner.

# Contents

# Acknowledgments

I took all the images in this book with a hand-held manual Minolta camera body and a Tamron 28-105 2.8 lens using Fuji Velvia 50 and 100 ASA or Provia 100 ASA professional films. All indentification was likewise done by me; however, thanks are due to those folks who helped with the never-ending job of slide filing: Cheryl Young, Ryan Moraski, and Matt Gardner.

Thanks to Nick Hemmerich and Cheryl Hilfer for reading the manuscript in draft and making valuable suggestions. Rick Darke and Tomasz Aniśko offered much helpful advice, and thanks to Ray Edwards for his computer expertise.

One recognizes that people who nurture and love gardens are nice. But as one who has followed the sun through countless public gardens, nursery display gardens, and home landscapes with camera in hand, it bears repeating: plant people are great! If any of the pictures in this collection cause the reader to pause, or if the reader is motivated to want to grow a specific selection, it is a credit to those who have created these gardens and cared for these plants. The images were taken in many of the places listed in "Where To See Conifers," in the appendix. I am grateful to them all. Perhaps special mention is deserved by the staff of the Dawes Arboretum, Francie B. Hill of the amazing Bickelhaupt Arboretum, and Susan Martin from the United States National Arboretum. Special tribute is due to Frau Jeddeloh (who kept me supplied with cool water), Uwe Horstmann (who served me freshly picked strawberries), and the secretary at Hachmann Baumschule, all of whom tolerated my rudimentary German and gave me access to their wonderful display gardens. Similarly helpful were Gary and Kaye Gee of Gee Farms, Hugh Ferrar at Iseli Nursery, Don Howse of Porterhowse, and Talon Buchholz at his nursery. Thanks to Dave Thompson at Longwood, who early on offered me teaching responsibilities. One could not wish for a better soulmate than Marilyn Daly. And particular appreciation to that guy everyone admires, R. William Thomas.

# Introduction

## Rudiments of conifer botany

A brief glance into this book and one soon discovers that conifers cannot simply be described as evergreen trees with needles. "Conifer" comes from the Latin meaning "to bear cones." A conifer's seeds are held in its cones. If one shakes a typical cone as it matures and opens, seeds will fall out. Plants that produce seeds encompass most of the plants on earth and are placed into two divisions: angiosperms and gymnosperms. The angiosperms have so-called covered seeds. Think of an apple or a pumpkin, where the seeds are embedded in the fruit. This is the biggest group of plants. Gymnosperms have so-called naked seeds (the word is from the Greek: a gym was once a place to run around naked). Gymnosperms evolved before flowering plants. Conifers are gymnosperms. There are fewer than 1,000 species of gymnosperms—representing only 0.5 percent of known plant species.

The mature, fertilized cone is the conifer's female "fruit" (although technically conifers do not "flower" and therefore cannot bear "fruit"). In most species, cones are woody structures. Not all conifers produce cones that look like the classic pinecone, however. Sometimes the seed is simply enclosed in a fleshy coat. Separate male "flowers" grow in the shape of a tiny cone or a catkin and provide the pollen to fertilize the female cone. In this book these staminate cones (male) and pistillate cones (female) will be referred to (and often illustrated, because they are ornamental) as the pollen-bearing cones and seed-bearing cones, respectively. Pollination in conifers is always dependent on wind currents to blow the abundant yellow pollen from the pollen-bearing cones to the seed-bearing cones. Fertilization takes place, and the seeds mature. This can take a season or several years. The seeds are then released to drop or are dispersed by wind or by birds. Some seeds are held tightly in closed cones until prompted to open by a forest fire. Most species of conifers are monoecious: they produce both pollen- and seed-bearing cones on the same tree. But some,

Pollen-bearing cones of *Picea orientalis*

Clustered needle foliage and woody seed-bearing cone of *Pinus parviflora*

Scale-like foliage and fleshy cones of *Thuja orientalis*

such as junipers and yews, have them on different trees; these plants are dioecious. Some cones, such as those of the pines, carry numerous seeds, while the juniper "berry" cone, for instance, usually encloses only a single seed.

Not all conifers have needle-like leaves that are held singly or in bundles (examples are spruces and pines); many have tiny flat scale-like leaves that tightly surround the twig (as in arborvitaes). When conifer seeds germinate, they have juvenile or needle-like foliage. Sometimes this needle-like foliage is maintained throughout the life of the plant, but generally the adult or scale-like foliage develops. These leaves are exceedingly small, densely crowded, and overlapping (junipers are the best illustration of this). There are cultivars that retain their juvenile foliage, forms that have both juvenile and adult foliage, and those that have all adult foliage.

## Conifers in the landscape

Various species of conifers, especially those in the pine family (Pinaceae), are the dominant forest cover over much of the northern hemisphere. There are extensive forests of junipers and cedars in the Northwest. Many conifers have exceptionally wide natural ranges; *Juniperus communis*, for instance, is circumpolar. Others, such as the numerous conifers that occur only at specific elevations of California, have relatively restricted natural ranges; these are not adaptable as garden plants and are not discussed in this book. An exception would be *Picea pungens* (Colorado spruce), which is found only in mid- to high-elevation zones in five western states, yet is widely planted and adapted across Europe and North America.

Conifers include the oldest living plants in the world: certain specimens of bristlecone pine (*Pinus longaeva*), growing at 10,000 ft. (3,050 m) in the White Mountains of California, approach 4,500 years old. Conifers also claim the tallest tree, the coast redwood (*Sequoia sempervirens*), 400 ft. (122 m) tall, also in California.

## The naming of conifers

Latin is the universal language of plants. Common names can be useful but are often confusing, especially with conifers. A good example is the common term "cedar" which has been used for at least six different genera (*Calocedrus*, *Chamaecyparis*, *Cryptomeria*, *Juniperus*, *Taiwania*, and *Thuja*) besides the true cedars of the genus *Cedrus*.

The Latin name, consisting of two parts, places the conifer within a larger system of nomenclature. This binominal system was invented by Carolus Linnaeus (1707–1778) who cataloged in Latin all the plant and animal species known in his time. Translation of the Latin name often reveals characteristics of the plant. The first part of a plant's name is the genus: *Juniperus*, *Cedrus*, *Pinus*, etc. A genus is a group of plants with very similar characteristics. The second part of the name is the specific epithet, commonly called the species. A species is a group of genetically very similar plants that are distinct from other species in the genus. Some genera (the plural of genus) have dozens of different species; other genera contain only one species. The genus is capitalized and the species is not, both words are written in italics: *Pinus strobus*. There is often a third name. This could be a subspecies or variety—plants found under special circumstances in nature. However, the most common third part to the name is the designation of a cultivar, or cultivated variety. These plants are in some way different from the usual species, perhaps displaying blue foliage rather than green, or are slower growing, and are usually propagated by grafting or rooted cuttings in order to maintain this characteristic's ornamental interest. The cultivar name is in Roman type and is enclosed in single quotes: *Pinus strobus* 'Elf'. The cultivar name will thus often reveal a characteristic of the selection. Prior to 1959, cultivar names were designated in Latin: *Pinus strobus* 'Contorta'. Today the name must be in the language of the person who introduced or named the plant: *Abies koreana* 'Goldener Traum'. When two species interbreed naturally in the wild, a hybrid is produced. The offspring's name is written with an × between the genus and species to signify this: *Taxus ×media*.

There is no strictly right or wrong way to pronounce these Latin names, but every syllable must be spoken.

The earliest name is the one that has to be used. Occasionally a plant, or even a species, that has been published and sold under a familiar name for decades requires a name change because research has shown that it was recorded earlier with a different name. The experts who catalog plant names and characteristics and dictate these matters are called taxonomists. The Royal Horticultural Society (RHS) took responsibility as the international registration authority for conifers in 1964 and has since been accumulating and publishing information. Four parts of a proposed eight-part International Conifer Register (ICR) had been published as this book was being prepared. The ICR is an attempt to provide precise, stable, and internationally acceptable nomenclature. Other standards for conifer names include *The World Checklist of Conifers* by Humphrey Welch and Gordon Haddow from 1993, and the *RHS Plant Finder*, which is published annually. Some cultivar names will not be listed or considered legitimate with these authorities but will nevertheless be in widespread use. If I have observed plants so labeled in arboretums and collections and listed in several conifer specialty nursery catalogs, I have included them in this encyclopedia under the commonly accepted name.

Conifers are grown all over the world. Those who pursue unusual selections are naturally eager to introduce and sell them. Confusion, duplication, and discrepancies are bound to occur from time to time. My apologies for entry names that some factions might consider erroneous. The situation is likely to get even worse. DNA studies of plants are becoming a very important tool in resolving these issues and can lead to a total reordering of sections of botanical classifications.

## Why grow conifers?

Perhaps more than any other group of plants, conifers are selected without much thought and inappropriately placed in the home landscape. They are often considered merely utilitarian, low-maintenance shrubs to situate next to a building to hide its foundation. Or a single Colorado spruce is placed in the middle of the front yard and overshadows the house years later. However, garden conifers are available in a varied palette of forms, colors, and textures. With some care in selection, these evergreens can provide interest and color the whole year round, especially if dwarf and slow-growing cultivars are combined with deciduous shrubs and herbaceous plants.

Conifers are not particularly finicky. Some with variegated foliage appreciate a little shade; others need protection from drought or harsh winds. Most firs and spruces, certainly, do better in cooler climates and will sulk in areas with hot, humid summers. But most conifers are adaptable to a wide range of growing conditions. Conifers are generally not considered shade plants and will do best when given full sun exposure. Nonetheless, there are a few species suitable for the gardener wishing to place conifers in a shady spot. Like most plants, conifers do best in moist, well-drained, neutral to slightly acid pH conditions, but they are usually able to survive whatever circumstances the gardener provides. Newly planted specimens need to be watered, but once established, conifers tend to be rather drought-tolerant, an important consideration in this era of global warming. Depending on their branch structure, some conifers will suffer damage from heavy, wet snow. Most dislike poor drainage, but the bald-cypress, *Taxodium distichum*, will tolerate standing water part of the growing season. Cold hardiness zones are listed for each species, but hot, humid summers might affect a plant's survival more than low winter temperatures.

Unlike a deciduous tree, conifers (or at least most of them) do not have to grow a whole new set of leaves every spring; therefore their demands for nourishment are correspondingly less. There is seldom a need to fertilize. They lead rather frugal lives.

Attention to the details of the descriptions of the many conifers in this volume will show that there are possibilities for sun and shade, wet and dry situations, and even for alkaline soils. There is likely to be a suitable conifer for any design specification.

Growth rates and ultimate size are listed for most of the plants. I would have preferred to give precise dimensions and growth rates for every selection in the encyclopedia; however, many cultivars will be planted in markedly different conditions from the area that studied and introduced them. Sometimes a plant has been observed for only a few years before being made available for sale, and the ultimate size is not yet known. Descriptions based on nursery-grown plants are subject to error. Sometimes a gardener buys a mislabeled container. Occasionally slower growing cultivars will revert, that is, out of the desired, compact, congested foliage will appear a branch that is faster growing. These branches must be pruned off, or they will dominate the plant.

Conifers are best moved or planted when relatively

small. It is wise to plant conifers in late spring or in early fall. Select plants that display the proper shape and healthy foliage. Remember that most conifers will not regrow lost branches, especially at the base.

The same principles should be followed with conifers as with any plant a gardener wants to grow. First, assess the various aspects of the climate, site, and soil. Then choose a species that suits the site and intended purpose. Finally, grow the plant well, attending to its needs.

## Using conifers in the garden

Conifers come in all shapes and sizes. The classic shape of conifers is pyramidal, making them ideal as focal points in large formal gardens. Many are fine hedging plants, providing shelter, windbreaks, and sound barriers. Some would say they are overused as groundcovers. Conifers can be grown in containers and are widely grown as bonsai. They are a requisite in Asian-style gardens and indispensable for creating topiaries. There are limitless choices of slow-growing conifers of all shapes for suburban landscaping, urban vestpocket gardens, and grave plantings. Some will grow only several feet in 100 years, others 4 ft. (1.2 m) a growing season. Careful consideration must be given to the ultimate height and spread when placing them; unlike perennials, the gardener does not have the luxury of moving them here and there with each new growing year. These are not plants that are forgiving of crowding. They want space to make their statement. Branches will die when subjected to shade. However, most genera have slow-growing cultivars that will keep their scale over many years in a mixed border, where they provide structure throughout changing seasonal displays.

Conifers can exhibit many different shapes and are discussed with appropriate descriptive terms.

**columnar:** tall and narrow
**fastigiate:** ascending branches
**globose:** rounded
**pendulous:** with weeping branches
**prostrate:** growing close to and spreading over the ground
**pyramidal:** conical, broad at base, narrowing and tapering to the top

Conifers are also desirable to plant because of their varied foliage colors and textures. Colors range from different hues of green, gray, or blue to exotic golds and silvers. There

Conifers provide year-round interest when integrated into the border

Conifers in a trough garden

are even variegated forms. A few change color seasonally. Deciduous conifers add to the parade of fall colors. Textures vary, from needles that can act as effective barriers to soft flat fronds that invite touching. Several conifers could be grown for their beautiful bark, notably *Pinus resinosa* (red pine) and *P. bungeana* (lacebark pine). In climates that support them, conifers associate beautifully with heaths and heathers. The very slow-growing selections are indispensable in trough gardens and rock gardens.

These plants are more than ornamentals. Not to be over-

Conifers in a mixed border

Conifers provide year-round screening

Conifers in an Asian-style garden

Conifer topiary

Conifers used in large-scale plantings

Deciduous conifers add to the fall color display

looked is the considerable value of conifers for wildlife. They not only provide protection and shelter for birds, but many supply cones with edible seeds for birds and mammals. Many conifers are capable of producing both wood and non-wood products that have been of great benefit to society, and they provide flavorings and medicinal products. There have been traditional uses of every part of the tree—foliage, bark, roots, resin, seeds, cones. Pine bark mulch is now widely used to satisfy the mulching frenzy of suburbanites.

Conifers have been revered and utilized by many cultures, notably the First Nations peoples of the Northwest. Many conifers have a rich mythology and folklore. They appeared on colonial flags and are depicted in the visual arts (the cypress paintings of Van Gogh) and music (*The Pines of Rome* by Respighi).

## Origin of conifer cultivars

The countless available conifer cultivars, mostly dwarf or slow-growing, originate from several sources. Some are collected in the wild and propagated by seed or by rooting cuttings from the plant. Similarly, many are discovered among the rows of thousands of seed-grown container plants in nursery production. Occasionally distinct changes in color or growth rate occur on normal branches of an established tree. These sports can be propagated and nursery stock obtained. Perhaps the most celebrated way to find new types is by searching for witches' brooms. These are congested bundles of usually small-needled growths that are attached to normal branches, particularly those of pines and spruces. There are various explanations of why they occur, including bud mutations, parasites, viruses, fungi, insects, or other pathology. These are collected and propagated and will usually remain dwarf. Sometimes these brooms will produce cones and viable seed which, in turn, can result in other dwarf selections. Since the number of years (or decades) these plants are grown and evaluated before being made available for the home gardener will vary greatly, it is easy to understand that there will all too often be similarity of forms, confusion of names, and duplication.

## Pests and diseases of conifers

Good cultural practice is the most effective way to avoid problems with pests and diseases in conifers. Conifers growing under appropriate conditions can deal with peri-

A witches' broom on a pine

ods of excessive heat, cold, drought, storm damage, and minor infestations of pests and diseases. However, stressed plants cannot. Stress is caused by poor soil, poor drainage, air pollution, salt, damage to roots, damage to bark (usually from mowers or string trimmers), soil compaction, improper pruning, storm damage, and pesticides. With conifers, excessive moisture—rather than moisture deficiency—is a common circumstance that leads to disease problems.

Select conifers that are suitable to your site and practice proper planting methods. It is especially important that these trees not be planted any deeper than they were growing originally. It is essential to provide a regular supply of water during the first year while the plant is getting established. Most conifers grow best in slightly acid soil, a pH of 5 to 6. Disease problems are more likely at higher levels. Unnecessary supplemental fertilization should be avoided. Ironically, vigorous, fast-growing trees are more susceptible to fungus infestations, the most common of coniferous diseases. Most diseases are caused when fungi and other organisms enter the unprotected wood and the process begins.

Wounds caused by mowers repeatedly hitting a tree trunk take a long time to heal.

Inspect conifers regularly to detect pest and disease problems early, when straightforward procedures can avoid an escalation of the situation. Often disease-resistant varieties are available.

## Animal damage

Deer and other hoofed browsers can be the most troublesome pests in gardens and arboretums, particularly in eastern North America. Browsing occurs throughout the year, but especially during the cold seasons, when deciduous plants are bare. Deer are chiefly attracted to *Taxus* and *Thuja*, but one can never consider a "deer-resistant" plant list trustworthy. Fencing at least 8 ft. (2.5 m) high is the only reliable way to exclude these expert jumpers. One can cage prized plants. Many deer repellents are marketed; success with these products is apparently related to a willingness to reapply them regularly and after heavy rain.

Small rodents like mice, voles, squirrels, and rabbits damage conifers by chewing on trunks and roots under the snow and eating bark, twigs, and buds. Again, fencing and chemical repellents are useful. Many public gardens maintain cats in the garden to control these pests. Watchful dogs, perhaps especially beagles, are very good for keeping all intruders out of the garden, provided they are given proper housing and are in the garden at night.

## Insect pests

Most insects found in the garden are not pests at all, but are beneficial. Even those that are considered harmful will not be damaging unless they are present in large numbers. It is best not to reach for a pesticide immediately upon spotting a potentially damaging insect since this can lead to other problems. Most pesticides will be harmful to beneficial insects as well as to livestock, fish, and humans. Often physical methods of control or changing cultural practices will take care of the situation. Vigilant monitoring for the extent of a pest population before resorting to chemicals is sensible.

When chemicals are used to control damaging insects they should be the appropriate ones for the pest identified, applied at the correct time in the pest's life cycle, and in a proper dose. Pesticides are poisons. They are regulated by the federal government and by states. Before using a pesticide, check with local authorities, county agents, a University Cooperative Extension Service, or an Agricultural Experiment Station to determine current use regulations. Do not apply on windy days or when honeybees are pollinating plants. Wear protective equipment while you are spraying and wash exposed skin thoroughly when finished. These toxins should be stored in their original containers, out of reach of children, pets, and livestock, and away from food and feed. Dispose of empty containers in a safe manner.

## Seasonal needle drop

Home gardeners often become concerned when they observe needles on their "evergreen" turning brown and dropping off. The needles of conifers have varying life spans and will drop after one to several years. *Pinus strobus* (eastern white pine), for instance, will drop its two- to three-year-old needles in the autumn, and this will be quite obvious on a mature plant. The shedding of needles is less noticeable in other popular genera like spruces (*Picea*). One need only confirm that the needle loss is from old growth. Needle loss from the tips of branches would be a reason for concern.

## Pathogens

The most common disease-causing organisms in conifers are fungi. Other diseases are caused by bacteria or viruses. Fungi will often cause a conifer to shed needles. Yellow spots will appear on the needles, which eventually turn brown and are shed. Sometimes tiny black fruiting bodies of the fungus are noticed. Numerous blights can occur, including *Diplodia* and brown spot. The twig tips and needles are afflicted and eventually large areas of foliage turn brown, especially on the lower branches, and are shed. Dozens of fungi can infect an injured area of bark, causing a blistered area, or canker. These diseased areas are very noticeable and often have resin oozing from them. *Cronartium* (fusiform rust), *Phomopsis*, and *Cytospora* are some of the most troublesome pathogens of conifers. Canker diseases will weaken and kill branches as the fungal pathogen invades the sapwood. Canker diseases are difficult to manage. A fungicide spray program by a certified administrator might be necessary to control repeated cycles of infection. The best way to prevent these diseases is to grow your conifer under proper cultural conditions, provide good air circulation, and avoid bark wounds, drought, and environmental stresses.

## Conclusion

In recent decades many new conifer cultivars have been introduced, mostly for collectors. Some, however, have become common, even classic, garden plants: *Pinus cembra* 'Chalet', *P. strobus* 'Blue Shag' and *P. s.* 'Sea Urchin', *Sequoiadendron giganteum* 'Hazel Smith'. Unfortunately many recent introductions have not been evaluated for ultimate size, habit, and durability. It is impossible to list and illustrate every one. Occasionally, because of cultural conditions, the photograph will not match the description of the plant. Additionally, some of the photographs do not represent the cultivar at maturity or during the season of greatest interest (for instance, those with brighter foliage during a limited time of year). There is no doubt that even as this book goes to press commercial growers will be introducing "newer" and supposedly "better" cultivars. But there should always be a place for the old standbys, and my hope is that this guidebook will help the readers—whether beginning or avid gardeners, landscape designers, nursery tradespersons, or horticulture students—make better choices.

# Encyclopedia of
# Garden Conifers

### *Abies* fir

The firs are a genus of about 50 species; the nomenclature for some species is confused, and the number varies from author to author. Firs originate in the cooler zones of the northern hemisphere, particularly in eastern Asia and North America, with a few species in Europe and northern Africa. They prefer cool mountains with sufficient moisture (40 to 50 in. [100 to 125 cm] in their native ranges) and good drainage. Nine species are native to the United States. They inhabit many of the same places as the spruces, *Picea*, and are also conical or columnar in habit. They have splendid form: spear-like tips above regular layers of whorled branches and straight trunks from base to tip. They make impressive trees and can be used in groupings in public landscapes, near large buildings, or as screens. Firs shed huge weights of snow quickly and easily. Unfortunately, with advancing age they tend to lose their lower branches and become less attractive. Although most species are of forest size and too large for the home garden, there are numerous dwarf selections that are prostrate, compact, or pendulous.

The trunks of firs are smooth, gray, and dotted with resin blisters. These blisters sometime ooze a stream of sticky, aromatic resin. The leaves are evergreen, needle-like, and generally flat in cross section. The needles are arranged spirally. They are usually blunt-tipped. Many are green and grooved on one side and have numerous rows of white stomata below. When you pull a needle off, no piece of epidermis pulls off, and a round crater-like scar is left on the stem. The stems will be smooth. These ID features are in contrast to the spruces, *Picea*, where a sliver of epidermis comes off with the needle and the stems are warty. Fir needles usually have a citrusy odor when bruised.

Habit of typical fir

Firs are monoecious. The seed-bearing cones of firs are barrel-shaped and stand upright on the branches, usually high in the upper crown of the tree. As they mature over one year, they glisten with exuded drops of resin. They disintegrate on the tree, and only the scales are found on the ground, with the spike of the central cone axis persisting on the branch. The pollen-bearing cones occur on the same tree and are found on the underside of the lower crown branches.

Firs generally have few pests and diseases but do require care in their selection and cultivation. They have shallow roots and do not tolerate urban pollution. *Abies* species and cultivars require full sun and some prefer cool summers. They will be difficult to establish in areas that experience high humidity and hot summer nights. It has been suggested that a limiting factor is the lack in suburban soil of specific mycorrhizae that are endemic to their native mountain-

*Abies* bark

*Abies* seed-bearing cones disintegrate on the tree

The needles and smooth stem of a typical fir

Only the cone scales of *Abies* will be found under the tree

*Abies* seed-bearing cone

tops. In addition, soils that are high in organic matter might not be ideal for firs that normally grow in gravelly soil. Their preference for cool climates limits their use in the southern regions of the United States. Although many species are too large for small gardens, numerous dwarf forms are to be found, and they will flourish in a cooler garden site with excellent drainage.

The wildlife importance of firs is only moderate. The evergreen foliage of young trees is useful to mammals and game birds for cover, especially in winter. Firs are used for nesting by many bird species, notably robins and mourning doves, whose first nest of the season is normally built before hardwood trees produce leaves. The fir seed is readily eaten by chickadees, purple finches, and cross-bills. The seeds are also sought by squirrels and chipmunks. Grouses make fir needles a major part of their diet. Hoofed browsers, particularly northern deer and moose, resort to fir foliage as a large part of their winter menu.

The firs are not commercially important in the timber industry. Many are grown as holiday trees. They are ideal because of their natural shape, fragrant needles in shades of green or blue-green, good needle retention, and nice branching arrangement for holding ornaments.

This genus is sometimes difficult to identify from the foliage alone, and the cones often disintegrate quickly and are seldom available. Note that the so-called China-fir (*Cunninghamia lanceolata*) and Douglas-fir (*Pseudotsuga menziesii*) are not true firs.

### *Abies alba*  European silver fir
Zones 4 to 7

*Abies alba* (syns. *A. pectinata*, *A. nobilis*) is a native of central Europe, from the Pyrenees to the Carpathians and the Balkan Peninsula. Although a large tree, reaching 150 ft. (46 m) in its native sites, it is likely to be half that size in cultivation, where it prefers moist soil. It is slow-growing and conical when young but be-comes irregular and round-topped with maturity. The branches are horizontal and sweep upward at the tips. This species of fir is notable for tolerating some shade. The two-ranked needles are flat, ½ to 1¼ in. (1.2 to 3 cm) long, notched at the apex, shiny dark green above with two silvery-white bands beneath. The cones are 4 to 6 in. (10 to 15 cm) long, green turning to brown with exserted and reflexed bracts. They are found only high on the tree. The bark is smooth and gray when young and becomes scaly on old trees.

'Barabits' Star': globose, dwarf, and spreading, grows 2 to 4 in. (5 to 10 cm) a year, also listed as 'Barabits' Spreader'.

'Compacta': a densely branched dwarf globose form, wider than tall, glossy dark green needles are silver beneath, grows 2 to 4 in. (5 to 10 cm) a year.

'Green Spiral': a narrow, pendulous

*Abies alba* 'Barabits' Star'

*Abies alba*

*Abies alba* 'Green Spiral'

tree with side branches that spiral outward and down with dark green glossy needles, growing 6 to 12 in. (15 to 30 cm) a year.

'Pendula': a strongly weeping, graceful form, rich green color, soft texture, needs staking during early growth.

'Pyramidalis': a formal, tight, narrow column with lustrous dark green needles.

'Virgata': long slender branches that grow downward.

*Abies alba* 'Pendula'

*Abies alba* 'Pyramidalis'

## *Abies amabilis*   Pacific silver fir
Zone 6

The Pacific silver fir is found in Alaska and south to Oregon. This species usually grows at elevations between 2,000 and 5,000 ft. (609 and 1,524 m), where there is 60 in. (150 cm) of annual rainfall. It ascends slim and straight to a height of 200 ft. (60 m). It can live 500 years. In cultivation it will reach 60 ft. (18 m) and is more shade-tolerant than most firs. The needles are 1¼ in. (3 cm) long, flat and bluntly pointed or notched and grooved. They are a beautiful dark shiny green above (*amabilis* means "lovely") with two silvery bands of stomata beneath, which give the tree its common name. The needles grow in four irregular ranks, the lower pair appearing brushed upward from below, the upper pair brushed forward along the twig. Like many firs, the foliage at the cone-bearing top of the tree is stout and very sharp. The crushed leaves have a tangerine scent. The cones, which do not appear regularly, are 3½ to 6 in. (9 to 15 cm) long and a dark velvety purple. The bark, an ash-gray with white blotches, is thin, and since the Pacific silver fir has shallow roots, it is usually killed by forest fires. Despite the great size of the tree, the wood is soft and weak and useful only for pulp. This species has been grown in the highlands of Wales and Scotland but is unlikely to do well in the usual home landscape.

'Spreading Star': an attractive, silver-gray prostrate form, reaches 3 ft. (0.9 m) over many years.

*Abies amabilis* 'Spreading Star'

### *Abies balsamea*    balsam fir
#### Zones 3 to 6

The balsam fir is native to eastern North America. It is found from Labrador to Alberta, south to Pennsylvania, west to Minnesota and Iowa and south in the Appalachian Mountains as far as Virginia. It can reach 50 to 65 ft. (15 to 20 m) in height with a dense pyramidal crown and can live over 100 years. It grows best in full sun on well-drained, acid, moist soil. In cultivation it is adaptable to cold areas and grows best there. It is not tolerant of pollution and often looks unkempt. The flat needles, ¾ in. (2 cm) long, are arranged spirally but on young trees appear two-ranked and horizontally spreading. They leave circular scars on the branches when they are shed after several years. On mature specimens the needles tend to curve upward and more or less cover the upper sides of the branches. The soft, flexible needles are notched at the end, dark green above with two prominent whitish lines on their lower surfaces. They persist on the tree seven to ten years. The yellow-red pollen-bearing cones are in clusters below the crown of the tree. The 2 to 3 in. (5 to 7.5 cm) long seed-bearing cones appear in the spring at the top of the tree's crown but are hardly ever obvious. They ooze a sticky white resin. The upright cones mature the first year, but the scales drop during early fall and leave only the persistent spike of the cone axis. Another useful identification feature is the resin blisters on the bark. The bark is gray-brown, smooth, and covered with raised blisters containing a sticky, fragrant, liquid resin. These resin blisters produce a transparent fixative that has long been used for mounting and preserving specimens for the microscope. The balsam medium, the cover glass, and the microscope lenses turn into one optical system with the same refractive index.

The wood of balsam firs is light and soft and not particularly strong or durable but is worthwhile for use in making boxes and for paper pulp. This fir is often farmed as a holiday tree because it retains its fine-looking fragrant needles long after the tree is cut. The aromatic needles are often stuffed into small pillows and sold as souvenirs to visitors. Although it is handsome as a young tree with its long lower branches and peaked top, as it matures it is not the most desirable conifer because it is short-lived and typically loses its lower branches. It is vulnerable to forest fires. This species will do best in cooler climates with abundant soil moisture.

The ruffed grouse, among other species, eats the seeds of the balsam fir. Rabbits, deer and moose will browse on the branch tips. The dense foliage provides nesting sites for many bird species and the balsam resin is used by nuthatches to cement their nests of shredded bark and grasses. Through the years the resin of this and other firs has been claimed to have wide-ranging medical benefits for humans. *Abies balsamea* is often used for rootstock for grafting. It is the provincial tree of New Brunswick.

'Nana': a rounded compact dwarf form that is ideal for rock gardens, dark green needles radiate on the stems, prefers some shade and adequate moisture, grows 2 to 3 in. (5 to 7.5 cm) a year.

*Abies balsamea* 'Nana'

*Abies cephalonica*

### *Abies cephalonica*   Greek fir
Zones 5 to 7

The broadly pyramidal Greek fir is large, reaching 50 to 100 ft. (15 to 30 m) in its native habitat in northern and eastern Greece and Turkey. It will grow in part shade to full sun with adequate moisture. The shiny green needles are rigid and sharp-pointed, ⅝ to 1 in. (1.5 to 2.5 cm), white beneath, and distributed around the stem. The cones are 5 to 6½ in. (12 to 16 cm) with reflexed bracts.

'Meyer's Dwarf': a dwarf, round, flat plant that does not form a leader, short dark green needles are held radially, very slow-growing, a natural bonsai, also known as 'Nana'.

*Abies cephalonica* foliage

*Abies cephalonica* 'Meyer's Dwarf'

### *Abies concolor*   concolor fir
#### Zones 4 to 7

The concolor fir is native from Oregon to Colorado, Utah, Arizona, New Mexico, and California. It is a dense, pyramidal tree with a rather rigid, stiff appearance. It reaches 50 ft. (15 m) tall by 20 ft. (6 m) wide, growing 8 to 12 in. (20 to 30 cm) a year. The needles are 2 to 3 in. (5 to 7.5 cm) long. They are soft, flat, and waxy, bluish on both sides, and curve upward. They are sharp at the tip and two-ranked along the stem and have a citrus fragrance when crushed. The stem is smooth with disc-like leaf scars after the needles drop. The olive-colored cones are cylindrical, 3 to 4 in. (7.5 to 10 cm) long, and held erect on the branch. They disintegrate when mature and are rarely seen. The bark is gray and on aged specimens becomes thick and horny with deep furrows and ridges.

This is one of the most adaptable of the firs. It is somewhat drought- and salt-tolerant. It also withstands heat and air pollution better than most firs. It should do well on any well-drained soil in full sun. It should not be planted in heavy clay. This is an excellent choice for the designed landscape where a blue pyramidal tree is desired. It will remain far more attractive over its longer life span than a Colorado spruce and is softer to the touch. The wood is soft and very

*Abies concolor*

*Abies concolor* foliage

*Abies concolor* bark

*Abies concolor* 'Blue Cloak'

Abies concolor 'Candicans'

Abies concolor 'Compacta'

Abies concolor 'Conica'

Abies concolor 'Fagerhult'

light, useful only for making boxes and pulpwood.

'Blue Cloak': a weeping form selected for its blue foliage, grows to 30 × 15 ft. (9 × 4.5 m) tall and wide in 30 years and retains its lower branches.

'Candicans': one of the bluest forms, fast-growing, upright and conical, reaching 40 ft. (12 m).

'Compacta': irregularly rounded and slow-growing, reaching 2 ft. (0.6 m) after many years, nice for the rock or small garden.

'Conica': a compact, conical dwarf with steel-blue 1 in. (2.5 cm) needles, its leader grows 6 in. (15 cm) a year.

'Fagerhult': a very blue, slow-growing, ground-hugging form that can be trained upright.

*Abies concolor* 'Gable's Weeping'

*Abies concolor* 'Glauca Compacta'

### *Abies concolor* (continued)

'Gable's Weeping': a slow-growing dwarf that will be prostrate unless staked, displays short, thin needles on exposed stem structure, eventually reaches 30 × 15 ft. (9 × 4.5 m).

'Glauca Compacta': similar to 'Compacta'.

'Masonic Broom': a flat-topped bush form with blue needles.

'Pyramidalis': narrow and upright, remaining under 30 ft. (9 m) tall.

'Sidekick': compact, growing only 1 in. (2.5 cm) a year.

'Wattezii': prostrate and spreading with pale gray-blue needles, sometimes grafted as 'Wattezii Prostrata'.

'Wintergold': green needles that turn gold in winter, grows 6 in. (15 cm) a year.

*Abies concolor* 'Masonic Broom'

*Abies concolor* 'Wattezii'

*Abies concolor* 'Sidekick'

## *Abies firma*   momi fir
### Zones 6 to 9

The momi fir is a large, conical tree that grows 40 to 60 ft. (12 to 18 m) in cultivation and up to 150 ft. (46 m) in its native habitat in Japan. With age it can become quite broad. The leaves are strongly two-ranked, about 1½ in. (3.5 cm) long. They are yellow-green above and gray-green below. The lower surface has white bands. The cones are 4½ in. (11 cm) long. The bark is dark gray, rough, and scaly. *Abies firma* does best in moist, well-drained soils in full sun. It is more adaptable to hot environments than one expects of a fir and is said to be the easiest to grow in the south of the United States, provided it has plenty of moisture. One would grow this fir only as a large landscape specimen.

*Abies firma*

*Abies firma* foliage

### *Abies fraseri*  Fraser fir
Zones 4 to 7

This is the southern counterpart of the balsam fir. It is found in the Appalachians from Virginia to North Carolina, Tennessee, and Georgia. It was named after John Fraser (1750–1811), a Scot botanist who explored that area in the 18th century. To see it at its best, one needs to look at it in its native habitat since it does not always do well in cultivation. It grows slowly to 40 ft. (12 m), occasionally to 70 ft. (21 m) in the wild. It is pyramidal with straight, rigid branches. It prefers to grow in a sunny area that is moist and well drained. The needles are ½ to 1 in. (1.2 to 2.5 cm) long and look as if they've been brushed upward on the stems. They are dark green above and whitish beneath. The gray trunk is covered with resin-filled blisters. On the cones the papery bracts project beyond the woody cone scales and bend downward at their tips; this distinguishes this species from *Abies balsamea*. The cones are small, 2 to 2½ in. (5 to 6 cm) long. The wood of the Fraser fir is very light and soft. The needles are not as fragrant as the balsam fir; nevertheless, it is often grown as a holiday tree.

'Julian Potts': a true miniature, growing less than 1 in. (2.5 cm) a year, it likes a cool site.

'Klein's Nest': low and spreading with short, rich green needles, also listed as 'Kline's Nest'.

'Prostrata': a vigorous, dense, low-growing, flat form reaching 2 × 5 ft. (0.6 × 1.5 m) high and round, growing 6 to 12 in. (15 to 30 cm) a year.

*Abies fraseri* 'Julian Potts'

*Abies fraseri* 'Klein's Nest'

*Abies fraseri* 'Prostrata'

## *Abies grandis*  grand fir   Zone 6

This fir is found from British Columbia into Montana and Idaho and south through Oregon into California. It generally grows in valleys below 3,000 ft. (900 m). Aptly named, it can rise 150 to 200 ft. (46 to 60 m); some have been measured up to 300 ft. (90 m), making it one of the tallest firs. In its native stands, this species can grow as much as 3 ft. (0.9 m) a year. Its form is distinctive. The crown displays dense flat branches that sweep down and then level out toward the tips. The top is a narrow dome. Older trees are often symmetrical to the ground. The roots extend deep and wide, anchoring the trees against wind. This species does not live more than 250 years.

The blunt-tipped, flat, glossy green needles, 1½ to 2 in. (3.5 to 5 cm) long, are grooved above with two white lines beneath and spread in distinctly even rows on opposite sides of the stem. The sparsely produced cones are 2 to 4½ in. (5 to 11 cm) long, a purplish green color, and found only at the top of the tree. The bark of young plants is thin and smooth and ashy brown with white streaks. Older plants become furrowed with pale brown ridges. There are the usual fir resin blisters under the bark, which will release their aroma when cut. It should be sited in moist, well-drained, acid soil with protection from harsh winds.

The wood is suitable only for pulping. The First Nations peoples wove its branches into headdresses and costumes and used the bark to make canoes. The boughs were burned as purifying incense.

'Van Dedem's Dwarf': a rounded dwarf, growing 1 in. (2.5 cm) a year, displaying rich dark green needles with a silver reverse.

*Abies grandis* 'Van Dedem's Dwarf'

### *Abies homolepsis*  Nikko fir
Zones 4 to 7

The Nikko fir is native to Japan. It has a formal habit, pyramidal with crowded branches to the base. Although it reaches 125 ft. (38 m) in the wild, in the garden it will peak at 50 ft. (15 m). The glossy dark green needles are ⅓ to 1⅛ in. (0.8 to 2.8 cm) long with two white bands underneath. The cones are 4 to 6 in. (10 to 15 cm) long and are purple when young. This species has proved tolerant of pollution.

'Prostrata': a low-spreading dwarf that will eventually reach 6 ft. (1.8 m) tall with wide, glossy dark green foliage.

*Abies homolepsis*

*Abies homolepsis* foliage

*Abies homolepsis* 'Prostrata'

## *Abies koreana*   Korean fir   Zones 5 to 8

This garden-worthy fir is native to the mountains of southern Korea. It grows slowly to 15 to 35 ft. (4.5 to 10.5 m) in a pyramidal form with horizontal branches. The needles are ½ to ¾ in. (1.2 to 2 cm) long with a rounded or notched apex, dark green above with two distinct white bands on the underside. This elegant species is admired for the silvery underside of the foliage of many cultivars and its 1½ to 3 in. (3.5 to 7.5 cm) long, cylindrical, round-ended cones, which range in color from dark purple to blue and often appear even on trees under 3 ft. (0.9 m), a very appealing quality. The bark is dark tan-brown and slightly resinous. Grow the Korean fir in full sun in a cool, moist location. It will tolerate wind but does not like wet feet or compacted soil. It is more heat-tolerant than most firs and is an excellent accent choice for the home landscape.

'Aurea': nest form or can be staked more upright, displays lemon-yellow color on the top of the needles in part shade, grows only 2 in.(5 cm) a year.

*Abies koreana*

*Abies koreana* foliage

*Abies koreana* seed-bearing cones

*Abies koreana* 'Aurea'

*Abies koreana* 'Aurea' foliage

## *Abies koreana* (continued)

'Blauer Eskimo': a low-spreading dwarf with gray-blue needles, grows 1 in. (2.5 cm) a year.

'Blaue Zwo': slow-growing and upright with gray-blue needles and numerous small showy cones, growing 1 to 2 in. (2.5 to 5 cm) a year.

'Blue Cones': grows slowly to 30 ft. (9 m) in a dense cone shape, produces purple-blue cones at an early age.

'Blue Standard': slow-growing, produces numerous deep violet cones.

'Bonsai Blue': dwarf with rich blue foliage.

'Cis': miniature and bushy with rich dark green needles, growing 1 in. (2.5 cm) a year.

*Abies koreana* 'Blauer Eskimo'

*Abies koreana* 'Blaue Zwo'

*Abies koreana* 'Blue Cones'

*Abies koreana* 'Bonsai Blue'

*Abies koreana* 'Cis'

*Abies koreana* 'Compact Dwarf'

'Compact Dwarf': slowly spreads horizontally without a leader, unlikely to produce cones.

'Doni-Tajuso': dark green foliage on a flat round plant, grows 1 in. (2.5 cm) a year, similar to 'Silberkugel'.

'Goldener Traum' ('Golden Dream'): dwarf and low-spreading with golden foliage in winter.

'Horstmann': dwarf and cone-shaped, growing 4 in. (10 cm) a year.

'Nanaimo': compact form with outstanding purple cones in youth.

*Abies koreana* 'Doni-Tajuso'

*Abies koreana* 'Goldener Traum'

*Abies koreana* 'Horstmann'

*Abies koreana* 'Nanaimo'

### *Abies koreana* (continued)

'Oberon': a globose dwarf with short dark green needles and prominent white winter buds.

'Prostrate Beauty': spreads irregularly, grows slowly with no central leader, produces colorful cones early.

'Silberkugel': dwarf and rounded displaying bright green needles with silver undersides, good for troughs and rock gardens.

'Silberlocke': the tightly curved-in foliage exposes silvery undersides, becomes more dense with age and displays beautiful purple cones in spring. Choice.

*Abies koreana* 'Silberlocke'

*Abies koreana* 'Oberon'

*Abies koreana* 'Prostrate Beauty'

*Abies koreana* 'Silberkugel'

*Abies koreana* 'Silberlocke' foliage

*Abies koreana* 'Silberperl'

*Abies koreana* 'Starker's Dwarf'

*Abies koreana* 'Verdener Dom'

*Abies koreana* 'Tundra'

'Silberperl': a congested dwarf growing 1 to 2 in. (2.5 to 5 cm) a year, much wider than tall, short needles with silver undersides and buds that look like silver pearls in fall and winter, 'Silberzwerg' is possibly the same plant. Choice.

'Starker's Dwarf': dense and ground-hugging, eventually becoming conical, cones early, dark glossy green foliage.

'Tundra': dwarf and low-spreading.

'Verdener Dom': narrowly conical.

### *Abies lasiocarpa*  alpine fir
Zones 5 and 6(7)

The alpine fir is found from Alaska south to British Columbia and Alberta and south through the Rocky Mountains of Idaho, Montana, Wyoming, Colorado, Utah, and Nevada into Arizona and New Mexico. It is the most widespread fir in western North America. This slow-growing fir has a very distinct habit: very slender, erect, and rigid, like a pencil. All but the lowermost branches are extremely short. This is the tree so beloved by photographers to frame their views of snow-capped mountains. In those mountain meadows, it will reach 50 to 75 ft. (15 to 23 m); at high elevations, however, it can be hardly taller than a person (note the term "alpine" in a strict botanical or ecological sense applies to the tundra zone above the timberline). The stiff needles are 1 to 1¾ in. (2.5 to 4.5 cm) long, deep blue-green with a notched tip. The new growth has a silvery sheen with fine white bands on all sides. The foliage grows out from all sides of the twig and looks brushed upward on the twig. The cones are violet-purple, densely clustered, and 2¼ to 4 in. (5.5 to 10 cm) long. The bark is smooth, thin, and pale gray with resin blisters, sometimes with a reddish inner bark showing through fissures. It does not survive forest fires. The wood is light, soft, and knotty and useful only for wood pulp.

var. *arizonica*: the popular corkbark fir, found in the mountains of southern Colorado, into New Mexico and Arizona, grows to 75 ft. (23 m) with a thick trunk and corky creamy white branches, silvery gray needles are 1 to 1½ in. (2.5 to 3.5 cm) long, small cones.

*Abies lasiocarpa*

*Abies lasiocarpa* var. *arizonica*

var. *arizonica* 'Compacta': Rocky Mountain fir, slow-growing and densely pyramidal, soft gray-blue foliage, whitish bark, also listed as *Abies lasiocarpa* 'Arizonica Compacta'.

'Martha's Vineyard': a medium-sized selection with a neat habit and pale blue new growth, reaches 30 ft. (9 m).

'Mulligan's Dwarf': upright and conical with dense, dark green needles.

*Abies lasiocarpa* var. *arizonica* 'Compacta'

*Abies lasiocarpa* 'Mulligan's Dwarf'

### *Abies nordmanniana*
#### Nordmann fir   Zones (4)5 to (6)7

This stately and elegant fir is native to the Caucasus Mountains of southeastern Europe and western Asia. It has a dense pyramidal form with branches that tend to droop and fully clothe the tree to the base. It reaches 50 × 20 ft. (15 × 6 m) tall and wide, growing 8 to 12 in. (20 to 30 cm) a year. The needles are ¾ to 1¼ in. (2 to 3 cm) long. They are shiny dark green above with two white bands below. The flat needles are notched at the tip and often point toward the tip of the twig. There is an orange-peel fragrance when they are crushed. The stem is smooth,

Abies nordmanniana

*Abies nordmanniana* branching structure

*Abies nordmanniana* foliage

*Abies nordmanniana* ‘Barabits’

*Abies nordmanniana* 'Durham Dwarf'

*Abies nordmanniana* 'Münsterland'

*Abies nordmanniana* 'Golden Spreader'

*Abies nordmanniana* 'Tortifolia'

*Abies nordmanniana* 'Pendula'

with disc-like leaf scars. The cones are cylindrical, up to 6 in. (15 cm) long, and held erect on the branches. They are rarely seen since they disintegrate while on the tree. The bark is charcoal-gray. Grow the Nordmann fir in well-drained, acid soil in full sun. It will tolerate heat better than most firs and is an outstanding choice for a specimen or windbreak in the larger designed landscape.

'Barabits': dwarf and broad-spreading, also called 'Barabits' Compact' and 'Barabits' Spreader.

'Durham Dwarf': remains dwarf for decades.

'Golden Spreader': slow-growing, flat, round, spreading form with bright golden-yellow foliage in winter, grows 3 in. (7.5 cm) a year, leaders should be cut out. Choice.

'Münsterland': slow-growing, flat round bun, light green needles, 8 × 16 in. (20 × 40 cm) in ten years.

'Pendula': wide-spreading semi-prostrate form but can reach 20 ft. (6 m).

'Tortifolia': irregular, twisted upper needles.

### *Abies pinsapo*   Spanish fir
Zones 6 to 8

The Spanish fir is a relatively slow-grow-ing species that is native to both sides of the Strait of Gibraltar. It can reach 70 ft. (21 m) in the wild but is unlikely to ex-ceed 45 ft. (14 m) under cultivation. Since it is native to a region of hot sum-mers, it is a fir better suited for growing in more southern areas. These conical trees are usually branched to the ground and have beautiful short blue-green needles that spread radially from the branches at nearly right angles, ¼ to ¾ in. (0.6 to 2 cm) long, stiff (sharp and prickly to the touch), and plastic-like with white bands on the underside. The upright cones are ¾ in. (2 cm) long, light brown in color, and appear in spring. The best performance will be in full sun on well-drained soils. It is useful in for-mal garden designs because of its distinc-tive habit. Crushed in water, the twigs yield a kind of soap.

'Aurea': a weak-growing shrub form to 25 ft. (8 m), waxy needles are blushed golden yellow in full sun.

'Glauca': distinctive short, rigid, frosty blue, waxy needles that whorl around the stems, reaches 15 ft. (4.5 m) in 15 years and eventually 60 ft. (18 m), makes a distinctive focal point in the garden.

'Horstmann': an attractive low-spreading compact dwarf with stiff blue foliage, useful for trough planting, grows 4 in. (10 cm) a year.

*Abies pinsapo*

*Abies pinsapo* foliage and cones

*Abies pinsapo* 'Glauca'

*Abies pinsapo* 'Aurea'

*Abies pinsapo* 'Horstmann'

### *Abies procera*  noble fir
Zones 5 and 6(7)

The noble fir is appropriately named since it is probably the largest of all *Abies* species in terms of diameter, height, and wood mass. It is native to moist soils in the mountains of Washington and Oregon south to California. The trees soar up to 200 ft. (60 m) tall and are known to live 600 years, but usual specimens will be 50 to 75 ft. (15 to 23 m) tall. With age the lower limbs die and a very tall clear trunk remains with a conical crown. It has no tolerance for shade. It requires a cool, moist habitat. The pungent needles are curved and grooved, a bluish green with a whitish tinge, held stiff and erect on top of the branches, 1 to 1½ in. (2.5 to 3.5 cm) long, four-sided with sharp tips. There are two whitish bands on both upper and lower surfaces of the needles (*Abies lasiocarpa* has one broad band above and two below, while both *A. grandis* and *A. amabilis* have only the two lower bands). The barrel-shaped cones are 4½ to 7 in. (11 to 18 cm) long with olive-colored scales hidden by pale green reflexed bracts that are fringed with long points. With age the bark is a bright red-brown with vertical furrows and long irregular plates. This species in youth has a beautiful pyramidal crown and this, along with its dense foliage, makes it appreciated both as a holiday tree and for use in the landscape.

The wood has been harvested by the

*Abies procera*

*Abies procera* 'Glauca'

*Abies procera* 'Blaue Hexe'

lumber industry for use in interior construction. The R.A.F. bombers of World War II had frames made from noble fir because the wood is light and strong and can be bent far before breaking.

'Blaue Hexe': broad, flat, spherical habit, short, powder-blue needles, growing 1 to 2 in. (2.5 to 5 cm) a year.

'Glauca': eye-catching blue needles, produces loads of cones.

'Glauca Prostrata': steel-blue, slow-growing, occasionally produces leaders, which should be cut out.

'La Graciosa': dense and often strongly weeping and low-growing, forms a broad mound at 6 in. (15 cm) a year.

'Sherwoodii': golden yellow foliage, tends to be prostrate but can form a leader.

*Abies procera* 'Glauca' foliage

*Abies procera* 'La Graciosa'

*Abies procera* 'Glauca Prostrata'

### *Abies veitchii*   Veitch's silver fir
### Zone 3

Veitch's silver fir is native to Japan. This conical tree usually displays short horizontal branches to the ground. It has smooth gray bark and dense needles that point forward and upward. There are two chalk-white bands beneath. The cones are 1¾ to 2½ in. (4.5 to 6 cm) long and are blue-violet when young.

'Hedergott': very dwarf and low-spreading with silver undersides to the needles.

'Pendula': slow-growing and pendulous, reaching 8 ft. (2.5 m) in seven years. This is not considered a valid name.

'Rumburg': cushion-shaped, growing 1 to 2 in. (2.5 to 5 cm) a year with dense light blue needles, sometimes listed as 'Rümbürk'.

*Abies veitchii*

*Abies veitchii* foliage

*Abies veitchii* 'Hedergott'

*Abies veitchii* 'Pendula'

*Abies veitchii* 'Rumburg'

### *Araucaria araucana*   monkey puzzle tree   Zones 7 to 9

The unusual monkey puzzle tree (or Chile-pine, although it is not actually a pine) is native to the hilly slopes of the former Arauco Province of Chile, where it can grow to 100 ft. (30 m) in height.

In cultivation it seldom exceeds 30 ft. (9 m). It dates back to the time of the dinosaurs: around 190 million years ago it was a dominant species in the southern hemisphere. It always has a single very straight stem with the branches whorled around it. It is slow-growing and very open and symmetrical in youth.

With age the top becomes dome-shaped above bare trunks. It has sharp, spiny-tipped dark green leaves that are arranged spirally around the stem. The leaves are leathery and overlapping and persist for many years. Mature specimens tend to lose their lower branches. The trunk is said to resemble an elephant's foot. It will sucker from its roots. The horizontal branches become downward-sweeping branches that curve up at the tip like the tail of a monkey. The cones are very large, 5 to 8 in. (12.5 to 20 cm) long, and mature over three years. They break apart while on the tree. The pollen- and seed-bearing cones are usually on separate trees. The large seeds (up to 300 per cone) were an important food source to indigenous peoples, who roasted them.

The monkey puzzle tree prefers moist soil and protection from harsh winds. It does not tolerate pollution. It is often grown as a garden specimen in the Pacific Northwest and California and is frequently planted in England. Apparently the common name implies that even a clever monkey would be puzzled trying to climb such a prickly tree (there are no monkeys in the forests of Chile). The tree is usually grown as a specimen or in a grove.

Another plant in this genus, *Araucaria heterophylla* (Norfolk Island pine), is often grown as a conservatory or house plant.

*Araucaria araucana* cones at top of tree

*Araucaria araucana* leaves

*Araucaria araucana* whorled branches

*Araucaria araucana* mature trunk

### *Calocedrus decurrens*
incense-cedar    Zones 5 to 8

Incense-cedar (not a true cedar, of course) is native to the Cascade Mountains in Oregon southward into California and Nevada. This species (formerly *Libocedrus decurrens*) can live more than 500 years and grows to 150 ft. (46 m) under favorable conditions in its native habitat. In cultivation it rarely exceeds 50 ft. (15 m). It is a slender tree with a spire-like top. The trunk is straight and will taper from a broad base. The trunks are often fluted and buttressed. The branches emerge perpendicular to the trunk and then ascend abruptly upward. In time the crowns become open and irregular. The lush and lacy deep glossy green foliage has closely overlapping, scale-like leaves that look like they were pressed with an iron. The leaves are arranged in a whorl of four around the branchlet, giving it a jointed appearance. Some of these leaves can be ½ in. (1.2 cm) long. The foliage is held erect and is similar on both sides, with no apparent top or bottom. The leaves give off a pungent spicy aroma when crushed. The bark is cinnamon-red, fibrous, furrowed, and reportedly 3 to 8 in. (7.5 to 20 cm) thick; this enables mature trees to survive wildfires. The pollen-bearing cones appear on the ends of lateral branches and shed their pollen in December. The ¾ to 1 in. (2 to 2.5 cm) seed-bearing cones appear at the tips of the previous season's growth and have six pointed scales with two large scales that bend back from the axis of the cone, looking like a duck's bill. The seeds germinate readily, even in shade.

Incense-cedar will grow in a wide range of soils. It is very drought-tolerant; it inhabits areas that receive as little as 15 in. (38 cm) of annual rainfall. Nevertheless, young plants should be watered during dry spells. It grows well in sun or light shade, in a wide range of conditions.

*Calocedrus decurrens*

*Calocedrus decurrens* foliage

*Calocedrus decurrens* seed-bearing cones

*Calocedrus decurrens* bark

*Calocedrus decurrens* fluted and buttressed trunk

*Calocedrus decurrens* 'Aureovariegata'

*Calocedrus decurrens* 'Berrima Gold'

*Calocedrus decurrens* 'Aureovariegata' foliage

It is the world's leading wood in the manufacture of pencils and, because it is so durable in the ground, is used for greenhouse benches, fence posts, and coffins. The deeply furrowed bark of ancient trees provides habitat for crevice dwellers like bats and brown creepers. The First Nations peoples used many parts of this species: the wood for construction, the boughs for aromatic brooms, the roots and bark for basketry.

*Calocedrus decurrens* makes a very handsome tree in the designed landscape and deserves to be more widely planted. A single specimen lends a formal effect. A grove of these is dazzling.

'Aureovariegata': slow-growing, columnar, variegated form with leaves splashed with yellow and green.

'Berrima Gold': slow-growing, bright gold form that looks deep gold to orange in the winter, popular in England.

'Compacta': a flat globose dwarf.

'Maupin Glow': a yellow-tipped form.

'Pioneer Sentry': a very narrow vigorous form that reaches 40 × 4 ft. (12 × 1.2 m).

## *Cedrus* cedar

The genus *Cedrus* has only four species, and although widely planted they are mainly suitable for large gardens or public landscapes. Frail-looking young specimens develop into wide-spreading stately trees with massive trunks as they age. Although they will adapt to a wide range of soils, they are not reliably hardy colder than zone 5. The needles are arranged in spirals on the growing shoots and appear in rosettes on spur shoots on older stems. Cedars vary in the length and the color of their needles, depending on the provenance of the tree. *Cedrus* species are difficult to identify by their cones, which are all the same shape.

Three species will be illustrated; the fourth, *Cedrus brevifolia*, is a rare species found on Cyprus. *Cedrus atlantica* is difficult to distinguish from *C. libani*; both can achieve enormous size. In cultivation all the true cedars will hybridize.

Cedar wood has been prized since antiquity; it is sweet-scented, oily, durable, uniform, and easily worked. It has poor steam-bending qualities but dries easily with a tendency to warp. The heartwood is light brown in color. It is durable but resistant to preservative treatment. It is used for construction, bridges, garden furniture, fences, gates, and paneling in railroad sleeping cars.

Cedars are large trees

Typical *Cedrus* foliage and erect cones

*Cedrus* pollen-bearing cones appear in the fall

*Cedrus* cones shatter on the tree, and their scales cover the ground below

## Cedrus atlantica   Atlas cedar
### Zones 6 to 9

*Cedrus atlantica* is considered by some authorities to be a variety or subspecies of *C. libani*, to which species it is closely related. Native to the Atlas Mountains of Morocco and Algeria in northern Africa, the Atlas cedar is pyramidal when young but becomes wide-spreading with age, to 60 ft. (18 m) tall by 40 ft. (12 m) wide. It grows a bit faster during youth than in maturity. It is open and skeletal-looking early on, but after several decades is handsome beyond description. It typically grows with one trunk, with branches extending off the main trunk at a 45° angle. The branches become horizontal as they extend, but the tips are pendulous. It grows 6 to 12 in. (15 to 30 cm) a year. The prickly needles are ¾ to 1 in. (2 to 2.5 cm) long and are borne spirally on young shoots and then whorled, 30 to 45 needles on spur shoots, further back on the stem. The foliage is green to blue-green in color. There is no change of color in winter. The erect pollen-bearing cones are relatively large, 1 in. (2.5 cm), and appear in late summer. The much smaller immature seed-bearing cones are hidden among the needles on spur shoots. The mature cones are egg-shaped, 3 in. (7.5 cm) long, and borne upright. Like those of all *Cedrus* species, they disintegrate when ripe the third year. The bark is charcoal-gray and becomes rugged with age. Rows of sapsucker holes are often seen.

*Cedrus atlantica* should be grown in full sun on well-drained soils. It will not accept shade. It tolerates drought and some salt. It is especially tolerant of chalky soil since in its native habitat it grows on dry limestone. It will suffer some winter injury occasionally in colder zones and should be protected from winter winds. It is considered difficult to transplant. Trees that have been regularly root-pruned prior to moving will do best.

*Cedrus atlantica* is not very attractive in youth but in 20 years' time becomes an imposing and picturesque silvery specimen in the larger landscape. It is also frequently seen as an espalier and in bonsai. In cultivation the blue-foliage forms are preferred, but the wild stands have green foliage. Dwarf, weeping, and fastigiate cultivars are available.

*Cedrus atlantica* in youth

*Cedrus atlantica* bark showing sapsucker holes

*Cedrus atlantica* in maturity

### *Cedrus atlantica* (continued)

'Argentea Fastigiata': narrowly conical with gray needles.

'Aurea': conical, short golden yellow needles in first year's growth, reaches 25 ft. (8 m).

'Aurea Robusta': upright and broadly conical with golden tips to branches, more vigorous than 'Aurea', reaches 30 to 60 ft. (9 to 18 m).

'Fastigiata': large and dense, branches ascend sharply forming upright column, blue-green needles, reaches 40 ft. (12 m) tall by 30 ft. (9 m) wide.

*Cedrus atlantica* bonsai over 50 years old

*Cedrus atlantica* 'Aurea'

*Cedrus atlantica* 'Argentea Fastigiata'

*Cedrus atlantica* 'Aurea Robusta'

*Cedrus atlantica* 'Fastigiata'

*Cedrus atlantica* f. *glauca*

f. *glauca*: a group name of commonly planted selections with powdery blue needles, reaches 8 to 10 ft. (2.5 to 3 m) in ten years, matures at 60 ft. (18 m) tall by 40 ft. (12 m) wide, many clones in cultivation.

'Glauca Pendula': serpentine leader with weeping branches and steel-blue needles, needs to be supported and well positioned, once established grows 8 to 16 in. (20 to 40 cm) a year, stunning trained to form an archway or embrace a pergola or fence. A living sculpture.

'Silberspitz': silvery white tips.

*Cedrus atlantica* f. *glauca* foliage

*Cedrus atlantica* 'Glauca Pendula'

*Cedrus atlantica* 'Glauca Pendula' foliage

*Cedrus atlantica* 'Glauca Pendula' trained on an arbor

*Cedrus atlantica* 'Silberspitz'

### *Cedrus deodara*  Deodar cedar
Zones 7 and 8(9)

Also known as the Himalayan cedar, this species, the least hardy of the true cedars, is native to high elevations in the Himalayas of Afghanistan, Pakistan, Kashmir, and western Nepal. Although variable, the habit is generally pyramidal with a drooping leader, a horizontal branching pattern, and gracefully pendulous branch tips. The mature plants are flat-topped. They reach 50 to 70 ft. (15 to 21 m) in cultivation but have been recorded as tall as 150 ft. (46 m). The needles are 1¼ to 2 in. (3 to 5 cm) long (longer than *Cedrus atlantica* or *C. libani*) and have a bluish cast. They are arranged alternately and singly on current growth and spirally on short spurs with 15 to 30 needles per whorl on older growth. The needles are diamond-shaped (not square) in cross section. The long soft foliage, graceful overall appearance, and more pendulous, whip-like leader are good ID features with which to distinguish it from the other cedars. Pollen-bearing cones appear in autumn at the end of short shoots and are 2½ in. (6 cm) long. The more limited seed-bearing cones ripen in the autumn following pollination and break apart the next year. They are barrel-shaped, 3 to 5 in. (7.5 to 12 cm) long. The bark is smooth and gray on young trees but with maturity has wide black to pink-gray furrows with short scaly ridges.

*Cedrus deodara* should be planted in full sun in well-drained, average soil. It tolerates heat well but should be protected from winter winds in colder areas. It grows vigorously as a young tree with a narrow crown and branch tips that hang down noticeably. They can become rather ragged-looking after 20 years, especially if they are denied sufficient moisture. Give it space. It should be grown as a large specimen for its magnificent,

*Cedrus deodara*

*Cedrus deodara* foliage

graceful habit with hanging branches. The timber of this tree was traditionally used for shipbuilding in India.

'Aurea': fast-growing, golden yellow needles in spring turn yellow-green, best color in full sun.

'Blue Dwarf': compact and rounded but eventually more loose and open than 'Pygmy', gray-blue needles.

'Bracken's Best': vigorous, consistent habit, pyramidal with graceful pendulous branchlets, reaches 60 × 30 ft. (18 × 9 m).

'Cream Puff': a shrub with white-tipped young foliage, 1 × 3 ft. (0.3 × 0.9 m) in ten years.

*Cedrus deodara* 'Aurea'

*Cedrus deodara* 'Blue Dwarf'

*Cedrus deodara* 'Aurea' foliage

*Cedrus deodara* 'Bracken's Best'

### *Cedrus deodara* (continued)

'Crystal Falls': soft blue foliage, elegant pendulous habit, fine-textured, reaches 30 ft. (9 m) tall and wide.

'Devinely Blue': wide-spreading, flat-topped mound with pale gray-green new growth, drooping branch tips, usually listed this way although it is named for a person named Divine.

'Feelin' Blue': dwarf spreading form with gray-blue foliage, reaches 1 × 3 ft. (0.3 × 0.9 m) in ten years.

'Glacier': slowly spreading mound, icy blue.

*Cedrus deodara* 'Crystal Falls'

*Cedrus deodara* 'Glacier'

*Cedrus deodara* 'Devinely Blue'

*Cedrus deodara* 'Feelin' Blue'

*Cedrus deodara* 'Glauca Pendula'

*Cedrus deodara* 'Gold Cascade'

*Cedrus deodara* 'Harvest Gold'

*Cedrus deodara* 'Hollandia'

'Glauca Pendula': weeping form that can be trained.

'Gold Cascade': slow-growing, compact weeper, golden foliage.

'Golden Horizon': semi-prostrate and flat-topped with gracefully weeping branches, spreads 2 to 4 ft. (0.6 to 1.2 m), golden foliage in full sun, often listed as 'Gold Horizon'.

'Gold Mound': broadly conical, young foliage bright golden yellow, 1 × 2 ft. (0.3 × 0.6 m) in five years.

'Harvest Gold': more intense yellow color than 'Aurea'.

'Hollandia': a dense blue mounding dwarf, grows 3 in. (7.5 cm) a year.

### *Cedrus deodara* (continued)

'Karl Fuchs': more cold hardy and narrower than species, very blue.

'Kashmir': habit of the species but hardier, foliage silver blue-green.

'Limelight': lime-green branches fading to pale green, conical.

'Montrose Veil': upright weeper but usually wider than tall.

'Pendula': a small weeping tree when trained on a stake, spreading slender branches.

*Cedrus deodara* 'Limelight'

*Cedrus deodara* 'Kashmir'

*Cedrus deodara* 'Montrose Veil'

*Cedrus deodara* 'Pendula'

*Cedrus deodara* 'Prostrate Beauty'

'Prostrate Beauty': slow-growing spreader, soft and light textured, striking blue color, eventually forms a leader.

'Pygmy': extremely slow-growing dwarf, less than ⅔ in. (1.7 cm) a year, useful for trough garden, blue-green needles ½ in. (1.2 cm) long, also called 'Pygmaea'.

'Raywood's Contorted': branchlets contorted at acute angles to stem, grows 4 to 6 in. (10 to 15 cm) a year.

'Raywood's Prostrate Dwarf': vigorous groundcover with blue needles.

*Cedrus deodara* 'Pygmy'

*Cedrus deodara* 'Raywood's Contorted'

*Cedrus deodara* 'Raywood's Prostrate Dwarf'

### *Cedrus deodara* (continued)

'Repandens': procumbent with pendulous branches and blue-green needles.

'Sander's Blue': one of the bluest weepers, reaches 50 × 30 ft. (15 × 9 m).

'Shalimar': soft blue color and graceful habit, upright tree form, selected for hardiness.

'Silver Mist': dense conical habit with soft whitish needles, grows 6 in. (15 cm) a year.

'Snow Sprite': creamy white to yellow new growth, small and mounding, eventually forms a leader, give it some shade.

'Wells Golden': dense bright golden yellow foliage, broad irregular cone.

'White Imp': slow-growing, dwarf with white foliage.

*Cedrus deodara* 'Silver Mist'

*Cedrus deodara* 'Repandens'

*Cedrus deodara* 'Wells Golden'

*Cedrus deodara* 'White Imp'

***Cedrus libani***   cedar of Lebanon
   Zones 5 to 7

The cedar of Lebanon is native to Lebanon, Syria, and the western side of the Taurus Mountains in southern Turkey. It was cultivated in Europe by the 17th century and was planted all across England to commemorate Napoleon's defeat at the battle of Waterloo in 1815. Hence, many great English manors have a cedar of Lebanon that is more than 200 years old. It is stiffly pyramidal in youth but develops a stately flat-topped crown in maturity. It will slowly reach 50 to 60 ft. (15 to 18 m) in cultivation and 125 ft. (38 m) in the wild. The trunks can be massive. It is usually multistemmed. The foliage is typically held on large branches that grow outward almost horizontally. The needles are alternate and typically appear in rosettes of 10 to 20 until, after two to three years, they are in whorls of 30 to 60 needles per spur, ¾ to 1 in. (2 to 2.5 cm) long. The needles are four-sided, stiff, and dark green to gray-green in color. The needles have white lines on all four sides and are pointed. They are borne for only two growing seasons. The upright yellow pollen-bearing cones appear in autumn on the end of short shoots. They are erect, up to 2 in. (5 cm) long, with yellow pollen. They shed their pollen in mid-September. The immature seed-bearing cones are cylindrical, green, ¾ in. (2 cm) long also at the end of short shoots. The mature cones are held upright. They are single, 3 to 5 in. (7.5 to 12 cm) long, and stalked. The apex of each cone is flat or slightly depressed. They mature the first autumn and break apart over the next year to release the seeds and bract scales. A spiky stalk remains on the shoot. The bark is dark gray or brown and smooth on young trees but

*Cedrus libani*

*Cedrus libani* foliage

*Cedrus libani* seed-bearing cones

*Cedrus libani* 'Beacon Hill'

*Cedrus libani* bark

### *Cedrus libani* (continued)

becomes black with a pebble-like appearance with maturity.

This cedar should be grown in an open, sunny location in loose, well-drained, acid soil. It will grow in clay soil if the drainage is adequate. It has a shallow root system and should not be mulched with alkaline materials like maple leaves or wood ashes. It does not appreciate pollution. This species needs to be 50 years old to look its best. It is a tree for the large property. It could be maintained on a small property by root pruning to restrict its size.

The timber is light, durable, and fragrant. It has been used for centuries for building. King Solomon's temple was said to be constructed from this wood 3,000 years ago.

'Aurea': slow-growing pyramidal, needles golden yellow with green base, best color in winter.

'Beacon Hill': large irregular shrub,

*Cedrus libani* 'Aurea'

*Cedrus libani* 'Brevifolia'

*Cedrus libani* 'Nana' with *Picea omorika* 'Pendula'

*Cedrus libani* subsp. *stenocoma*

often upright and narrow, with bright yellow growth, fading to yellow-green.

'Brevifolia': not as tall as species with short needles.

'Glauca': silvery bloom to needles, branches shorter than species.

'Glauca Pendula': pendulous habit with distinctly blue needles.

'Golden Dwarf': slow-growing and horizontal with yellow needles, sometimes called 'Aurea Prostrata'.

'Green Prince': slow-growing, 1 in. (2.5 cm) a year, deep green dwarf that becomes an open-branched pyramid giving the appearance of great age, excellent choice for trough gardens or bonsai.

'Nana': very slow-growing, dense and conical, wider than tall, will reach 4 ft. (1.2 m) in ten years.

'Pendula': a narrow upright form with sweeping pendulous branches, slow-growing, 8 ft. (2.5 m) in ten years.

'Sargentii': mounded slow-growing dwarf, short trunk with weeping branches, a groundcover form, does not appreciate staking, will form a thick blue-green mat in the rock garden.

subsp. *stenocoma*: a hardier form that grows in higher elevations throughout the native range of *C. libani*, strong horizontal branching habit, a tough plant, zone 5.

### *Cephalotaxus*   plum-yew

This is a genus of a half-dozen or more species, all from Korea, China, and Japan, and only a few hardy enough to be commonly found in gardens. There exists some confusion with the taxonomy of this genus.

One cannot avoid making comparisons between *Cephalotaxus* and *Taxus*. The plum-yews might look like their relatives, the common yews, on first glance, but they are much larger-leaved, have completely different cones, and are perhaps not so versatile. However, they are eminently garden-worthy plants, and the cultivars are becoming more commonly available.

They will grow in sun or part shade but typically grow best as understory shrubs and have the huge advantage to the home gardener of not being so palatable to hoofed browsers as yews famously are. They tend to tolerate wetter soils than yews. Very variable, *Cephalotaxus* can be a large bush or a small tree. The branches are arranged opposite or in whorls. Some specimens will have either pollen-bearing or seed-bearing cones, others have both kinds. *Cephalotaxus* tolerates shearing well and is remarkably heat-tolerant. The cultivars can be grown as specimens in a mixed border, as foundation plantings, or, in the case of *C. harringtonia* 'Fastigiata', in a formal setting. Like some *Taxus* species, *Cephalotaxus* has been found to contain anticancer compounds.

*Cephalotaxus fortunei*

### *Cephalotaxus fortunei*   Chinese plum-yew
Zones 7 to 9

This rare species is native to Burma and China, where specimens can be 40 ft. (12 m) tall. In cultivation it is usually a large, shade-tolerant, multistemmed shrub or small tree with dark green glossy needles, 2½ to 3½ in. (6 to 9 cm) long, displayed spirally in upright shoots and in two opposite rows on spreading branches. The olive-brown seed-bearing cones are ¾ to 1¼ in. (2 to 3 cm) long.

*Cephalotaxus fortunei* foliage

*Cephalotaxus harringtonia* 'Duke Gardens'

*Cephalotaxus harringtonia* 'Fastigiata'

*Cephalotaxus harringtonia* 'Fastigiata'
foliage

*Cephalotaxus harringtonia* 'Korean Gold'

### *Cephalotaxus harringtonia*
Japanese plum-yew
Zones 6 to 9

This species is usually represented by the following garden forms.

'Duke Gardens': a dense, spreading, shade-tolerant shrub with glossy dark green needles whorled around the stem, ascending branches give it a more upright form than 'Prostrata', equally slow-growing, reaches 2 to 3 ft. (0.6 to 0.9 m) tall and wide, a female form.

'Fastigiata': markedly upright male selection, grows slowly, eventually distinctly vase-shaped, can reach 16 ft. (5 m) but is usually seen less than 10 ft. (3 m), deep green, almost black-green, 1½ to 2½ in. (3.5 to 6 cm) long needles are arranged spirally around the stem and facing upward, can be difficult to place, but works well in a formal setting or at an "inside" corner of a structure.

'Korean Gold': a fastigiate form, with new growth appearing yellow, then turning pale green, and green with season's end, foliage in whorls, should be protected from winter winds.

### *Cephalotaxus harringtonia*
(continued)

'Prostrata': a low-growing form with spreading branches, 2 to 3 ft. (0.6 to 0.9 m) high and wide, leaves arranged more or less opposite, 1½ to 3 in. (3.5 to 7.5 cm) long, deep dark green with two gray-green bands on the underside displayed in ranks on each side of the stem, pollen-bearing cones are borne hanging under the stem at the leaf axils, nutmeg-shaped seed-bearing cones are about 1 in. (2.5 cm) long, hanging on drooping stalks, maturing over two years from a pale green to a light plum color.

*Cephalotaxus harringtonia* 'Prostrata' seed-bearing cones

*Cephalotaxus harringtonia* 'Prostrata'

*Cephalotaxus harringtonia* 'Prostrata' foliage

*Cephalotaxus harringtonia* 'Prostrata' pollen-bearing cones

## *Chamaecyparis*  falsecypress

Although it contains many of our mainstay garden conifers with all possible shapes, sizes, and foliage variants, this genus is rather small, with only about a half-dozen species. Three are native to North America, one in the east and two in the west, and three are found in eastern Asia. Many are slow-growing and therefore useful in mixed borders, and there are countless genuinely dwarf cultivars. They generally prefer moist, well-drained soil, and most are easily transplanted. They commonly appreciate shielding from harsh winds early on. The foliage can be juvenile (needle-like) or adult (scale-like, often in flat sprays). Pollen- and seed-bearing cones are on the same tree. The former are barely visible but usually yellow; the latter are round with 6 to 12 shield-like cone scales (they look like exploding soccer balls) that mature the first year (except *Chamaecyparis nootkatensis*). In their native stands these trees are characteristically found in closely packed growths in moist forests. They have traditionally been valued for their wood, which was widely utilized by First Nations peoples and later exploited by the colonists. In earlier descriptions those species with pointed, spreading juvenile leaves were classed in the genus *Retinispora*. Like various other conifers, two of the three species native to North America (*C. nootkatensis* and *C. thyoides*) bear the common name cedar because *Chamaecyparis* was unknown to the arriving colonists, and the fragrant wood evidently reminded them of the familiar *Cedrus*.

There is a chamaecyparis available to fill practically any landscape requirement one could think of. They are generally container-grown by nurseries and are not a problem to transplant.

The many established nursery selections of *Chamaecyparis* (with names like 'Compacta', 'Nana', or 'Minima' in various combinations with 'Aurea' or 'Variegata' and the like) have developed from similar source species plants and are only relatively stable. The distinctions among them are often rather subjective, some would say capricious.

It is easy to confuse *Chamaecyparis* with *Thuja* (arborvitae), but the most obvious difference for the novice to observe is the cones.

*Chamaecyparis lawsoniana*

### *Chamaecyparis lawsoniana*
Lawson falsecypress
Zones 5 to 7

Native from southern Oregon to northern California at lower elevations than *Chamaecyparis nootkatensis*, this species should be grown in full sun in cool, moist soil similar to its native habitat along the

### *Chamaecyparis lawsoniana*
(continued)

Pacific Coast. It is commonly known also as the Port-Orford-cedar and Lawson-cypress. It is a pyramidal tree with horizontal spreading branches that often droop. In native stands it will grow to 180 ft. (55 m) but usually reaches no more than 60 ft. (18 m) in cultivation. The foliage is scale-like, in flat fan-like sprays with a blue cast. There are faint white marks on the underside. It is often pendulous at the tips. Some say it smells like parsley. The pollen-bearing cones are bright red in the spring. The seed-bearing cones are ⅓ in. (0.8 cm) round, maturing from blue-green to a reddish brown. A projection from the cone scale is reflexed. They mature the first year but are often retained on the tree. The very thick 6 to 10 in. (15 to 25 cm) bark is silvery brown to red-brown and deeply ridged and furrowed in maturity. It has a flaring base. *Chamaecyparis lawsoniana* can live more than a hundred years. This species is used as a specimen in gardens but also can be made into a hedge or screen and will tolerate some shade. It will not sprout from old wood; therefore it must be pruned cautiously if being trained into hedging. Selections are avail-able with blue, green, and even gold foliage. The loads of cultivars that are dwarf in size are particularly favored in British gardens. All prefer moist, well-drained soil and safeguarding from prolonged heat and drought for best growth. Generally speaking these selections are relatively stable and do not revert to the species forms. In the main the variegated gold and white forms should be given some protection from harsh winter sun and winds, although the gold color usually is most prominent in sunny situations. Forms with bluish or plain green foliage are typically hardier and will tolerate some shade.

The wood has been used for everything from household items to posts and boat construction. Nearly all the old-growth forests have been logged.

A serious problem for *Chamaecyparis lawsoniana* is a root disease caused by the fungus *Phytophthora lateralis*. Other (Asian) *Chamaecyparis* species and *C. nootkatensis* seem to be resistant. Losses from this disease have been severe in the Pacific Northwest especially along water courses and rural roads. The disease enters in the rootlets and spreads through the inner bark and cambium. The infected tissue dies and effectively girdles the tree. Later the foliage is affected and withers. The disease is spread through earth movement by construction and logging operations as well as along moving water. The fungus also moves on the feet of domestic and wild animals. Many cultivars have disappeared from the nursery trade because of losses, and many mature trees have had to be replaced with other species. *Chamaecyparis lawsoniana* can still be enjoyed in low-risk sites with attention to minimizing introduction of the disease. Genetically resistant stock has not been developed.

'Alumnigold': deep golden foliage in spring.

*Chamaecyparis lawsoniana* 'Glauca' foliage

*Chamaecyparis lawsoniana* seed-bearing cones

*Chamaecyparis lawsoniana* bark

*Chamaecyparis lawsoniana* 'Alumnigold'

*Chamaecyparis lawsoniana* 'Columnaris'

*Chamaecyparis lawsoniana* 'Columnaris Glauca'

*Chamaecyparis lawsoniana* 'Dik's Weeping'

*Chamaecyparis lawsoniana* 'Glauca'

'Alumnii': columnar tree to 25 ft. (8 m) with densely ascending branches, soft-textured gray-blue adult foliage in flat sprays.

'Columnaris': a tight narrow column 15 to 20 ft. (4.5 to 6 m) high with blue-green foliage in dense flat sprays, good for an accent or hedging.

'Columnaris Glauca': bluish form of above.

'Dik's Weeping': an open-growing green tree with pendulous branchlets, not very vigorous.

'Elwoodii': slow-growing narrow columnar form with several leading shoots of dense prickly juvenile foliage, gray-green turning steel-blue in cold weather.

'Filiformis Compacta': broad, rounded dwarf with drooping secondary branches, white markings on blue-green foliage, will reach 5 ft. (1.5 m).

'Fletcheri': persistent juvenile foliage on a slow-growing dense column with ascending main branches, reaches 6 ft. (1.8 m), gray-green, bronzes in winter.

'Glauca': a dense grayish column.

'Golden Showers': compact growth with drooping tips of yellow variegated foliage, fast-growing.

### *Chamaecyparis lawsoniana* (continued)

'Green Globe': a dense rounded compact dwarf eventually reaching 1 to 2 ft. (0.3 to 0.6 m), perfect for rock garden or trough.

'Green Hedger': uniform-growing, dense, and erect pyramidal form with bright green color, branches from the base, ideal for hedging.

'Imbricata Pendula': an open conical tree to 25 ft. (8 m) with whip-like drooping branchlets.

'Intertexta': upright and open with pendulous branchlets and coarse blue-green foliage, reaches 30 ft. (9 m).

'Little Sprite': slow-growing narrow columnar form, fern-like sprays of blue-gray foliage, use as an accent plant.

'Mini Globus': dwarf and globose.

'Minima': a rounded dwarf with ascending branches and yellow-green adult foliage, reaches 2 ft. (0.6 m) high and wide.

'Minima Aurea': a broad cone with soft golden yellow foliage, reaches 2 to 3 ft. (0.6 to 0.9 m), needs winter protection.

*Chamaecyparis lawsoniana* 'Green Globe'

*Chamaecyparis lawsoniana* 'Intertexta'

*Chamaecyparis lawsoniana* 'Green Hedger'

*Chamaecyparis lawsoniana* 'Imbricata Pendula'

*Chamaecyparis lawsoniana* 'Minima Aurea'

'Oregon Blue': a broad column with outstanding silver-blue foliage, drooping branch tips, grows fast, reaching 50 ft. (15 m).

'Pelt's Blue': like 'Columnaris' but a more intense blue.

'Pembury Blue': perhaps the best bright silver-blue foliage held in upright vertical sprays, in a 25 to 50 ft. (8 to 15 m) column.

'Pixie': a broadly rounded dwarf with dense blue-green foliage.

*Chamaecyparis lawsoniana* 'Oregon Blue'

*Chamaecyparis lawsoniana* 'Pembury Blue'

*Chamaecyparis lawsoniana* 'Oregon Blue' foliage

*Chamaecyparis lawsoniana* 'Pelt's Blue'

*Chamaecyparis lawsoniana* 'Pixie'

## Chamaecyparis lawsoniana
(continued)

'Schneeball': a white variegated globose dwarf.

'Silver Threads': a narrow pyramidal dwarf with creamy variegation.

'Stardust': upright and vigorous with clear yellow foliage throughout.

'Stewartii': regular and conical to 30 ft. (9 m), golden yellow glossy foliage in large, flattened, drooping sprays on ascending branches.

'Summer Snow': bright ivory-white foliage in warm season fading to green.

'White Spot': upright and dense with whitish new growth on blue-green foliage.

'Winston Churchill': small to mid-sized dense cone with golden yellow foliage in all seasons.

'Wissel's Saguaro': slow-growing with odd branching habit reminiscent of a giant cactus.

'Yvonne': upright cone with bright golden yellow foliage reaches 3 ft. (0.9 m).

Chamaecyparis lawsoniana 'Schneeball'

Chamaecyparis lawsoniana 'Silver Threads'

Chamaecyparis lawsoniana 'Stardust'

Chamaecyparis lawsoniana 'Summer Snow'

Chamaecyparis lawsoniana 'White Spot'

Chamaecyparis lawsoniana 'Wissel's Saguaro'

Chamaecyparis lawsoniana 'Yvonne'

Chamaecyparis nootkatensis foliage and seed-bearing cones

Chamaecyparis nootkatensis bark

## *Chamaecyparis nootkatensis*
Alaska-cedar     Zones 4 to 7

Also called Nootka-cypress, Nootka falsecypress, yellow-cypress, and yellow-cedar, this species is found from Alaska south to British Columbia and south along the Cascade Mountains to northern California. In its native habitat it will reach the greatest size, up to 150 ft. (46 m). Considering its nativity, where the annual precipitation exceeds 60 in. (150 cm), it is no revelation that this plant demands plenty of moisture. It will tolerate some shade. It is a slow-growing species and can live 2,000 years or more. In cultivation it is faster growing and displays denser foliage. The tree has a weeping habit with the secondary branchlets draped toward the ground from the principal branches, which sweep in a graceful upward curve. Typically the tree's leading shoot will droop. The dark blue-green foliage is in flat

sprays. The foliage can feel prickly to the touch because the scale-like leaves are sharply pointed. There are no white markings on the underside. The foliage emits an unpleasant resinous odor when crushed. To some observers it smells like a cut potato. The pollen-bearing cones are yellow and on side branches of the previous year's growth. They are shed in early spring. The ½ in. (1.2 cm) thick seed-bearing cones are found near the tips of branchlets and are red-brown, maturing during the second year. Each scale has a noticeable horny point. These scales separate and release the seeds when mature. The young bark is scaly and with maturity the bark becomes gray with narrow intersecting ridges. The bark does not peel off in long strips as does that of *Thuja plicata*, a species sometimes confused with this one. The tree trunk is buttressed at the base. The bark is only ½ in. (1.2 cm) thick and provides no protection from fires, though these are not

common in the moist areas this tree inhabits. The tree carries snow loads well.

*Chamaecyparis nootkatensis* is propagated by cuttings generally. When grafted it does not "take" onto *Chamaecyparis* but is successful on *Cupressus* or *Thuja orientalis*. It is one of the parents of the intergeneric hybrid ×*Cupressocyparis leylandii*. Some authorities have recently reclassified this species, placing it in the genus *Xanthocyparis*. It will likely be some time before standard publications and nursery catalogs recognize and adjust to this change.

The wood was favored by the First Nations peoples for boat construction, long house construction, and totems. It is strong despite being light in weight and is very durable when exposed to moisture. This is a tree to celebrate in the larger landscape; there are only a few selections for the mixed border.

### *Chamaecyparis nootkatensis* (continued)

'Aurea': pyramidal, slower growing and denser than the species, foliage is yellow in youth, later becoming more yellow-green.

'Aureovariegata': variegated branchlets are brighter in summer.

'Compacta': a dense rounded bushy habit with light green foliage in dense flat sprays, reaches 6 ft. (1.8 m).

'Glauca Aureovariegata': a rare conical tree with blue cast and gold variegation.

'Glauca Pendula': conical tree with pendulous blue-green foliage.

*Chamaecyparis nootkatensis* 'Aureovariegata'

*Chamaecyparis nootkatensis* 'Aurea'

*Chamaecyparis nootkatensis* 'Compacta'

*Chamaecyparis nootkatensis* 'Glauca Aureovariegata'

*Chamaecyparis nootkatensis* 'Glauca Pendula'

Chamaecyparis nootkatensis 'Green Arrow'

Chamaecyparis nootkatensis 'Jubilee'

Chamaecyparis nootkatensis 'Pendula'

Another form of *Chamaecyparis nootkatensis* 'Pendula'

*Chamaecyparis nootkatensis* 'Pendula' foliage and seed-bearing cones

'Green Arrow': a narrow form with branches that sweep straight downward close to the trunk, often forming a skirt at the base, could be planted in groups to cause a commotion.

'Jubilee': very narrow and fast-growing with descending branches of rich green foliage, more narrowly weeping than 'Pendula'.

'Pendula': an elegant weeping tree with pendulous secondary branches, two forms in cultivation, one slender and dense, the other fuller with widely spaced sweeping branches.

*Chamaecyparis nootkatensis* 'Pendula Variegata'

*Chamaecyparis nootkatensis* 'Strict Weeper'

### *Chamaecyparis nootkatensis*
(continued)

'Pendula Variegata': white mottling, also called 'Pendula Aureovariegata'.

'Strict Weeper': more narrowly weeping than 'Pendula', also listed as 'Strict Weeping'.

'Van den Akker': one of the narrowest forms. Striking.

'Variegata': habit like the species but blue-green foliage is speckled with white.

*Chamaecyparis nootkatensis* 'Variegata' foliage

*Chamaecyparis nootkatensis* 'Variegata'

*Chamaecyparis nootkatensis* 'Van den Akker'

*Chamaecyparis obtusa*

## *Chamaecyparis obtusa*   hinoki falsecypress   Zones 5 to 8

The hinoki falsecypress is native to Japan, where it is an important timber tree and is considered sacred by Shintos. A large, broad, and conical tree, 125 ft. (38 m) in the wild and 50 to 75 ft. (15 to 23 m) in cultivation, this species is rather more adaptable to heat and drought conditions than its cousins. The foliage, a rich dark green, is held in short flat sprays. The leaves are bluntly rounded at the tips (hence *obtusa*—sometimes the Latin names are helpful!), and there are white × markings on the undersurface. The solitary, rounded, seed-bearing cones are held on short stalks. They mature to an orange-brown color the first year. The bark at maturity is a bright red-brown, furrowed and peeling off in long, thin strips. Like *Chamaecyparis lawsoniana*, the species is more apt to be seen in arboreta and large landscapes. However, there are myriad cultivars to

*Chamaecyparis obtusa* cultivars are popular in mixed borders

### *Chamaecyparis obtusa* (continued)

satisfy every imaginable need of the home gardener and landscape designer, many of them challenging to differentiate from one another. No Asian-style garden would be authentic without the inclusion of this species, and it is a favorite (dare I say darling?) of bonsai enthusiasts. Many of the slow-growing selections are good choices for container culture. In earlier times this species was included in the genus *Retinispora*.

'Aurora': similar to 'Nana Gracilis' with a pale yellow color.

'Baldwin Variegated': a slow-growing dwarf, open and somewhat variegated with yellow.

'Blue Feathers': narrow and compact, feathery powder-blue foliage, often used for bonsai, reaches 4 ft. (1.2 m).

*Chamaecyparis obtusa* foliage

*Chamaecyparis obtusa* showing the white marking on the underside and "exploding soccer ball" seed-bearing cones

*Chamaecyparis obtusa* bark

*Chamaecyparis obtusa* bonsai

*Chamaecyparis obtusa* 'Aurora'

*Chamaecyparis obtusa* 'Baldwin Variegated'

*Chamaecyparis obtusa* 'Blue Feathers'

*Chamaecyparis obtusa* 'Compacta'

*Chamaecyparis obtusa* 'Contorta'

*Chamaecyparis obtusa* 'Coralliformis'

*Chamaecyparis obtusa* 'Coralliformis' foliage

'Chilworth': a slow-growing bun-shaped dwarf with bright green recurved foliage, useful for bonsai but will eventually reach 6 ft. (1.8 m), bronzes in winter.

'Compacta': dense and broadly conical, reaching 16 ft. (5 m).

'Contorta': a slow-growing conical dwarf with dense, dark green twisted and contorted foliage, reaches 6 ft. (1.8 m), bronzes in winter.

'Coralliformis': dwarf and bushy mound with unique dark green, twisted, cord-like foliage, reaches 5 ft. (1.5 m) after 25 years.

### *Chamaecyparis obtusa* (continued)

'Crippsii': slow-growing, wide-spreading branches with drooping tips, golden yellow, ferny frond foliage with good winter color, broadly conical to 15 × 8 ft. (4.5 × 2.5 m). A choice accent plant.

'Elf': a fine-textured very slow-growing dwarf with ascending main branches, reaches only 4 in. (10 cm).

'Elmwood Gold': bright yellow in summer, bronze in winter, reaches 4 × 3 ft. (1.2 × 0.9 m) in ten years.

'Ericoides': conical form with dense blue-green, mostly needle-like foliage, bronzes in winter, reaches 6 ft. (1.8 m).

'Fernspray Gold': slender and slow-growing, reaches 10 ft. (3 m) after many years, bright yellow foliage all year, use as an accent or can be sheared, benefits from wind protection.

*Chamaecyparis obtusa* 'Crippsii'

*Chamaecyparis obtusa* 'Crippsii' foliage

*Chamaecyparis obtusa* 'Elmwood Gold'

*Chamaecyparis obtusa* 'Elmwood Gold' foliage

*Chamaecyparis obtusa* 'Ericoides'

*Chamaecyparis obtusa* 'Fernspray Gold'

*Chamaecyparis obtusa* 'Filicoides' foliage

*Chamaecyparis obtusa* 'Filicoides'

*Chamaecyparis obtusa* 'Gold Drop'

*Chamaecyparis obtusa* 'Flabelliformis'

*Chamaecyparis obtusa* 'Goldilocks'

'Filicoides': a small open-growing bush with long thin branches and flat fern-like foliage, in time will reach 5 ft. (1.5 m).

'Flabelliformis': slow-growing dwarf, emerald-green cupped foliage, airy appearance.

'Gold Drop': compact and rounded dwarf, yellow-green, brighter in winter, grows 2 in. (5 cm) a year.

'Goldilocks': similar to 'Crippsii' but smaller.

### *Chamaecyparis obtusa* (continued)

'Gracilis': dense dark green foliage in shell-shaped sprays, the branch tips droop, pyramidal form can reach 40 ft. (12 m).

'Graciosa': an upright globose form with a loose habit and bright green foliage, to 9 ft. (2.7 m), needs wind protection.

'Green Cushion': a very dwarf bun.

'Hage': a dense and globose form with small bright green leaves, grows slowly to 4 ft. (1.2 m).

'Intermedia': a flat-topped rounded form with light green dense foliage, which grows slowly to 1 ft. (0.3 m), useful for trough gardens.

'Jean Iseli': a miniature hummock with deep green compact foliage.

'Kamakurahiba': a dwarf, low-growing, and graceful shrub with cock's-comb-like branchlets tipped yellow-white.

'Kosteri': an upright bushy form with bright green, twisting, mossy foliage that

*Chamaecyparis obtusa* 'Gracilis'

*Chamaecyparis obtusa* 'Green Cushion'

*Chamaecyparis obtusa* 'Hage'

*Chamaecyparis obtusa* 'Kosteri'

*Chamaecyparis obtusa* 'Lemon Twist'

*Chamaecyparis obtusa* 'Little Ann'

*Chamaecyparis obtusa* 'Little Marky'

bronzes in winter, eventually reaches 5 × 4 ft. (1.5 × 1.2 m), appreciates protection from drought and harsh winds, a favorite of gardeners.

'Lemon Twist': thread-like flattened and twisted foliage with yellow highlights.

'Little Ann': vigorous, dense and conical to 5 ft. (1.5 m) tall and wide, with tufted dark green foliage.

'Little Marky': dense pyramidal dwarf, chartreuse-yellow foliage, reaches 30 in. (75 cm) in 15 years.

'Lycopodioides': a rounded dwarf shrub to 6 ft. (1.8 m) with irregular spreading branches with dark green cock's comb tips.

'Lycopodioides Aurea': golden form.

'Magnifica': elegant and broad-spreading, reaching 20 ft. (6 m) in 20 years.

'Mariesii': slow-growing, rounded, open cone shape with thready yellow-tipped scale-like foliage, generally reaches 4 ft. (1.2 m), protect from harsh wind and sun.

'Meroke Twin': dwarf and pillar-shaped with bright lemon-yellow foliage that turns deep gold, reaches 3 to 6 ft. (0.9 to 1.8 m).

'Nana': flat-topped dense layered form with fan-shaped foliage, grows very slowly to 4 ft. (1.2 m) after many years, a favorite for troughs, rock, and alpine gardens.

*Chamaecyparis obtusa* 'Lycopodioides' and 'Lycopodioides Aurea'

*Chamaecyparis obtusa* 'Magnifica'

*Chamaecyparis obtusa* 'Meroke Twin'

### *Chamaecyparis obtusa* (continued)

'Nana Aurea': bright yellow cupped sprays of foliage, to 6 × 3 ft. (1.8 × 0.9 m).

'Nana Gracilis': glossy dark green dense cupped foliage, conical when mature, reaching 3 ft. (0.9 m), a universally admired cultivar that has been cultivated in gardens for over 100 years.

'Nana Lutea': a compact shrub with golden cupped foliage in sun.

'Opaal': similar to 'Nana Gracilis' but yellow-green, cones when young.

*Chamaecyparis obtusa* 'Nana Aurea'

*Chamaecyparis obtusa* 'Nana Gracilis'

*Chamaecyparis obtusa* 'Nana Gracilis' in a container

*Chamaecyparis obtusa* 'Nana Lutea'

*Chamaecyparis obtusa* 'Opaal'

*Chamaecyparis obtusa* 'Pygmaea'

*Chamaecyparis obtusa* 'Reis Dwarf'

*Chamaecyparis obtusa* 'Pygmaea Aurescens'

*Chamaecyparis obtusa* 'Repens'

'Pygmaea': a rounded, wide-spreading form with flat, fan-shaped glossy-green foliage, purple-tinged in winter, name not exactly appropriate since can reach 6 ft. (1.8 m).

'Pygmaca Aurescens': a broad-spreading, flat-topped dwarf, brown-green foliage in summer and orange-copper in winter, eventually reaches 15 × 7 ft. (4.5 × 2 m).

'Reis Dwarf': fine-textured and bright green with twisted branches that project from the plant creating irregular shapes that are not reversions and should not be pruned.

'Repens': low and wide-spreading with bright green, finely textured, closely held sprays of foliage.

*Chamaecyparis obtusa* 'Rigid Dwarf'

*Chamaecyparis obtusa* 'Spiralis'

*Chamaecyparis obtusa* 'Spiralis Aurea'

*Chamaecyparis obtusa* 'Split Rock'

### *Chamaecyparis obtusa* (continued)

'Rigid Dwarf': upright growth, with glossy dark green cupped foliage, very slow-growing to 15 ft. (4.5 m), protect from dry wind.

'Spiralis': upright conical shape with dark green, cupped, fine-textured foliage, very slow-growing, branches spiral outward and upward from the trunk.

'Spiralis Aurea': golden form.

'Split Rock': compact upright form, blue-green juvenile and adult foliage.

'Stoneham': slow-growing dwarf to 3 ft. (0.9 m), light green, dense, flat foliage sprays.

*Chamaecyparis obtusa* 'Stoneham'

Chamaecyparis obtusa 'Tempelhof'

Chamaecyparis obtusa 'Tsatsumi Gold'

Chamaecyparis obtusa 'Verdon'

'Sunspray': compact upright cone, grows only 2 to 4 in. (5 to 10 cm) a year, eventually reaching 6 ft. (1.8 m), pale gold color, needs wind protection.

'Tempelhof': broadly cone-shaped with dense olive-green fan-shaped foliage and orangish stems.

'Tetragona Aurea': compact upright but variable, moss-like foliage golden yellow when grown in sun, slow-growing, benefits from trimming.

'Torulosa': twisted and contorted branches with dark green yarn-like foliage, in 20 years reaches 6 × 4 ft. (1.8 × 1.2 m).

'Tsatsumi Gold': dwarf with gold-colored, thread-like, flat stems and irregular growth, 3 to 6 in. (7.5 to 15 cm) a year to 6 ft. (1.8 m), has also been called 'Golden Whorl' and 'Sanotome'.

'Verdon': compact upright cone with golden-colored soft appressed needles that resist winter sunburn, growth rate varies, reaches 10 × 4 ft. (3 × 1.2 m).

Chamaecyparis obtusa 'Torulosa' (right) with Abies pinsapo 'Glauca'

## *Chamaecyparis pisifera*
### sawara-cypress   Zones 4 to 8

The sawara-cypress is native to the southern islands of Honshu and Kyushu of Japan, where it is an important timber tree. In its native habitat it can reach 150 ft. (46 m) but is usually half that in cultivation. It is more likely to be found in arboreta than home landscapes. This species varies a great deal, from the large native trees to tiny garden selections with foliage in all shades of green, blue, yellow, white, and variegated. The foliage is scale-like, in flat sprays, with incurved tips. The leaves are sharply pointed and have white markings below. The Latin *pisifera* ("pea bearing") refers to the tiny, round, spiny cones, which are carried within the foliage or slightly beneath it. They mature in the first year. However, this species does not produce cones freely. The bark is smooth, dark red-brown, and peels in long narrow strips. Many cultivars of this species have "normal" foliage, but lots of the selections available for garden use are quite different from the type in personality, form, and appearance.

For unclear reasons, cultivars in this species have (Latinized) group names. Sorting out the nomenclature of some of these plants is difficult. The Squarrosa group has only juvenile foliage with soft, needle-like leaves. Often blue-toned, the plants have a fluffy appearance. Examples are 'Squarrosa Intermedia' and 'Boulevard'. The Plumosa group has part juvenile foliage with needle-like foliage or persistent semi-juvenile foliage ('Plumosa Aurea' and 'Snow', for example). The awl-shaped leaves stand out at a 45° angle to the stem and are soft. Filifera group selections have whip-like foliage; examples are 'Filifera Aurea', 'Golden Mop', 'Sungold', and 'Gold Spangle'. No white markings are detectable.

*Chamaecyparis pisifera*

*Chamaecyparis pisifera* foliage varies greatly among cultivars

*Chamaecyparis pisifera* 'Aurea Nana'

In earlier times this species was classed in the genus *Retinispora*. It is an important timber species in Japan.

'Aurea Nana': slow-growing globose dwarf, golden foliage.

'Aureovariegata': dwarf with mottled golden yellow foliage.

'Baby Blue': similar to 'Boulevard' but more diminutive.

'Boulevard': soft silver-blue juvenile foliage, dense conical habit, becomes purple-tinged in winter, usually develops patches of dead foliage which must be trimmed out and does not look good unless sheared into a bun or poodled, useful in containers, withstands heavy pruning.

*Chamaecyparis pisifera* 'Aureovariegata'

*Chamaecyparis pisifera* 'Baby Blue'

*Chamaecyparis pisifera* 'Boulevard'

*Chamaecyparis pisifera* 'Boulevard'
showing dead foliage

*Chamaecyparis pisifera* 'Boulevard'
poodled

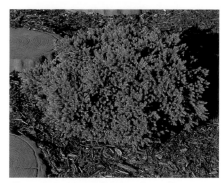

*Chamaecyparis pisifera* 'Boulevard'
withstands pruning

### *Chamaecyparis pisifera*
(continued)

'Compacta': compact, low-growing, dense adult foliage, reaches 4 ft. (1.2 m) in ten years, sometimes unstable.

'Compacta Variegata': open and slow-growing, green with flecks of yellow-white, reaches 1 ft. (0.3 m) in ten years, sometimes unstable.

'Curly Tops': similar to 'Boulevard' but lateral shoots have a twisted and curled appearance, juvenile leaves are glaucous blue with white bands, persistent interior brown needles, rounded, reaches 6 ft. (1.8 m).

'Ericoides Aurea': compact, dense, pyramidal, light green juvenile foliage bronzes to brown in winter.

*Chamaecyparis pisifera* 'Compacta'

*Chamaecyparis pisifera* 'Compacta Variegata'

*Chamaecyparis pisifera* 'Compacta Variegata' foliage

*Chamaecyparis pisifera* 'Curly Tops'

*Chamaecyparis pisifera* 'Curly Tops' foliage

*Chamaecyparis pisifera* 'Ericoides Aurea'

*Chamaecyparis pisifera* 'Filifera Aurea' foliage

*Chamaecyparis pisifera* 'Filifera Aurea' with *Hydrangea quercifolia* in fall

*Chamaecyparis pisifera* 'Filifera'

*Chamaecyparis pisifera* 'Filifera Aurea Nana'

'Filifera': dense and broadly pyramidal, finely textured string-like sprays of green foliage draped on whip-like pendulous branches, reaches 6 to 8 ft. (1.8 to 2.5 m) tall and up to 15 ft. (4.5 m) wide, easy to grow, adds a delicate look to a border.

'Filifera Aurea': form like 'Filifera' but with golden yellow foliage that is maintained year-round if not shaded, shape and size can be controlled by pruning, a great contrast in the winter landscape.

'Filifera Aurea Nana': slow-growing dwarf, but eventually reverts to full size.

*Chamaecyparis pisifera* 'Filifera Aurea'

*Chamaecyparis pisifera* 'Filifera Aureovariegata'

*Chamaecyparis pisifera* 'Filifera Flava'

*Chamaecyparis pisifera* 'Golden Mop'

### *Chamaecyparis pisifera* (continued)

'Filifera Aureovariegata': whip-like branches are splashed with yellow, slower growing than 'Filifera Aurea', very showy.

'Filifera Flava': foliage sulphur-yellow.

'Golden Mop': dwarf, low and mounding, bright golden color, fine thready foliage, slow to establish, protect from harsh sun, also listed as 'Filifera Golden Mops'.

'Gold Spangle': bright yellow, thread-like foliage with some sections more congested, broadly pyramidal habit, fast-growing to 7 × 3 ft. (2 × 0.9 m), protect from harsh sun.

*Chamaecyparis pisifera* 'Gold Spangle'

*Chamaecyparis pisifera* 'Juniperoides'

*Chamaecyparis pisifera* 'Nana'

*Chamaecyparis pisifera* 'Lemon Thread'

*Chamaecyparis pisifera* 'Plumosa'

'Juniperoides': low-growing, compact, fine-textured, foliage emerges creamy yellow, give full sun, also listed as 'Plumosa Juniperoides'.

'Lemon Thread': fine-textured rich gold foliage, fast-growing to 20 ft. (6 m) tall and wide.

'Nana': blue-green adult foliage in sprays, flat-topped and rounded, to 2 ft. (0.6 m) in 40 years.

'Plumosa': semi-juvenile, soft-textured feathery foliage, medium green with white bands beneath, grows 30 to 60 ft. (9 to 18 m).

*Chamaecyparis pisifera* 'Plumosa Aurea'

*Chamaecyparis pisifera* 'Plumosa Aurea Nana'

*Chamaecyparis pisifera* 'Plumosa Aureovariegata'

*Chamaecyparis pisifera* 'Plumosa Compressa'

### *Chamaecyparis pisifera* (continued)

'Plumosa Aurea': fine-textured new growth is soft golden yellow and persists through summer, grows slowly to 30 ft. (9 m).

'Plumosa Aurea Nana': dwarf form.

'Plumosa Aureovariegata': feathery sprays of semi-juvenile mottled foliage.

'Plumosa Compressa': compact, irregular, flat-topped cushion, mossy juvenile gray-green foliage tipped in light yellow, slow-growing to 10 × 12 in. (25 × 30 cm) in ten years, good for rock gardens.

*Chamaecyparis pisifera* 'Plumosa Compressa' bonsai

*Chamaecyparis pisifera* 'Plumosa Juniperoides'

*Chamaecyparis pisifera* 'Plumosa Rogersii'

*Chamaecyparis pisifera* 'Snow'

*Chamaecyparis pisifera* 'Squarrosa'

*Chamaecyparis pisifera* 'Snow' in fall with *Fothergilla gardenii*

*Chamaecyparis pisifera* 'Spaan's Cannon Ball'

*Chamaecyparis pisifera* 'Squarrosa' foliage

'Plumosa Juniperoides': deep green wavy juvenile foliage, golden yellow in summer, compact and slow-growing, never taller or wider than 2 ft. (0.6 m).

'Plumosa Rogersii': conical and slow-growing with upright branching, golden yellow foliage, reaches 3 ft. (0.9 m) tall and wide, needs protection from wind.

'Snow': mossy, blue gray, ferny, semi-juvenile foliage, whiter at tips of new growth, vigorous and dense, reaches 6 ft. (1.8 m) unless pruned.

'Spaan's Cannon Ball': dwarf rounded habit, blue-green foliage with hint of yellow, bronzes in winter, reaches 2 ft. (0.6 m) in ten years, morning shade is helpful, plant away from wind.

'Squarrosa': conical tree with irregular branchlets, soft feathery silver-green foliage, reaches 30 ft. (9 m).

*Chamaecyparis pisifera* 'Squarrosa Intermedia'

*Chamaecyparis pisifera* 'Squarrosa Minima'

*Chamaecyparis pisifera* 'Sungold'

*Chamaecyparis pisifera* 'Tama-himuro'

*Chamaecyparis pisifera* 'Tsukumo'

### *Chamaecyparis pisifera*
(continued)

'Squarrosa Intermedia': tight gray-blue juvenile foliage, fast-growing, becomes open and rangy to 6 × 4 ft. (1.8 × 1.2 m) unless trimmed annually, outstanding for creating topiaries.

'Squarrosa Minima': a derivative of above with tight blue-green foliage.

'Sungold': dwarf and mounding, threadleaf foliage with gold new growth, turning green in winter, vigorous, does not need protection from sun.

'Tama-himuro': rounded dwarf with tight blue-green juvenile foliage.

'Tsukumo': a tight low mound, very small green leaves, stays small enough to be used in troughs and forms a stout trunk making it good for bonsai, spelling varies.

'Vintage Gold': will reach 15 to 20 ft. (4.5 to 6 m).

'White Pygmy': fine-textured tiny bun with white-tipped foliage, grows slowly to 1 ft. (0.3 m).

*Chamaecyparis pisifera* 'Vintage Gold'

## *Chamaecyparis thyoides*
### Atlantic white-cedar
Zones 4 to 9

Other common names for this species are quite informative: southern white-cedar, swamp-cedar, post-cedar, and coast white-cedar. Its wood has been traditionally used for boat-building, roof shingles, and posts because of its durability in contact with moisture. It is native along the Atlantic coast of North America from Maine to northern Florida and west along the coast to Mississippi.

This is a tree of freshwater swamps and boggy low-lying areas. It is frequently found growing in dense pure stands in areas suiting it. It grows with a straight trunk and at maturity has a rather narrow pointed top with short lateral branches.

It reaches 30 to 50 ft. (9 to 15 m) and under ideal conditions can get to 90 ft. (27 m). It should be grown in full sun. The foliage displays both needle-like and scale-like leaves. The small needle-like leaves are found on seedlings and vigorous shoots. The scale-like leaves are often bluish green with distinct white × patterns on the undersurface. Some observers say the crushed leaves smell of ginger. Unlike its *Chamaecyparis* relatives, the foliage does not grow in flat sprays. The pollen-bearing cones are terminal and yellowish. The numerous seed-bearing cones, ¼ in. (0.6 cm) spheres, appear in clusters and are blue turning blue-purple and finally liver-colored. Many selections of this species tend to cone like mad, even the dwarfs. The bark is gray-brown to red-brown, shredding in narrow strips. It is on the short list of conifers that will tolerate moist soils. It is often grown as a hedging plant.

The Atlantic white-cedar is the state tree of New Jersey, where there is a 900-acre swamp of giant trees at Green Bank State Forest. It has traditionally been an important timber tree because of the durability of the wood in contact with the soil. During the American Revolution against the British Crown this tree was made into charcoal used in the making of gunpowder. Many coniferites think this species should be utilized more in ornamental gardens.

*Chamaecyparis thyoides* growing in a wet site

*Chamaecyparis thyoides* foliage and seed-bearing cones

*Chamaecyparis thyoides* 'Ericoides'

*Chamaecyparis thyoides* 'Glauca'

*Chamaecyparis thyoides* 'Heatherbun'

*Chamaecyparis thyoides* 'Little Jamie'

*Chamaecyparis thyoides* 'Red Star' in spring

### Chamaecyparis thyoides
(continued)

'Andelyensis': a compact and slow-growing columnar form to 10 ft. (3 m), gray-green adult foliage with random juvenile foliage, bronzes in winter when it has tiny red pollen-bearing cones.

'Ericoides': oval, compact shrub with soft gray-green juvenile foliage, turns a deep violet-brown in winter, needs protection from harsh winter sun and wind.

'Glauca': slow-growing compact and conical shrub with silver-blue foliage.

'Heatherbun': dwarf globe with soft, fuzzy, medium green juvenile foliage turning a hazy heather-purple in winter, reaches 6 to 8 ft. (1.8 to 2.5 m), contrasts nicely with other conifers.

'Hopkinton': large and narrow with blue-gray needles, vigorous to 40 × 20 ft. (12 × 6 m), useful for hedges.

'Little Jamie': a slow-growing narrow cone with dark green foliage turning purple-brown in winter, also called 'Little Jamey'.

'Qiana': compact with uniform branching form, rich green color, use as accent, hedge, or windbreak, deer do not favor.

'Red Star': upright column of plum-purple in winter that changes to deep sage-green in summer, reaches 10 ft. (3 m), also called 'Rubicon'.

'Variegata': loose and open conical form to 10 to 12 ft. (3 to 3.6 m) tall and 10 ft. (3 m) wide, bright gold-splashed foliage, does well in moist sandy soil in part shade.

## *Cryptomeria japonica*  Japanese-cedar  Zone 5

*Cryptomeria japonica* is native to and planted throughout Japan. It is the only species in its genus. It is very important there both as an ornamental plant and as a source of wood. It can grow to 160 ft. (49 m). Japanese-cedars are the oldest and largest living trees of Japan. There are said to be more than 200 cultivars, including many dwarf forms. Cryptomerias are valuable in the designed land-scape because of their graceful habit, shade tolerance, and beautiful foliage. The species appreciates well-drained, moist soil, and protection from harsh winter winds. It can be sheared (it will even grow from the stump if cut off) and is not prone to any common pests or diseases. Most of the cryptomerias available were selected in Japan. "Sugi" is the Japanese common name for the species and is often part of the name of numerous cultivars that were introduced prior to 1959. However, there is a good deal of inconsistency in the naming of cryptomerias: sometimes the original Japanese name is applied, sometimes it is westernized, and in other instances the cultivar names have been contracted.

In youth cryptomerias are cone-shaped, but with age they open out and spaces appear among the branches, giving them a poodled look. They usually have a pointed or sometimes broadly domed top. The foliage is needle-like, soft, dark green, surrounding the stem, and awl-shaped ("keeled"). The base of

*Cryptomeria japonica* foliage

*Cryptomeria japonica* foliage in winter

*Cryptomeria japonica* showing dead foliage

*Cryptomeria japonica* with age can develop a poodled look

### *Cryptomeria japonica* (continued)

the needle clasps the stem; the needle it-self diverges from the shoot and points toward the growing tip. The stem of the new growth is green. Many forms change color in the winter, commonly varying from a light bronze to a deep purple, but then quickly green up again in spring. The pollen-bearing cones appear in spring in the axils of the leaves and are yellow-green in clusters of 20 or more, at the ends of branchlets. The immature seed-bearing cones are globular and soli-tary at the ends of branchlets. The ma-ture seed-bearing cones are round and prickly, green when immature and ma-turing to brown in one season. They are at the ends of shoots and remain on the tree for months even after shedding their seeds. The bark is red-brown, fibrous, and soft. With maturity the bark peels off in long strips. The trunk is usually straight, sometimes buttressed at the base.

The timber is economically important in Japan. The wood is very rot-resistant and easily worked; it is used for build-ings, bridges, ships, posts, and pulp. Cryptomerias are often planted around temples.

Leaf blight, a fungus disorder, can cause interior foliage to turn brown and unsightly. Fungicide sprays can be ap-plied. It is best to avoid the problem by providing good air circulation and plant-ing specimens where they get the drying morning sun.

'Albospicta': new growth is white.

'Araucarioides': typical awl-shaped needles are densely crowded on slender whip-like branches, yellows slightly in winter, needs protection from harsh winds, reaches 15 ft. (4.5 m) tall and wide.

*Cryptomeria japonica* pollen-bearing cones

*Cryptomeria japonica* seed-bearing cones

*Cryptomeria japonica* mature persistent seed-bearing cones

*Cryptomeria japonica* bark

*Cryptomeria japonica* 'Albospicta'

*Cryptomeria japonica* 'Araucarioides'

*Cryptomeria japonica* 'Barabits' Gold'

*Cryptomeria japonica* 'Benjamin Franklin'

*Cryptomeria japonica* 'Birodo'

*Cryptomeria japonica* 'Black Dragon'

*Cryptomeria japonica* 'Compacta'

'Bandai-sugi': slow-growing, globose, dense bright green moss-like foliage turns deep bronze in winter, irregular growth with some branchlets growing strongly, others are short, reaches 4 ft. (1.2 m) in ten years.

'Barabits' Gold': indistinguishable from 'Sekkan-sugi'.

'Benjamin Franklin': vigorous upright habit, remains green during the winter, salt-tolerant, reaches 20 ft. (6 m).

'Birodo': globose and compact, medium green in summer, turning purple in winter.

'Black Dragon': vigorous, dense, upright conical habit to 6 ft. (1.8 m), pale green spring growth ages to deep dark green, which is retained in winter.

'Compacta': densely branched, blue-green needles.

*Cryptomeria japonica* 'Cristata'

*Cryptomeria japonica* 'Elegans Aurea'

*Cryptomeria japonica* 'Cristata' foliage

*Cryptomeria japonica* 'Elegans Nana'

*Cryptomeria japonica* 'Elegans Nana' foliage

### *Cryptomeria japonica*
(continued)

'Cristata': slow-growing narrow bush or small tree with ascending branches, branch tips appear as if pasted together, giving a twisted, deformed look, reaches 10 ft. (3 m), can be pruned to call attention to the cock's combs.

'Elegans': bushy with spirally arranged branchlets, dense, soft, ferny foliage that turns from pale green in sum-mer to purplish brown in winter, does not cone, needs corrective pruning, can reach 10 to 12 ft. (3 to 3.6 m).

'Elegans Aurea': slow-growing, strongly conical to 10 to 15 ft. (3 to 4.5 m), soft light green foliage (not yellow despite the name) that is brighter in winter.

'Elegans Nana': compact globe to cloud-shaped, slow-growing to 3 to 4 ft. (0.9 to 1.2 m), soft billowy blue-green foliage turns purple-brown in winter, protect from winter sun and wind.

*Cryptomeria japonica* 'Elegans Nana' winter color

*Cryptomeria japonica* 'Enko-sugi'

*Cryptomeria japonica* 'Giokumo'

*Cryptomeria japonica* 'Globosa'

'Elegans Viridis': foliage remains green in winter.

'Enko-sugi': slow-growing to 12 ft. (3.6 m), irregular shape with long whip-like deep green branches, possibly the same as 'Araucarioides'.

'Giokumo': slow-growing shrub with coarse green foliage.

'Globosa': low-growing, broadly rounded to 5 ft. (1.5 m), dense blue-green foliage turning bronze-red in winter.

'Globosa Nana': broadly rounded, 3 to 4 ft. (0.9 to 1.2 m) tall and wide, pendulous branchlets, deep green foliage with tightly pressed needles, bronzes in winter, needs protection from winter sun and wind.

*Cryptomeria japonica* 'Globosa Nana'

### *Cryptomeria japonica* (continued)

'Gracilis': erect and narrow to 16 ft. (5 m), light green all seasons.

'Gyokuryu': irregular globe to 3 ft. (0.9 m) tall and wide, dark green foliage turning bronze in winter, protect from winter wind.

'Hino': compact globe, bronzes in winter.

'Jindai-sugi': upright and spreading, slow-growing to 4 ft. (1.2 m) in ten years, bright green, dense foliage all year.

'Kilmacurragh': cushion-shaped with distinctive branch tips like cock's combs, reaches 4 ft. (1.2 m) tall.

'Kitayama': narrow upright selection, attractive green winter color.

'Knaptonensis': slow-growing, upright and mounding, creamy white new growth, prefers some shade and wind protection.

'Koshyi': spreading habit, reaching 6 × 20 in. (15 × 50 cm) in 20 years, pale green, protect from afternoon sun and winter wind.

*Cryptomeria japonica* 'Gyokuryu'

*Cryptomeria japonica* 'Kilmacurragh'

*Cryptomeria japonica* 'Knaptonensis'

*Cryptomeria japonica* 'Hino'

*Cryptomeria japonica* 'Hino' in winter

*Cryptomeria japonica* 'Koshyi'

*Cryptomeria japonica* 'Little Champion'

*Cryptomeria japonica* 'Little Diamond'

*Cryptomeria japonica* 'Majiro'

*Cryptomeria japonica* 'Manhishmi-sugi'

*Cryptomeria japonica* 'Nana'

'Little Champion': low cushion of apple-green foliage.

'Little Diamond': dense globose bush, slower growing than 'Globosa Nana'.

'Majiro': reaches 6 ft. (1.8 m) with gold variegated leaves, brightest in winter, protect from wind and sun.

'Manhishmi-sugi': wide globe, branch ends in tight clusters of short-needled branchlets.

'Nana': slow-growing to 3 ft. (0.9 m), horizontal branchlets with drooping tips, green all seasons.

### *Cryptomeria japonica* (continued)

'Ogon-sugi': broad pyramidal form with drooping branch tips, also called 'Aurea'.

'Pom Pom': dwarf with little tufts at ends of branches.

'Pygmaea': slow-growing, similar to 'Nana' but more compact, flat-topped, and broad, often more than one leader, deep green foliage turning red-bronze in winter.

'Rein's Dense Jade': formal-looking with jade-green closely appressed needles, bronzes in winter.

'Sekkan-sugi': dense, upright to 30 ft. (9 m), foliage cream to bright yellow-gold tipped in summer, less in winter, needs protection from drying winds and full sun.

*Cryptomeria japonica* 'Pom Pom'

*Cryptomeria japonica* 'Pygmaea'

*Cryptomeria japonica* 'Sekkan-sugi'

*Cryptomeria japonica* 'Rein's Dense Jade'

*Cryptomeria japonica* 'Spiralis'

*Cryptomeria japonica* 'Spiralis' foliage

*Cryptomeria japonica* 'Spiraliter Falcata'

*Cryptomeria japonica* 'Tansu'

*Cryptomeria japonica* 'Vilmorin Gold'

'Spiralis': broad and pyramidal, foliage pressed against stem so tightly that the stems appear twisted like yarn, bright green year-round, benefits from shaping.

'Spiraliter Falcata': more dwarf and upright than 'Spiralis', branches twist and curve and are thinner.

'Taisho Tama': broad cone with dark green foliage.

'Tansu': small and rounded with dense light green foliage, bronzes in winter, grows 2 to 3 in. (5 to 7.5 cm) a year, reaches 2 ft. (0.6 m), good for bonsai and rock gardens.

'Vilmorin Gold': rounded with yellow-gold foliage in summer.

### *Cryptomeria japonica* (continued)

'Vilmoriniana': very slow-growing to 20 in. (50 cm) in ten years, dense, deep green short needles that bronze in winter, good for trough gardens.

'Yatsubusa-sugi': dwarf and congested.

'Yoshino': beautiful pyramidal form reaching 20 ft. (6 m) tall by 8 ft. (2.5 m) wide, growing 1 ft. (0.3 m) a year, rich green foliage all year round, retains branches to ground. Choice.

*Cryptomeria japonica* 'Yatsubusa-sugi'

*Cryptomeria japonica* 'Vilmoriniana' in summer

*Cryptomeria japonica* 'Yoshino' foliage

*Cryptomeria japonica* 'Yoshino'

*Cryptomeria japonica* 'Vilmoriniana' foliage in winter

*Cryptomeria japonica* 'Yoshino' in a college landscape

*Cunninghamia lanceolata*

## *Cunninghamia lanceolata*
### China-fir   Zones 6 to 9

This species is a forest tree of China, where it is valued as a timber tree. It is not actually a fir, or even in the same family as the true firs, *Abies*. It grows to 75 ft. (23 m) tall and 30 ft. (9 m) wide with a single stem. The habit is often broadly pyramidal with a rounded top. The branches are usually widely spaced and droop somewhat. The bright glossy green needles are lance-shaped (hence its epithet), 1 to 2½ in. (2.5 to 6 cm) long. They are very flexible but have a wickedly sharp tip. They are usually displayed in two ranks, often curving upward a bit. There are two white bands beneath. The pollen-bearing cones are small and in terminal clusters (occasionally at the base of seed cones), through which the new shoots grow. The ovoid seed-bearing cones are green, maturing to brown; they are solitary and terminal. The attractive bark is cinnamon-brown and hard, peeling off in long irregular strips. *Cunninghamia lanceolata* will sucker from the base and can be grown as a shrub by pruning. It does best in areas of mild winters and appreciates plentiful moisture. It is adaptable to a wide range of soils and will withstand salt spray but should be given protection from harsh winds. This species is not practical for the home landscape but will be found in

*Cunninghamia lanceolata* foliage

*Cunninghamia lanceolata* underside of foliage

*Cunninghamia lanceolata* lighter new growth

### *Cunninghamia lanceolata*
(continued)

most arboretum collections. It is a bit of a horticultural oddity. Old specimens often look rather ragged. The needles fall while still attached to large twigs, thus it is usually covered with conspicuous clumps of dead foliage that likewise litter the ground under it. These dead needles are very flammable.

The wood is soft but durable, easily worked, and resistant to rot. It is used for general construction, bridges, ships, posts, furniture, and coffins.

*Cunninghamia lanceolata* pollen-bearing cones

*Cunninghamia lanceolata* seed-bearing cones

*Cunninghamia lanceolata* bark

*Cunninghamia lanceolata* litter beneath, sprouts from old wood

*Cunninghamia lanceolata* grown as a shrub

'Chanson's Gift': neater than the species, single-stemmed, more compact and pyramidal, with glossy darker green foliage.

'Glauca': more silvery blue new foliage and often has a pendulous habit, considered hardier than the species and makes a very attractive specimen when well grown, best to clip to encourage new growth.

var. *konishii* 'Little Leo': cushion-shaped plant with short leaves, needs some shelter, grows 1½ in. (3.5 cm) a year.

*Cunninghamia lanceolata* 'Chanson's Gift'

*Cunninghamia lanceolata* var. *konishii* 'Little Leo'

*Cunninghamia lanceolata* 'Glauca'

*Cunninghamia lanceolata* 'Glauca' foliage

## ×*Cupressocyparis leylandii*
### Leyland cypress   Zones 6 to 10

This is another conifer with a story. It is an intergeneric hybrid. That means it has parents of two different genera. Hybrids quite commonly occur between closely related species; it is not often that a cross occurs naturally between trees of different genera. Both parents are from western North America: *Chamaecyparis nootkatensis* (Alaska-cedar) and *Cupressus macrocarpa* (Monterey cypress). These two trees originally coupled in a British garden in 1888. They would never have met in the wild because their natural ranges are thousands of miles apart.

The Leyland cypress is a versatile and adaptable tree that combines the rapid growth of the Monterey cypress and the hardiness and habit of the Alaska-cedar. It is a very attractive tree with a dense columnar habit. It grows much faster than either parent, 2 to 4 ft. (0.6 to 1.2 m) a year, to a height of 60 ft. (18 m). It will tolerate coastal conditions and most soils. It is said to withstand salt better than any other conifer. Give it full sun, or it will be less vigorous. It is very pollution-tolerant. The soft foliage is carried in flat sprays that radiate in all directions from the stem and are slightly drooping. The foliage color is held during the winter. Cones are said to be common on most selections except 'Haggerston Grey', but, in fact, are hard to find. They are ½ in. (1.2 cm) round, with shield-like scales and a small spine. The mature bark is dark brown with shallow ridges.

Its numerous selections make handsome, fine-textured specimens. ×*Cupressocyparis leylandii* has become especially valued in England because it will withstand trimming and has become a common conifer for hedging. It is unequaled for tall screens but can quickly outgrow its space in residential landscapes. It is widely grown as a holiday tree, although

*×Cupressocyparis leylandii*

it is not fragrant and the branches do not hold ornaments well. It does not set seed and must be propagated by cuttings. It is best container-grown. In areas with cold winters the best success with this species is by buying small, container-grown specimens and planting them in the spring. This allows the plants to distribute their fibrous roots in the gardener's soil. Larger specimens planted in the

fall in exposed sites are subject to heaving out of frozen soil or being blown over by winds.

The most important disease that affects Leylands is caused by several fungal species of *Seiridium*. Cankers form at damaged bark and resin will be seen; oozing causes dieback of leading shoots. Bagworms (see the discussion at *Thuja*) can be a problem also.

×*Cupressocyparis leylandii* cones

×*Cupressocyparis leylundii* bark

If *Chamaecyparis nootkatensis* is re-classified as *Xanthocyparis nootkatensis*, the Leyland cypress will become ×*Cupro-cyparis leylandii*.

'Castlewellan': dense columnar habit, bronzy yellow tips, interior dark green, color best in cooler weather, popular for hedging because somewhat slower-growing.

'Golconda': fine-textured lemon-yellow foliage throughout the compact tree, burns in winter, reaches 20 ft. (6 m).

×*Cupressocyparis leylandii* at planting

×*Cupressocyparis leylandii* 'Golconda'

×*Cupressocyparis leylandii* ten years later

### ×*Cupressocyparis leylandii* (continued)

'Gold Rider': fast-growing with a narrow crown to 70 × 12 ft. (21 × 3.6 m), golden foliage not burned by sun.

'Green Spire': narrow and columnar with dense, bright green foliage.

'Haggerston Grey': columnar but more open than some cultivars, vigorous, gray-green foliage.

*×Cupressocyparis leylandii* 'Gold Rider' foliage

*×Cupressocyparis leylandii* 'Gold Rider'

*×Cupressocyparis leylandii* 'Green Spire'

*×Cupressocyparis leylandii* 'Haggerston Grey'

'Harlequin': foliage has creamy white patches.

'Leighton Green': vigorous, tall narrow column, rich green flat ferny foliage, frequently produces cones. Popular.

'Naylor's Blue': vigorous, tall columnar form to 50 ft. (15 m) with open branching, gray-blue foliage turns bluer in cold weather, provide good drainage and protection from wind.

'Picturesque': large spreading tree with contorted branches and twisted sprays of blue-green foliage.

×*Cupressocyparis leylandii* 'Leighton Green'

×*Cupressocyparis leylandii* 'Harlequin'

×*Cupressocyparis leylandii* 'Naylor's Blue'

×*Cupressocyparis leylandii* 'Naylor's Blue' foliage

*×Cupressocyparis leylandii* 'Robinson's Gold'

*×Cupressocyparis leylandii* 'Stapehill'

## ×*Cupressocyparis leylandii* (continued)

'Robinson's Gold': fast grower, variable gold color but often brighter and more uniform than 'Castlewellan'.

'Silver Dust': columnar tree with creamy white variegation.

'Stapehill': dense columnar tree with rich green foliage in flattened sprays, not tolerant of drought or shade, not the best cultivar.

'Star Wars': tall and pyramidal, dense foliage with uniform white variegation.

*×Cupressocyparis leylandii* 'Silver Dust'

## *Cupressus*  cypress

This is a group of trees or large shrubs that grow in North America (mainly California, Mexico, and Central America), southern Europe, Africa, and Asia. Many of the cypresses occur in small isolated stands. Authorities cannot agree on the classification of plants in this genus; some of the 13 to 25 present species have been moved back and forth between

*Cupressus* (true cypress) and *Chamaecyparis* (falsecypress). Cypresses may be distinguished from *Chamaecyparis* species by their larger cones and lesser hardiness. *Cupressus* has been cultivated for thousands of years in the Mediterranean region and near Buddhist temples in China, Tibet, and India. It is not a genus that has been the subject of much study; indeed, it does not contain many species of horticultural importance for the home

gardener but is admired in public gardens and arboreta in the West.

This is a genus for full sun. It is tolerant of almost any soil condition that is not constantly wet. These plants are considered difficult to transplant and should be purchased container-grown. The foliage is scale-like. Many species have resinous glands on the leaves that are aromatic and sticky when crushed. Cones appear on the tips of shoots. Pollen-bearing cones are evident in late winter. The seed-bearing cones usually mature in two years and are round and woody with projections on the surface. The cones can remain on the tree for years. The seeds are sometimes not released until opened by fire. Generally, this genus has rather large cones. The wood is prized for its sweet scent and resistance to decay. Legend has it that this wood was used to construct Noah's ark.

## *Cupressus arizonica*  Arizona cypress  Zones 7 to 9

Given that the Arizona cypress is native to southwest Arizona, New Mexico, and Mexico, it is obvious it will tolerate hot, dry conditions and should be grown in full sun. It is a small to medium-sized tree 40 to 50 ft. (12 to 15 m) tall and half as wide with a broadly columnar rounded crown. The dense foliage is scale-like, pointed, and blue-green. The cones are 1¼ in. (3 cm) round with pointed scales. The bark is red-brown and peeling.

The species is not often found in gardens, but selections from its several varieties, notably var. *glabra* (smooth cypress), are valued. Over the species as a whole there is intergradation between smooth and fibrous barks, and these variations of bark texture as well as foliage features have been used to segregate species. Some of the following cultivars are no doubt actually selections of var. *glabra* (and

*Cupressus arizonica*

### *Cupressus arizonica* (continued)

could even be listed as *Cupressus glabra*: some authorities consider *C. arizonica* and *C. glabra* synonymous). Regardless of their specific epithet, a single plant of many of these cultivars will make a dramatic statement in the garden. They are very popular in Australia and New Zealand.

'Arctic': upright and pyramidal with horizontal branching, rich green foliage with white tips early in the season, slow-growing to 20 ft. (6 m).

'Blue Ice': upright habit, frosty blue-gray color, showy red-brown stems, grows slowly to 15 ft. (4.5 m), wind-tolerant.

*Cupressus arizonica* 'Blue Ice'

*Cupressus arizonica* foliage

*Cupressus arizonica* cone

*Cupressus arizonica* bark

*Cupressus arizonica* 'Blue Ice' tailored

'Blue Pyramid': compact, symmetrical pyramid, silver-gray foliage, reaches 20 to 25 ft. (6 to 8 m).

'Carolina Sapphire': upright broadly pyramidal form with silver-blue foliage, rapid growing.

'Chaparral': dense broad column, creamy white foliage.

'Golden Pyramid': gold-tinted foliage, strong grower, 15 × 5 ft. (4.5 × 1.5 m) in 15 years.

*Cupressus arizonica* 'Blue Pyramid'

*Cupressus arizonica* 'Golden Pyramid' foliage

*Cupressus arizonica* 'Chaparral'

*Cupressus arizonica* 'Golden Pyramid'

*Cupressus arizonica* 'Limelight'

*Cupressus arizonica* 'Raywood's Weeping'

*Cupressus arizonica* 'Silver Smoke'

*Cupressus arizonica* 'Sapphire Skies'

*Cupressus arizonica* 'Sulfurea'

### *Cupressus arizonica* (continued)

'Limelight': compact narrow conical habit, light yellow to lime-green all seasons, 10 × 5 ft. (3 × 1.5 m) in ten years.

'Raywood's Weeping': narrow, upright with downward hanging branches, reaches 20 ft. (6 m) in ten years.

'Sapphire Skies': narrow, pyramidal, rich blue-green foliage.

'Silver Smoke': narrow with open branching and drooping tips, blue-gray.

'Sulfurea': dense, columnar to 50 ft. (15 m), frosted yellow over blue-green foliage.

## *Cupressus bakeri*  Siskiyou cypress  Zone 6

The Siskiyou cypress is native to Oregon and California at 3,600 to 6,500 ft. (1,100 to 2,000 m) elevation in the Siskiyou Mountains. It is a broadly columnar tree up to 80 ft. (24 m) tall. The aromatic scale-like foliage is a gray-green. The seed-bearing cones are ⅓ to ¾ in. (0.8 to 2 cm) round with a silvery sheen and prominent projections. The bark is cherry-red and peeling, maturing to gray.

*Cupressus bakeri*

*Cupressus bakeri* foliage

## *Cupressus cashmeriana*  Kashmir cypress  Zones 8 and 9

This is a small tree in cultivation with a pyramidal habit and rounded crown. It has upright branches with long and pendulous branchlets. The leaves are often an attractive iridescent blue-green in flattened sprays. The seed-bearing cones are ½ in. (1.2 cm) round, pale green maturing to dark brown. It can be a beautiful and elegant tree, growing to 60 ft. (18 m), but is usually grown as a conservatory plant. It reaches 16 ft. (5 m) high and 7 ft. (2 m) wide in ten years. It is sometimes listed as *Cupressus torulosa* var. *cashmeriana*.

*Cupressus cashmeriana*

### *Cupressus macrocarpa*
#### Monterey cypress    Zones 7 to 9

This beautiful tree is found near the Monterey Peninsula of California. Its habit depends on growing conditions. Those overlooking the Pacific are densely foliaged, stunted, and irregular in habit, whereas those further from shore are taller and straighter. It grows fast and makes a nice hedge plant in areas with a mild and humid climate. It will not tolerate drought. This is a good species for growing near the sea because of its salt tolerance. Under good conditions it will grow to 75 ft. (23 m) and develop a broad flat crown and live for hundreds of years. The dense foliage is a rich bright green and is not resinous. The persistent solitary or sometimes paired cones are 1 to 1⅓ in. (2.5 to 3.3 cm) wide, maturing in two years with shield-like scales. The bark is red-brown and ridged with maturity. This species is often grown in New Zealand and Australia and is perhaps best known as one of the parents of ×*Cupressocyparis leylandii* (Leyland cypress).

'Aurea': upright irregular pyramid with gold foliage.

'Lutea': narrow and pyramidal with bright yellow new growth that turns green, slow-growing, seed cones are yellow.

*Cupressus macrocarpa* 'Lutea'

### *Cupressus sempervirens*
#### Italian cypress
##### Zones 7 to 9

The Italian cypress is native to the eastern Mediterranean across to Iran. Most common in cultivation is var. *stricta*, the very narrow vertical tree always featured on postcards from Tuscany. It is 60 to 90 ft. (18 to 27 m) in height with a spread of only 8 ft. (2.5 m). It will tolerate long hot summers. The leaves are scale-like and dark green in short flat sprays.

The pollen-bearing cones are small and yellow. The glossy brown-gray seed-bearing cones are 1⅓ in. (3.3 cm) round with little round knobs on the scales. They mature in two years but often persist on the tree. The species is said to live up to 1,000 years and to be tolerant of drought, wind, and dust and not fussy about soil pH. The fragrant wood is moth-repellent, durable, and easily worked.

'Swane's Gold': slender compact column, slow-growing to 4 ft. (1.2 m) in ten years, ultimately 12 ft. (3.6 m), golden yellow in youth, bronzes in winter, ideal for small gardens.

'Totem': a very narrow upright column, deep green foliage, reaches 12 ft. (3.6 m) by 20 in. (50 cm) in ten years, also listed as 'Totem Pole'.

*Cupressus sempervirens*

*Cupressus sempervirens* cone

*Cupressus sempervirens* 'Totem'

### *Ginkgo biloba*  maidenhair tree
Zones 4 to 8

This tree is a loner, not related to anything else in the encyclopedia. It is a tree that, based on fossil records, was found over a large part of the earth 200 million years ago. It preceded the dinosaurs. It is thought to have originated in eastern China, where it has been grown in temple gardens for thousands of years. This tree grows rather slowly at first but can reach 80 ft. (24 m) and live for a thousand years. In youth the tree is rather spare-looking, but it becomes very wide-spreading with maturity. Except for full sun it has few requirements. It is tolerant of urban and industrial conditions and has been widely used as a street tree. Wet sites should be avoided; otherwise, it will grow from Montreal to New Orleans. It is also free of insect pests or diseases. The distinctive alternate leaves are fan-shaped, usually two-lobed (that is, with a deep central notch), on spur shoots. They are apple-green on both sides and scalloped along the margins. Very fine parallel veins radiate from the base of the leaf. The leaves are clustered three to five on small shoots. Both long and short shoots are produced. The short shoots have leaves in a tight spiral and are covered with circles of leaf scars; each marking a year's growth. There are long shoots with leaves spirally arranged. The foliage turns a clear yellow in the autumn. It has been observed that the leaves all seem to fall at once, carpeting the ground in a circle under the tree. The bark on mature plants is thick, gray-black with shallow fissures.

*Ginkgo* is dioecious. The pollen-bearing cones are catkin-like in small clusters, pendulous from the spur shoots, and appear in the spring. The "sperm" are motile and depend on water to travel to the seed-bearing cone. Seed-bearing cones, ¾ to 1 in. (2 to 2.5 cm) round, develop

*Ginkgo biloba*

*Ginkgo biloba* foliage

*Ginkgo biloba* spur shoots

*Ginkgo biloba* pollen-bearing cones

*Ginkgo biloba* seed-bearing cones

*Ginkgo biloba* bark

*Ginkgo biloba* fall color

*Ginkgo biloba* watch your step!

*Ginkgo biloba* don't step!

on the dwarf shoots, usually carrying only one seed that is covered by a thick, oily flesh. They are produced in pairs or threes and mature and fall in autumn the first year. *Ginkgo* cones can be produced without pollination. The seeds (kernels) themselves are smooth and silvery white, covered by a hard shell with a thick fleshy coat, and are a special delicacy roasted in Asian cooking. The seeds are steamed until the shell cracks, then the kernel is removed and eaten or used in baked dishes. They are said to taste like baked potatoes or chestnuts.

*Ginkgo* takes decades to begin to produce cones. Thus, it can take some time before owners are unhappy to learn they have a female tree. When crushed, the ripe seed-bearing cones smell like carrion. Putrid. For that reason, male trees should be selected and planted. The common name arises from the resemblance of the leaf to the maidenhair fern, *Adiantum pedatum*. It is regarded as a sacred tree in Asia. It has been considered a symbol of changelessness, hope, love, protection, and longevity. The topknots worn by samurais and sumo wrestlers are shaped like a ginkgo leaf. Some consider ginkgo extracts valuable medicinally for improving brain function. The light, fine-grained wood of the tree is of little economic value; it is often used to make tea utensils and chessmen.

'Autumn Gold': upright branching, excellent autumn color, reaches 50 × 30 ft. (15 × 9 m), male selection.

'Beijing Gold': spring growth is yellow, outstanding fall color, reaches 50 ft. (15 m).

'Chase Manhattan': very slow-growing with smaller leaves than the species, striking yellow fall color, ideal for bonsai and rock gardens.

'Chi-chi': dwarf, dense, multi-stemmed habit, reaches 4 ft. (1.2 m) in ten years, male.

### *Ginkgo biloba* (continued)

'Fairmount': dense, upright pyramidal, fall color not exceptional, male.

'Gresham': horizontally spreading habit to 30 ft. (9 m) high and wide, male.

'Jade Butterfly': dwarf, vase-shaped shrub.

'Lakeview': narrowly conical, grows slowly to 50 ft. (15 m), handsome fall color, male.

'Magyar': uniform, upright-branching habit, reaches 50 ft. (15 m) after many years.

'Mariken': compact with pendulous branches.

'Princeton Sentry': columnar fastigiate form, male.

'Saratoga': distinctly upright habit, dense ascending branches with distinct central leader, male.

'Tit': same as 'Chi-chi'.

*Ginkgo biloba* 'Magyar'

*Ginkgo biloba* 'Jade Butterfly'

*Ginkgo biloba* 'Mariken'

'Tremonia': narrowly fastigiate, large leaves, female, reaches 30 ft. (9 m).

'Tubifolia': slow-growing, compact, slender leaves form sort of a tube shape, also listed as 'Tubiformis'.

'Variegata': variegated green and gold, not robust, often reverts, female.

'Yadkin Gold': upright, multi-stemmed, and shrubby, good for smaller garden or bonsai.

*Ginkgo biloba* 'Tremonia'

*Ginkgo biloba* 'Tubifolia'

*Ginkgo biloba* 'Variegata'

### *Juniperus*  juniper

More than 60 species of junipers are found over most of the northern hemisphere. Over a dozen are native to North America. Many are useful in public landscapes and private gardens, some because of their ornamental qualities but most because they are of undemanding cultivation, drought resistant, and often appropriate for tough situations with poor soil and harsh climates. Most are even tolerant of lime. It is a very varied genus. The home gardener usually thinks of junipers as providing a prostrate and creeping groundcover in sunny locations, but there are many selections that are shrubby or upright in habit and even some tall columnar landscape trees. They are widely available and have con-

tributed greatly to the enhancement of gardens the world over.

The foliage of *Juniperus* is often indistinguishable from that of *Cupressus*, and identifying and sorting through this genus is difficult even for the trained eye. Some junipers have sharply pointed needle-like foliage (prickly juvenile) and others have flat and scale-like (smooth adult) foliage that hugs the stem. Many have both types. All young plants will bear needle-like leaves. The juvenile foliage is more likely to be retained on the trees that are pruned or grown in thin soil. Juniper foliage can be seen in every shade of green as well as silver and yellow. The awl-shaped needles have white bands on the upper inner surface, which sometimes look like they are on the lower side because of the makeup of the

branches. Almost all junipers are dioecious, that is, the pollen- and seed-bearing cones appear on different plants. The female plants bear fleshy bluish cones—juniper "berries" in everyday speech. The tastiness of these "berries" to birds helps to explain the wide colonization of junipers. Birds especially attracted to junipers include cedar waxwings, robins, and mockingbirds.

Although some exceptions will be noted, most junipers prefer full sun with good drainage, and most are not finicky about soil conditions. Junipers can withstand shaping and can be developed into hedges. All are readily raised from seed, and most cultivars propagate readily from cuttings.

Many named cultivars lack satisfactory descriptions. It is thought that many

Junipers are available in a variety of habits, textures, and colors

selections of *Juniperus chinensis* (Chinese juniper) are actually hybrids with *J. sabina* (savin juniper). Many sources list them as *J. ×media*; however, recent analysis recommends that these be listed as *J. ×pfitzeriana*. A good number of *J. ×pfitzeriana* are listed as *J. ×media* in Europe and in the United States as *J. chinensis*. Most of the selections in this group of junipers are groundcovers or spreading and shrub-sized. There appears no handy resolution to this situation, and coniferites will dispute a number of the listings. To quote the legendary Humphrey Welch: "The nomenclature of [*J. chinensis*] has a long record of confusion."

Many junipers, especially newly transplanted ones, are susceptible to tip blights. A common one is phomopsis tip blight, a fungus infection caused by *Pho-*

*mopsis juniperivora*, which first presents as yellow spots on young needles but will eventually cause dieback of new shoots and entire branches. The fungus is spread by splashing rain and wind or by insects and is persistent in dead foliage. Overhead watering in a nursery situation should be avoided. Infected twigs and branches should be pruned during dry weather and destroyed. Chemical control is usually not needed. One should select resistant cultivars, provide good air circulation, and avoid planting junipers in shaded areas. *Juniperus chinensis* 'San Jose' and *J. horizontalis* 'Plumosa' are widely grown junipers that often suffer from tip blight. Junipers are also frequently infested with bagworms (see the discussion at *Thuja*).

Junipers are popular for bonsai

Needle-like juniper foliage

Scale-like juniper foliage

Typical fleshy juniper cones ("berries")

Many junipers turn bronze in winter

### *Juniperus chinensis*   Chinese juniper   Zones 4 to 9

This dioecious species is native to Japan and China. It is a variable species, confounding even to the most authoritative botanists. Some forms can grow to 50 ft. (15 m) but most are shrubby or creeping groundcovers. Many exhibit both juvenile foliage with a spiny point borne in sets of two or three and blunt-tipped adult foliage, but numerous named selections have only one type of foliage or the other. The foliage is green to blue-green and gray-green. The pollen- and seed-bearing cones are carried on separate plants. The seed-bearing cones are fleshy and berry-like, violet-brown, and about ½ in. (1.2 cm) in diameter.

Chinese junipers are easy to grow and will tolerate both acid and alkaline soils. They tolerate light dappled shade but will do best in full sun. Those with yellowish foliage require sun. Established plants will tolerate dry situations.

Selections of this species are much confused in the trade, often listed as *Juniperus ×pfitzeriana* or even *J. ×media*. Whatever their name, the 85 or more cultivars of this species are widely grown as ornamentals in North America and Europe. There is a form to satisfy every design requirement, including hedging. The Chinese juniper is commonly associated with Asian-style gardens, where it is clipped annually into various shapes. This species of juniper is commonly made use of by bonsai enthusiasts. The wood is used for carving and posts.

'Armstrongii': slow-growing, dense spreading shrub to 5 ft. (1.5 m), soft gray-green foliage, variously listed as ×*media* and ×*pfitzeriana*.

'Aurea': golden columnar form, dense and narrow, mixture of prickly juvenile and smooth adult foliage, bright all sea-

*Juniperus chinensis* 'Aurea'

*Juniperus chinensis* 'Armstrongii'

*Juniperus chinensis* 'Blue Alps'

*Juniperus chinensis* 'Blue Point'

*Juniperus chinensis* 'Excelsior'

sons, protect from wind and harsh summer sun, reaches 15 ft. (4.5 m), male.

'Blaauw': vigorous with strongly ascending branches and short outer branches, dense gray-blue adult foliage, reaches 5 ft. (1.5 m), nice for small garden.

'Blue Alps': upright and vigorous spreading shrub with slightly pendulous prickly silvery blue-green foliage, red-brown bark, reaches 20 × 10 ft. (6 × 3 m).

'Blue Point': conical with dense blue-green foliage, grows to 12 ft. (3.6 m) high and 8 ft. (2.5 m) wide, good for hedges.

'Daub's Frosted': low-growing groundcover, two-toned, blue-green frosted with gold, quickly reaches 15 in. (38 cm) by 5 ft. (1.5 m).

'Dropmore': very slow-growing mounding shrub with dense gray-green adult foliage.

'Excelsior': columnar with mixed foliage, female.

*Juniperus chinensis* 'Daub's Frosted'

*Juniperus chinensis* 'Dropmore'

### *Juniperus chinensis* (continued)

'Fairview': narrow pyramid with bright green prickly foliage, vigorous.

'Globosa': slow-growing pale green female form, not actually naturally globose.

'Globosa Cinerea': broadly irregular habit with dense gray-green foliage, possibly identical to 'Shimpaku'.

'Golden Glow': low-growing with bright gold foliage, 3 × 4 ft. (0.9 × 1.2 m).

'Gold Lace': vigorous and spreading with soft feathery bright gold foliage, reaches 2 × 4 ft. (0.6 × 1.2 m), variously listed under ×*pfitzeriana* and ×*media*.

*Juniperus chinensis* 'Fairview'

*Juniperus chinensis* 'Globosa Cinerea'

*Juniperus chinensis* 'Golden Glow'

*Juniperus chinensis* 'Gold Lace'

*Juniperus chinensis* 'Gold Sovereign'

*Juniperus chinensis* 'Gold Star'

*Juniperus chinensis* 'Japonica'

*Juniperus chinensis* 'Kaizuka'

'Gold Sovereign': compact and slow-growing with bright yellow foliage all seasons, reaches up to 20 ft. (6 m) with wider spread.

'Gold Star': compact with prickly golden yellow foliage in full sun, reaches 4 ft. (1.2 m) tall with a 6 ft. (1.8 m) spread.

'Hetz Columnaris': probably the same plant as 'Fairview'.

'Japonica': a dense plant with prickly foliage on a low shrub that will eventually become more upright and develop adult foliage.

'Kaizuka': irregular and upright with upward shoots that twist in various directions, dense mop-like clusters of bright rich green scale-like foliage, violet-blue cones, interesting accent or specimen plant, reaches 20 ft. (6 m), can be trained against a wall, also known as Hollywood juniper and 'Torulosa'.

### *Juniperus chinensis* (continued)

'Keteleeri': vigorous, narrowly pyramidal with upward reaching branches of scale-like blue-green foliage, abundant sizable light green cones even on young plants, useful for hedging and for full-sun, dry, and tough situations, reaches 50 ft. (15 m).

'Kohankie's Compact': compact with blue-green prickly foliage, reaches 4 ft. (1.2 m).

'Maney': a semi-erect vase-shaped shrub form with blue-green prickly foliage, profuse blue cones, reaches 7 × 12 ft. (2 × 3.6 m).

'Mint Julep': spreading plant to 7 ft. (2 m) tall with drooping tips to the branches, bright green (one of the best) mixed foliage, female, sometimes listed as ×*pfitzeriana*.

'Mordigan Aurea': a spreading 3 ft. (0.9 m) high bush with olive-green prickly foliage, also listed under ×*media* and as *Juniperus* ×*pfitzeriana* 'Mordigan Gold'.

*Juniperus chinensis* 'Kohankie's Compact'

*Juniperus chinensis* 'Mint Julep'

*Juniperus chinensis* 'Maney'

'Obelisk': dense, prickly, blue-green narrow column, reaches 8 to 10 ft. (2.5 to 3 m).

'Oblonga': slow-growing to 3 ft. (0.9 m) tall and wide in six years, prickly juvenile foliage, eventually develops adult foliage.

'Old Gold': compact to 3 ft. (0.9 m) high and a bit wider, yellow scale-like foliage in warm season, bronzes in winter, some list as ×*media*.

'Olympia': slender and columnar with blue-green mixed foliage, reaches 10 ft. (3 m).

*Juniperus chinensis* 'Obelisk'

*Juniperus chinensis* 'Old Gold'

*Juniperus chinensis* 'Oblonga'

*Juniperus chinensis* 'Olympia'

### *Juniperus chinensis* (continued)

'Owen': dense and low-growing.

'Parsonsii': spreading and flat-topped, 3 × 9 ft. (0.9 × 2.7 m), dark green with waxy blue cones.

'Plumosa Albovariegata': slow-growing, adult blue-green foliage with splashes of creamy white.

'Plumosa Aurea': flat-topped spreading form in arching sprays of adult foliage, golden yellow in summer, turning bronze in winter.

*Juniperus chinensis* 'Owen'

*Juniperus chinensis* 'Parsonsii'

*Juniperus chinensis* 'Plumosa Albovariegata'

*Juniperus chinensis* 'Plumosa Aurea' in August

*Juniperus chinensis* 'Plumosa Aurea' in February

*Juniperus chinensis* 'Plumosa Tremonia'

*Juniperus chinensis* 'Robust Green'

*Juniperus chinensis* 'San Jose'

*Juniperus chinensis* 'Saybrook Gold'

*Juniperus chinensis* 'Rosefield Perfect'

'Plumosa Tremonia': upright with rich golden yellow foliage.

'Robust Green': broad, informal and craggy, ascending branches with blue-green prickly foliage in dense tufts, produces lots of cones, reaches 15 × 3 ft. (4.5 × 0.9 m).

'Rosefield Perfect': narrow with dense blue-green foliage on erect branches.

'San Jose': low-growing, irregularly spreading, very hardy, gray-green mixed foliage, 12 in. (30 cm) tall, tough.

'Saybrook Gold': low and wide-spreading with center depression, horizontal branches arch slightly and droop at tips, persistent soft bright yellow juvenile foliage, doesn't always age well, 30 in. (75 cm) tall by 6 ft. (1.8 m) wide, also listed as a selection of *Juniperus ×media* or *J. ×pfitzeriana*.

*Juniperus chinensis* 'Sea Spray'

*Juniperus chinensis* 'Shimpaku'

### *Juniperus chinensis* (continued)

'Sea Spray': low and wide-spreading, blue-green soft foliage.

'Shimpaku': vase-shaped, fine-textured with gray-green color, used for bonsai.

'Spartan': fast-growing dense narrow column to 16 ft. (5 m), rich dark green adult foliage, cones well, useful for hedges and screening.

'Stricta': pyramidal, branches ascend to a point, prickly gray-blue foliage.

'Torulosa Variegata': probably the same as 'Variegated Kaizuka'.

'Trautman': compact and slow-growing, narrowly upright with blue-green foliage and abundant blue cones, reaches 12 × 4 ft. (3.6 × 1.2 m).

'Variegated Kaizuka': similar to 'Kaizuka' in habit but slower growing and with creamy yellow variegation.

*Juniperus chinensis* 'Spartan'

*Juniperus chinensis* 'Stricta'

*Juniperus chinensis* 'Trautman'

*Juniperus chinensis* 'Variegated Kaizuka'

### *Juniperus communis*  common juniper  Zones 2 to 6

There is a reason this is called the common juniper. It is found across the northern hemisphere from North America through Europe and Asia to Japan and Korea. It is one of only three conifers native to Great Britain. It is found in every possible site, from high and dry and alkaline to marshy and acid. This species sometimes is a small tree but more often is a large shrubby plant with a flat top. It typically has a rather slow growth rate. Its entirely juvenile awl-shaped needled (prickly) foliage is very stiff and in whorls of three with a blue-white strip on the upper surface. The needles always grow straight out from the stem, never embracing it as in some other species. The fleshy seed-bearing cones are twice the size of *Juniperus virginiana* and are often used in the production of gin. Garden selections like full sun and will tolerate windy conditions. They will also thrive in poor, rocky soils. Many dwarf forms exist with variations of foliage color. There are many "varieties" of this species listed in the literature; sorting it out is disturbing for the botanist not to mention an encyclopedia compiler. There are around 105 cultivars. Note that this species is not tolerant of heat.

The wood of the common juniper has been used to produce charcoal and to smoke meat. The "berries" are used to flavor game and gin.

'Anna Maria': foliage pale green, reaches 6 × 4 ft. (1.8 × 1.2 m) in ten years.

'Arnold': a dense narrow column, silver-green foliage.

'Berkshire': slow-growing little bun, prickly dark green foliage with striking silver white bands, which give it a gray-green to blue-green appearance, bronzes in winter, to 1 ft. (0.3 m) tall.

*Juniperus communis* 'Arnold'

*Juniperus communis* bonsai 240 years old

*Juniperus communis* 'Anna Maria'

*Juniperus communis* 'Berkshire'

## *Juniperus communis* (continued)

'Compressa': slow-growing narrow upright dwarf, cone-shaped without shearing, fine-textured silvery blue-green foliage, grows 2 in. (5 cm) a year to 3 ft. (0.9 m).

var. *depressa*: vigorous and tough, grows 4 ft. (1.2 m) tall and 12 ft. (3.6 m) broad, gray-green, browns in winter, tolerates poor soil, native to the eastern United States and Canada.

'Depressa Aurea': yellow spring foliage fades to green, vigorous and tough, broad-spreading to 4 ft. (1.2 m) high.

'Echiniformis': tiny, tight, prickly foliage in soft-appearing mounds, very slow-growing, syn. 'Hemispherica', sometimes listed as *J. chinensis*, also known as hedgehog juniper.

'Effusa': low mounded carpeting mat of soft overlapping branches, forms a wide-spreading circle, shade-tolerant, pale brown new growth matures to blue-green, 1 × 6 ft. (0.3 × 1.8 m).

'Gold Cone': slow-growing narrow and columnar shrub or small tree, dense foliage, golden in summer, yellow-green in winter, protect from sun and wind.

*Juniperus communis* 'Compressa'

*Juniperus communis* 'Gold Cone'

*Juniperus communis* var. *depressa*

*Juniperus communis* 'Depressa Aurea'

*Juniperus communis* 'Effusa'

---

---

---

---

---

*Juniperus communis* 'Green Carpet' grown as standard

*Juniperus communis* 'Hornibrookii'

*Juniperus communis* 'Horstmann'

*Juniperus communis* 'Haverbeck'

'Green Carpet': a slow-growing prostrate mat of bright green juvenile foliage, hardy and adaptable, ideal for slopes, rock gardens, or troughs.

'Greenmantle': ground-hugging, dense rich green foliage, grows 2 in. (5 cm) a year.

'Haverbeck': dense blue-gray mixed foliage, reaches 1 ft. (0.3 m) in eight years.

'Hibernica': pillar-shaped with dense and compact vertical branches to 25 ft. (8 m) high, pale green needles with silver band on upper surface produces a blue-green effect, protect from wind and heavy snow, also known as Irish juniper.

'Hornibrookii': spreading and ground-hugging, prickly green needles are silver below, true plant is slow-growing and male but various forms are found in the trade.

'Horstmann': spreading and irregular with prickly pendulous blue-green foliage, grows up to 12 in. (30 cm) a year, accepts pruning.

*Juniperus communis* 'Miniatur' with *J. c.* 'Green Carpet'

*Juniperus communis* 'Oblonga Pendula'

*Juniperus communis* 'Nana Aurea'

### *Juniperus communis* (continued)

'Miniatur': slow-growing and upright.

'Nana Aurea': ground-hugging with drooping branches, mixed foliage, yellow beneath all seasons.

'Oblonga Pendula': upright wide bush to 11 ft. (3.4 m), horizontal branches with pendulous tips, mixed foliage.

'Pencil Point': pillar-shaped, tight light green foliage with silver bands giving a blue-green appearance, probably same as 'Sentinel'.

*Juniperus communis* 'Pencil Point'

*Juniperus communis* 'Prostrata'

'Prostrata': ground-hugging form, reaches 1 ft. (0.3 m) by 4 to 6 ft. (1.2 to 1.8 m).

'Repanda': vigorous creeping form, sets new roots as it scrambles and forms a uniform circle, tips of branches nod, soft dark green foliage in summer, bronzy in winter, 15 in. (38 cm) high and 8 ft. (2.5 m) wide.

'Schneverdingen Goldmachangel': slow-growing, broad and open, pendulous gold-tipped branches, also called 'Golden Showers'.

'Sentinel': upright and columnar, almost pointed without shearing, blue-green foliage, reaches 5 ft. (1.5 m).

'Sieben Steinhäuser': slow-growing and upright with blue foliage.

'Tage Lundell': columnar dwarf with yellow variegation, to 3 ft. (0.9 m) in ten years.

'Vase': vigorous, prickly foliage turns chocolate-brown in winter, avoid harsh winds.

*Juniperus communis* 'Sentinel'

*Juniperus communis* 'Sieben Steinhäuser'

*Juniperus communis* 'Tage Lundell'

*Juniperus communis* 'Vase'

### *Juniper conferta*   shore juniper
Zones 5 to 9

The shore juniper is native to the sea-sides of Japan. This slow-growing but generally vigorous species is most often used as a groundcover for sunny, well-drained or sandy seaside conditions. It will tolerate poor soil but not moist soil. It is salt-tolerant. The foliage is needle-like, soft, but sharp-tipped and deeply grooved, with a white band above. It is usually a bushy, procumbent shrub that spreads across the ground with the tips of the advancing growth pointing upward. The seed-bearing cones are spherical, about ½ in. (1.2 cm) round, silvery or blue-black, with a waxy bloom. Many of the cultivars are useful for container or rock gardens.

'Blue Lagoon': dense spreading mat with prickly foliage, green needles with blue overtones, single white band on each needle, turns plum in winter, 1 × 9 ft. (0.3 × 2.7 m).

'Blue Pacific': spreading mat with prickly foliage, green with blue and silver overtones, does not bronze in winter, also listed as a selection of *Juniperus rigida* subsp. *conferta*.

'Blue Tosho': same as 'Silver Mist'.

'Silver Mist': salt-tolerant prostrate form with densely growing intensely silvery blue prickly foliage.

'Sunsplash': prostrate groundcover, blue-green foliage with bright yellow patches in all seasons, 5 ft. (1.5 m) wide in three years, sometimes labeled 'Variegata'.

*Juniperus conferta* 'Blue Lagoon'

*Juniperus conferta* 'Blue Lagoon' foliage

*Juniperus conferta* 'Blue Pacific'

*Juniperus conferta* 'Silver Mist'

*Juniperus conferta* 'Sunsplash'

### *Juniperus davurica*
daurian juniper
Zones 6 to 9

The daurian juniper is native to eastern Asia. It is usually a spreading shrub with adult and juvenile foliage on thick ascending branches. Grow in full sun. It is drought-tolerant and has a very high salt tolerance. The species is seldom grown, but several cultivars are used as groundcovers and for bonsai. Some sources list the following cultivars as *Juniperus chinensis*.

'Expansa': fast-growing groundcover, gray-green foliage on rigid horizontal branches, reaches 2 to 3 ft. (0.6 to 0.9 m) by 4 to 7 ft. (1.2 to 2 m).

'Expansa Aureospicata': prickly foliage with butter-yellow variegation.

'Expansa Variegata': rich blue-green mixed foliage with splashes of white on mounding, low-spreading form.

*Juniperus davurica* 'Expansa'

*Juniperus davurica* 'Expansa Aureospicata'

*Juniperus davurica* 'Expansa Variegata'

### *Juniperus deppeana*   alligator juniper
Zones (6)7 to 9

Since it is native to the southwestern United States and northern Mexico, this species does well in hot, dry situations and sometimes suffers in colder areas. The adult foliage is tightly appressed to the stem, forming a four-sided branchlet. Some selections are bushy, and others upright and columnar. In its native habitat this species will reach 60 ft. (18 m). Preferring full sun, the alligator juniper will tolerate both limestone soils and moderately heavy soils. Like most junipers, it will not do well in poorly drained, wet soils. The common name derives from the appearance of the bark on mature specimens. Many display the brightest silver or blue foliage of any juniper.

'Davis Mountain Weeping': a small cone-shaped tree with deeply furrowed red-brown bark, pendulous habit, can be trained into a cascading specimen.

*Juniperus deppeana* 'Davis Mountain Weeping'

### *Juniperus horizontalis*   creeping juniper
Zones 4 to 9

The creeping juniper is native to the North American continent from Newfoundland to Alaska, and south to Wyoming, Nebraska, northern Illinois, and northern New York. It is common in the Adirondacks in open, dry, sandy, and rocky habitats. Most selections of this species are prostrate. They are hardy enough to grow in areas as different as the seashore and mountain slopes. They typically have long main branches with many short, dense branchlets. The leaves on the cultivated forms are mainly needle-shaped, often in whorls of three, green or blue-green, and frequently turn mauve in the winter. The soft adult foliage can be found on older growth. Many are slow-growing at first but become vigorous groundcovers useful for massing. They tolerate all types of soil but, typical of junipers, prefer full sun and good drainage. There are many more cultivars of this species in the catalogs than actually needed.

'Bar Harbor': dense mat of soft steel-blue scale-like foliage, turns a delicate mauve-purple in winter, branches spread and root in all directions with ascending tips, tolerates salt spray, does not cone.

'Blue Chip': a dense mounded carpet of soft and feathery bright silver blue-green foliage all seasons, reaches 10 in. (25 cm) by 6 ft. (1.8 m).

'Blue Forest': upward-turning branch tips make it look like a miniature forest, blue-green foliage in summer, almost blue-purple in winter, spreading form to 18 in. (46 cm) tall.

*Juniperus horizontalis* 'Bar Harbor'

*Juniperus horizontalis* 'Blue Chip'

*Juniperus horizontalis* 'Blue Horizon' in October

'Blue Horizon': low-growing creeping plant, does not mound up, blue-green, bronzing in winter, male.

'Blue Prince': ground-hugging form with blue needles, reaches 6 in. (15 cm) by 5 ft. (1.5 m).

'Blue Rug': one of the best ground-hugging forms, scale-like foliage, glaucous blue maintained throughout the year, female, also listed as 'Wiltonii'.

'Douglasii': wide-spreading and low-growing with mixed foliage, gray-green in summer, bronzed in cold weather, very small needles clasp the stem on semi-erect branchlets, useful in dune gardens, also known as Waukegan juniper.

'Glauca': ground-hugging with long straight branches, steel-blue adult foliage, possibly just a European version of 'Bar Harbor'.

*Juniperus horizontalis* 'Blue Prince'

*Juniperus horizontalis* 'Blue Rug'

*Juniperus horizontalis* 'Douglasii'

*Juniperus horizontalis* 'Glauca'

### *Juniperus horizontalis* (continued)

'Golden Carpet': prostrate with greenish yellow foliage.

'Green Acres': trailing and dense with dark green foliage all seasons.

'Grey Pearl': dense shrub with upright branches to 1 ft. (0.3 m), gray-green foliage, gradually becomes wider than high.

'Hughes': vigorous, low-growing and wide-spreading with ascending branches, blue-green, turns slightly purple in winter, 1 × 7 ft. (0.3 × 2 m) in ten years.

'Icee Blue': the name says it all, reaches 4 in. (10 cm) by 8 ft. (2.5 m).

*Juniperus horizontalis* 'Golden Carpet'

*Juniperus horizontalis* 'Green Acres'

*Juniperus horizontalis* 'Grey Pearl'

*Juniperus horizontalis* 'Hughes'

*Juniperus horizontalis* 'Icee Blue'

*Juniperus horizontalis* 'Limeglow'

'Limeglow': billowy foliage with brilliant chartreuse color even in hot summers.

'Mother Lode': brilliant gold in summer turning to shades of deep gold and salmon-orange with green overtones in winter, provide full sun with good drainage, very slow-growing, similar to 'Golden Carpet'.

'Planifolia': rapidly growing, dense and low to 10 in. (25 cm), silver-blue needle foliage.

'Plumosa': vigorous flat-topped spreading shrub, branches radiate from center of plant, dense prickly foliage gray-green in summer, bronze-purple in winter, to 20 in. (50 cm) high, also known as Andorra juniper.

'Prince of Wales': low-growing and broad-spreading, dense, soft-appearing bright green foliage with a hint of blue, 4 to 6 in. (10 to 15 cm) high.

*Juniperus horizontalis* 'Mother Lode'

*Juniperus horizontalis* 'Planifolia'

*Juniperus horizontalis* 'Plumosa'

*Juniperus horizontalis* 'Prince of Wales'

*Juniperus horizontalis* 'Prostrata' bonsai

*Juniperus horizontalis* 'Webber'

## *Juniperus horizontalis* (continued)

'Prostrata': dense blue-gray mat, 12 in. (30 cm) high.

'Venusta': ground-hugging, dense dark blue-gray summer foliage, turns plum-purple in cold weather, spreads 6 to 8 ft. (1.8 to 2.5 m) wide but under 1 ft. (0.3 m) high, similar to 'Wiltonii'.

'Webber': low and spreading, glaucous green.

'Wiltonii': slow-growing, ground-hugging, glaucous blue scale-like foliage on long branches, color maintained throughout the year, produces cones, 6 in. (15 cm) tall by 6 ft. (1.8 m), also known as 'Blue Rug'.

'Youngstown': groundcover with tightly knit branches that turn up at a 45° angle, takes limited shade, bronzes in winter.

*Juniperus horizontalis* 'Venusta'

*Juniperus horizontalis* 'Wiltonii'

## *Juniperus* ×*pfitzeriana*  Pfitzer juniper  Zones 4 to 9

The Pfitzer junipers are considered by most authorities to be hybrids between *Juniperus chinensis* and *J. sabina*. A good number of *J.* ×*pfitzeriana* are listed as *J. chinensis* in the United States and as *J.* ×*media* in Europe; however, despite widespread use the label ×*media* has not been unanimously accepted. Most of the selections in this group of junipers are groundcovers or spreading and shrub-sized. They usually have both prickly juvenile and soft adult scale-like foliage. These hardy plants will tolerate most any soil condition in heat and cold as long as they are provided good drainage. Colors vary from green to blue to silver to yellow and variegated. The following cultivars are correctly identified ×*pfitzeriana*. Additional studies will no doubt be done to confirm the relationships of other cultivars alleged to be in the Pfitzer group.

'Fruitlandii': vigorous spreading groundcover, coarse, dense green foliage, reaches 24 in. (60 cm).

'Gold Coast': fast-growing, semi-prostrate, flat-topped, and wide-spreading, bright yellow adult foliage holds color in winter.

'Hetzii': branches extend up and out of this bushy selection, easy to train, tough, gray-blue adult foliage through the seasons.

'Kallay's Compact': flat-topped globe, deep green prickly foliage.

'Pfitzeriana Glauca': wide-spreading with gray-blue prickly foliage.

'Wilhelm Pfitzer': wide-spreading shrub, ascending branches with pendulous tips, juvenile and adult green foliage, widely planted.

*Juniperus* ×*pfitzeriana* 'Fruitlandii'

*Juniperus* ×*pfitzeriana* 'Gold Coast'

*Juniperus* ×*pfitzeriana* 'Kallay's Compact'

*Juniperus* ×*pfitzeriana* 'Pfitzeriana Glauca'

### *Juniperus pingii* ping juniper
Zone 7

The ping juniper is native to China. It is a broadly pyramidal, graceful, semi-weeping tree with pendulous branch tips. The foliage is light green. It reaches 7 ft. (2 m) in ten years and eventually 20 ft. (6 m). It is usually found only in collections. The species is closely related to *Juniperus squamata*.

### *Juniperus procumbens*
garden juniper   Zones 4 to 8(9)

This popular and useful species of juniper for garden use is native to Japan. It slowly forms a mat of layered foliage, growing to 1 ft. (0.3 m) tall and up to 8 ft. (2.5 m) wide. The stiff branches turn upward at the ends. The very prickly foliage is a pale green (the white bands on the needles makes it look slightly bluish in some light) in all seasons. The species is never found, but the cultivar 'Nana' is widely planted and a good choice. It is a compact mat with layered branches that vary in length. The needle-like foliage is very prickly and remains distinctly blue-green in all seasons. This is an ideal conifer for placing at the top of a low stone wall or at the corner of steps to soften sharp corners. It is often used for bonsai.

*Juniperus pingii*

*Juniperus procumbens* 'Nana'

*Juniperus procumbens* 'Nana' foliage

*Juniperus procumbens* 'Nana' bonsai

*Juniperus rigida* 'Pendula'

## *Juniperus rigida*   needle juniper
Zones 6 and 7

The needle juniper is native to China, Korea, and Japan. This large shrub or small tree, to 20 ft. (6 m), has a broad and irregular habit. The sharply pointed needles are in threes, ½ to 1 in. (1.2 to 2.5 cm), and displayed on softly pendulous branches. The ¼ in. (0.6 cm) cones are brown-black. This species will tolerate hot, dry conditions. It is too open-growing to use as a screen.

'Pendula': downswept branches with straight branchlets, possibly no different from the species.

*Juniperus rigida* 'Pendula' foliage

## *Juniperus sabina*   savin juniper
Zones 3 to 7

The savin juniper is widely distributed in the mountains of southern and central Europe to the Caucasus. It is a variable species; most selections are low and spreading shrubs to 6 ft. (1.8 m) high and 10 ft. (3 m) wide. Plants can have both scale-like and needle-like foliage that has an unpleasant odor when crushed. The small cones are blue-black. This juniper usually does not turn bronze in winter. Although not a very ornamental species, the cultivars would be particularly useful for gardens in colder climates.

'Broadmor': dense and low-spreading, blue-green, reaches 3 × 10 ft. (0.9 × 3 m).

'Fastigiata' dense, columnar with ascending branches, dark green.

'Monard': flat and wide-spreading, tiered branches, 1 × 6 ft. (0.3 × 1.8 m).

'Skandia': soft deep green foliage, tolerates some shade, 1 × 10 ft. (0.3 × 3 m).

'Von Ehren': vase-shaped, reaches 5 ft. (1.5 m) tall and wide.

*Juniperus sabina*

*Juniperus sabina* 'Broadmor'

*Juniperus sabina* 'Fastigiata'

*Juniperus sabina* 'Monard'

*Juniperus sabina* 'Skandia'

*Juniperus scopulorum* 'Blue Arrow'

## *Juniperus scopulorum*   Rocky Mountain juniper
### Zones 3 to 7

The Rocky Mountain juniper is native from British Columbia and Alberta south to Texas. It is the most widespread juniper in western North America. It typically grows at elevations of 5,000 ft. (1,500 m) but can also be found near sea level. It is usually seen as a columnar tree up to 50 ft. (15 m) tall but is often a ragged little shrub on poor sites. It is a hardy species that prefers good drainage in sunny situations with dry air and is often seen on dry rocky ridges or sandy soils (the Latin *scopulus* means "cliff" or "rock"). It needs only 10 in. (25 cm) of rainfall annually. It is slow-growing and can live hundreds of years. The foliage is scale-like except in saplings, which will have awl-like foliage. Some selections have an arresting silver-blue appearance. The foliage is pungent when crushed. The branches can be spreading, ascending and/or drooping. The bark is thin, red or gray, and shreds in long strips. The wood is close-grained and very aromatic, like the eastern *Juniperus virginiana*. Unlike other junipers, this species is monoecious, with male and female cones on the same plant. Cones can persist for several years. There are over 100 cultivars.

'Blue Arrow': compact small tree with a narrow upright habit, 12 to 15 ft. (3.6 to 4.5 m) tall by 2 ft. (0.6 m) wide, blue-gray, similar to 'Skyrocket' but not quite as blue.

'Blue Heaven': erect column, compact rough adult foliage, silver-blue in warm seasons, blue-green in colder, to 6 ft. (1.8 m).

'Candelabra': upright weeper with silver-blue foliage.

'Moffetii': dense conical tree with coarse silver-green foliage.

*Juniperus scopulorum* 'Candelabra'

*Juniperus scopulorum* 'Moffetii'

### *Juniperus scopulorum* (continued)

'Pathfinder': narrowly pyramidal, blue-green in all seasons, foliage in flat sprays, reaches 20 × 8 ft. (6 × 2.5 m).

'Silver King': a wide-spreading 2 ft. (0.6 m) high groundcover with silver-green foliage all seasons.

'Skyrocket': very narrow, 15 × 2 ft. (4.5 × 0.6 m), blue-green, darkens in winter, use as a vertical accent or in a formal design, male, does not age well.

'Sparkling Skyrocket': similar but with scattered variegation and slower growing.

'Tolleson's Weeping': broad conical tree with pendulous branchlets, silver-gray, reaches 20 ft. (6 m).

'Wichita Blue': loose and irregular open pyramidal habit with ascending branches, intense silver-blue foliage all year, male, 12 × 6 ft. (3.6 × 1.8 m).

*Juniperus scopulorum* 'Sparkling Skyrocket'

*Juniperus scopulorum* 'Tolleson's Weeping'

*Juniperus scopulorum* 'Pathfinder'

*Juniperus scopulorum* 'Wichita Blue'

*Juniperus squamata* 'Blue Carpet'

*Juniperus squamata* 'Blue Carpet' foliage

*Juniperus squamata* 'Blue Pearl'

*Juniperus squamata* 'Blue Star'

### *Juniperus squamata*  flaky juniper  Zones 4 to 7

This species is not usually found in designed landscapes. It is more important for the characteristics it has passed on to its cultivars, some of which are the most popular conifers used in gardens today. *Juniperus squamata* is found in higher elevations in Afghanistan and east to central China. Quite variable in nature but usually shrub-sized, it is a drought-tolerant and resilient plant. The selections have needle-like foliage, and some a concentrated blue coloration. It usually displays nodding tips to the shoots. The cones are fleshy and glossy black and contain only a single seed (another common name is singleseed juniper). The reddish brown bark is scaly. There are a dozen or more cultivars.

'Blue Carpet': fast-growing horizontal sprays reach only 12 in. (30 cm) high but 6 ft. (1.8 m) wide, silver-blue turning gray-green in winter, easy to grow.

'Blue Pearl': dwarf cushion of prickly foliage less than 12 in. (30 cm) high, sometimes listed as *horizontalis*.

'Blue Star': irregular slow-growing mound of dense blue foliage changing to a purplish heather-blue in winter, does best in full sun, to 16 in. (40 cm) high, sometimes grafted on standards.

*Juniperus squamata* 'Dream Joy'

*Juniperus squamata* 'Holger'

### *Juniperus squamata* (continued)

'Dream Joy': dwarf, upright, spreading, foliage sulphur-yellow in warm season, grows 4 to 6 in. (10 to 15 cm) a year.

'Holger': dense and wide-spreading with sharply pointed pale yellow new foliage, turns gray-green in summer, reaches 3 × 4 ft. (0.9 × 1.2 m).

'Meyeri': upright branches arch out every which way with drooping tips, up to 20 ft. (6 m) tall, dense, prickly silver-blue foliage, slightly off-color in winter, beautiful when well grown and given renewal pruning.

'Prostrata': slow-growing, tips of branches droop.

'Wilsonii': spreading vase shape, silver gray-green foliage, slow-growing to 4 ft. (1.2 m) tall and wide in ten years.

*Juniperus squamata* 'Prostrata'

*Juniperus squamata* 'Wilsonii'

## *Juniperus virginiana* eastern red-cedar Zones 3 to 9

This is the most widespread of all the native conifers in the eastern United States. It is found from Nova Scotia to northern Florida and west to the Dakotas and Texas. Although commonly referred to as eastern red-cedar, the tree is really a juniper and not a true cedar. It will grow slowly to 20 to 50 ft. (6 to 15 m) in height. Younger trees are often narrow and columnar, but with age the species becomes rounder and irregular. It is found on hillsides and in abandoned fields, along roadsides, or in any dry, rocky situation. An undisturbed specimen can live 300 years. The adult foliage is mostly scale-like, but younger plants will have juvenile foliage as will the shadier and inner sections of mature specimens. On normal shoots, the scale-like blunt-tipped leaves are opposite, held at a 90° angle to one another, and four-ranked, closely appressed to the branchlet, dark bluish green, and persisting for a half-dozen years. The juvenile leaves are found on vigorous shoots and shady interior areas. They are ¼ to ½ in. (0.6 to 1.2 cm) long, sharply pointed and awl-shaped. They are primarily in pairs. The pollen-bearing cones, ⅛ to ¼ in. (0.3 to 0.6 cm) long and yellowish, appear terminally in early spring. The seed-bearing cones on different trees are ¼ in. (0.6 cm) in diameter, fleshy like a berry with a firm, waxy skin and sweet-tasting flesh. They mature in two to three years and contain one or two seeds. They smell like gin when crushed. The cones are pale green at first and mature to a dark blue and are covered with a whitish bloom. Trees begin producing cones at 10 to 15 years of age. The bark is light reddish brown and exfoliates in long narrow strips. The trunk is often buttressed and fluted at the base.

This species is not finicky about soil quality but will grow best in full sun with good drainage. This tough tree will tolerate drought, heat, and cold and difficult site situations where other conifers will struggle. It is especially valuable for gardeners in the Midwest and Plains states. Among the many cultivars are some that provide abundant blue seed-bearing cones. The species tends to bronze in the winter, so selection has been made for cultivars that stay green all year. Both upright and semi-prostrate forms can be had.

The wood is extremely durable in contact with the soil and has traditionally been used for fence posts and outdoor structures. The pungent deep red heartwood is easy to work with and is used for

*Juniperus virginiana* growing in old pasture

## *Juniperus virginiana* (continued)

making moth-proof chests for garment storage, interior paneling for spas, and pencils. Cedar oil, a component of popular furniture polishes, is extracted from the foliage and wood. Many birds feast on the berry-like cones during the winter, notably the cedar waxwing, which is named after this "cedar." The seed is dispersed by the birds everywhere.

As an ornamental plant, *Juniperus virginiana* is especially useful for very dry, full-sun locations. A tough plant. There are 85 cultivars.

Cedar-apple rust (*Gymnosporangium juniperi-virginianae*) is a fungal disease that spends part of its life cycle on the eastern red-cedar and another part on apple or hawthorn trees. Both hosts are necessary for the survival of the fungus and can be up to 5 miles (8.3 km) apart. The disease can cause defoliation of the apple and hawthorn species in periods of drought. Galls as large as golfballs are formed on the juniper host during the second year of the complicated cycle, causing small twig and tip dieback. One should select species, particularly crabapples, that are resistant to rust diseases. Resistant *Juniperus virginiana* cultivars include 'Burkii', 'Globosa', and 'Kosteri'. *Juniperus virginiana* can also be troubled with scale (see the discussion at *Thuja*).

'Blue Arrow': narrow and upright, retains lower branches, deep blue.

*Juniperus virginiana* juvenile foliage

*Juniperus virginiana* adult foliage and seed-bearing cones

*Juniperus virginiana* bark

*Juniperus virginiana* winter color

Outdoor structure made from *Juniperus virginiana*

*Juniperus virginiana* 'Blue Arrow'

*Juniperus virginiana* 'Burkii' in August

*Juniperus virginiana* 'Burkii' in March

'Burkii': columnar with a straight stem and ascending branches, dense blue-green mixed foliage, bronzes in winter.

'Canaertii': upright, eventually opens up, dense dark green foliage all seasons, tufted at the ends of the branches, abundant blue cones.

'Corcorcor': narrow and conical, remains a rich green all seasons, rapid growing, sturdy and dependable, reaches 25 to 30 ft. (8 to 9 m), also called 'Emerald Sentinel'.

*Juniperus virginiana* 'Canaertii' foliage and cones

*Juniperus virginiana* 'Canaertii'

*Juniperus virginiana* 'Corcorcor'

### *Juniperus virginiana* (continued)

'Essex Weeping': a weeping form that spreads along the ground but can be staked while young to desired height.

'Fastigiata': narrow columnar form with ascending branches, blue-green adult foliage.

f. *glauca*: narrow and columnar, silver-blue in spring, silver-green in summer, reaches 25 ft. (8 m).

'Globosa': dwarf rounded shrub to 5 ft. (1.5 m), bright green in summer, dulls in winter.

'Grey Owl': soft dusty silver-gray foliage and abundant silver-gray cones, grows slowly into a wide-spreading shrub 3 ft. (0.9 m) tall by 6 ft. (1.8 m) wide. Exceptional.

*Juniperus virginiana* 'Globosa'

*Juniperus virginiana* 'Grey Owl' foliage and cones

*Juniperus virginiana* 'Essex Weeping'

*Juniperus virginiana* f. *glauca*

*Juniperus virginiana* 'Grey Owl'

'Helle': dense column, deep green all seasons, reaches 8 to 12 ft. (2.5 to 3.6 m) in 15 years, possibly same as *Juniperus chinensis* 'Spartan'.

'Hillii': compact narrow column to 20 ft. (6 m) tall with silver-blue foliage, also called 'Hill's Silver'.

'Hillspire': upright conical habit, bright green foliage all seasons on densely packed branches, male, can reach 30 ft. (9 m).

'Kosteri': compact 4 ft. (1.2 m) tall but can spread to 30 ft. (9 m) wide in time, gray-blue foliage bronzes in winter.

'Manhattan Blue': compact, conical blue-green foliage, male, similar to 'Glauca'.

*Juniperus virginiana* 'Helle'

*Juniperus virginiana* 'Hillspire'

*Juniperus virginiana* 'Kosteri'

### *Juniperus virginiana* (continued)

'Nana Compacta': irregular rounded dwarf to 3 ft. (0.9 m), blue-green, bronzes in winter.

'Nova': columnar form with blue-green foliage, purplish in winter.

'Pendula': small tree with arching branches and drooping branchlets, mostly prickly needles, will reach 40 ft. (12 m), name is applied to many pendulous forms.

'Prostrata': name applied to various low-spreading forms.

'Pseudocupressus': narrow and columnar, branches erect along the stem to slender point, juvenile blue-green foliage, reaches 40 ft. (12 m).

*Juniperus virginiana* 'Nana Compacta'

*Juniperus virginiana* 'Nova'

*Juniperus virginiana* 'Pendula'

*Juniperus virginiana* 'Pseudocupressus'

*Juniperus virginiana* 'Royo'

*Juniperus virginiana* 'Silver Spreader'

*Juniperus virginiana* 'Woodlander's Weeping'

'Royo': spreading form with lacy silver foliage.

'Silver Spreader': low ground-covering shrub, bright silver-gray in summer, more gray-green in winter, thick and coarse foliage, undemanding.

'Woodlander's Weeping': markedly pendulous, prickly needles stay green year-round, male, benefits from staking in youth, can reach 12 ft. (3.6 m) tall and 8 ft. (2.5 m) wide.

## *Larix* larch

The larch (along with the dawn redwood, bald-cypress, ginkgo, and golden-larch) is another deciduous conifer, one that drops its foliage each winter. There are about ten species of larch in the colder sections of the northern hemisphere. They are widely distributed across North America, Asia, and Europe with fossil records that go back millions of years. Three are native to North America. They occur in every province and territory of Canada. Most are more important in forestry than as ornamental plants. Larches can be found growing from lowland habitats to subalpine conditions. Although the various species have many similarities in appearance to the casual observer, they differ in their cultural requirements and plant communities as well as in the details of their cones and needles. Still, some authorities disagree about the divisions of *Larix* species and subspecies. Most are rather fast-growing to heights of 100 ft. (30 m) and are too large for the average garden. Larches usually grow with one central trunk. Their branches are often pendulous with clusters of needles held on short shoots called spurs. Each of these clusters hold many needles, and the needles are of differing lengths. New shoots will have needles spiraling singly around the stem. The needles are generally an appealing lime-green in early spring and turn a luminous gold in the autumn. The small pollen-bearing cones are yellow and often appear on bare stems. The seed-bearing cones appear in early spring and are vibrantly colored; they ripen in one year and are held upright on the stem. The dark-colored mature cones of larches are often held on the tree for years. Full sun is recommended for all species.

The genus *Larix* is easy to recognize, but the various species are difficult to sort out and some are jumbled in the trade.

The species can be differentiated by cone characteristics. The European and Japanese larch cones are about the same size, 1 to 1½ in. (2.5 to 3.5 cm) long, but the cone scales of the Japanese larch are reflexed. The American larch cones are only ½ in. (1.2 cm) long. The foliage of larches looks a bit like that of *Cedrus*; but *Cedrus* needles are unkind to the touch and those of *Larix* are soft. Of course, the cones are completely different.

The great attraction of larches to the gardener is their light green foliage in the growing season, their golden flash of fall color, and, in some cases, their austere winter habit. Several of the larches

*Larix decidua*

are valued for their wood, which is strong, heavy, and durable. A number of *Larix* cultivars are suitable for the designed landscape.

The larch casebearer (*Coleophora laricella*), an insect from Europe, infects all species of larch in the United States. This pest eats the inside tissue of needles and causes defoliation. They live in cases made from sections of hollowed-out needles during part of their life cycle. It is the spring feeding on the new foliage that causes the most damage. Since larches are deciduous, they can tolerate repeated defoliations but eventually branch tips and entire branches will die. The pest is weakened by late frosts and is eaten by various insects, spiders, and birds. Several insect parasites have been introduced to reduce casebearer populations.

### *Larix decidua*  European larch
Zones 3 to 6(7)

The European larch is native to Europe east to Siberia. It is the only deciduous conifer native in Europe. This rapidly growing and very hardy tree is much planted in eastern North America for timber and occasionally as a specimen. It has a conical habit up to 75 ft. (23 m) tall with branches held horizontally but drooping at the tips. The twigs display short shoots that are brown-black with rings from each year's growth. The ½ to 1½ in. (1.2 to 3.5 cm) long needles are in 30- to 40-needle whorls on short spurs but held singly on tip growth. The needles are of unequal length, bright green when young, deeper green in summer, and turning mustard-yellow in autumn.

The pollen-bearing cones are rounded and yellow, appearing in spring. The seed-bearing cones are 1 to 1½ in. (2.5 to 3.5 cm) long with numerous scales that are rounded and not reflexed. They are stalkless with pubescent scales, mature reddish brown, and persist on the tree. The bark is red-brown and platy.

*Larix decidua* is adapted to much drier habitats than other larches. It will tolerate poor soil but not pollution. In the wild it is often found in wet areas. It demands full sun. One would grow this as a specimen in a large landscape to admire its beautiful pristine pale green spring foliage and lustrous gold fall dis-play. It is an important tree for reforestation. The durable wood is used for posts, shipbuilding, and general construction.

*Larix decidua* bark

*Larix decidua* foliage and seed-bearing cones through the seasons

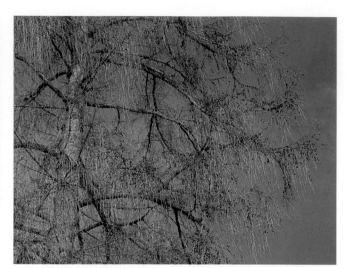

*Larix decidua* in winter

*Larix decidua* fall foliage

*Larix decidua* tailored

*Larix decidua* trimmed as hedge

*Larix decidua* 'Horstmann Recurved' foliage

*Larix decidua* 'Horstmann Recurved'

*Larix decidua* 'Krejci'

*Larix decidua* 'Julian's Weeper' in October

### Larix decidua (continued)

'Corley': slow-growing, low, leaderless, and densely branched in all directions, good golden autumn color, 2 × 12 ft. (0.6 × 3.6 m) after ten years.

'Horstmann Recurved': twisted and contorted branches on irregularly shaped tree, bright green in spring turning gold in autumn, reaches 7 ft. (2 m) in ten years.

'Julian's Weeper': pendulous, should be staked, some say the same as *Larix kaempferi* 'Pendula'.

'Krejci': not vigorous, slow-growing, conical, also listed as 'Krejcy' and often as a selection of *Larix kaempferi*.

'Little Bogle': mounding and spreading with a tiered pendulous habit, bright green turning golden brown in fall, reaches 4 × 3 ft. (1.2 × 0.9 m) in ten years.

### *Larix decidua* (continued)

'Pendula': fast growth, variable from wide-spreading to narrow, needs staking or could be used as a groundcover. Many specimens in the trade are actually *Larix kaempferi* 'Pendula'.

'Pesck': vigorous bushy dwarf.

'Polonica': tree form if staked with drooping branchlets, rare, found only in arboretums, reaches 12 × 4 ft. (3.6 × 1.2 m) in ten years, perhaps should be var. or subsp. *polonica*.

'Steinplatte': grows about 4 in. (10 cm) a year.

'Varied Directions': wider than tall, branches go out and up from this vigorous spreading plant, then arch down and cover the ground, sometimes grafted as a high standard, also listed as *Larix ×eurolepis* or *L. sibirica*, or said to be a hybrid between *L. decidua* and *L. kaempferi*.

*Larix decidua* 'Pesek'

*Larix decidua* 'Pendula'

*Larix decidua* 'Steinplatte'

*Larix decidua* 'Varied Directions'

## *Larix kaempferi*  Japanese larch
### Zones 4 to 7

The Japanese larch is native to Honshu. It is similar to *Larix decidua* except the needles have two distinct longitudinal bands on the bottom, young branches are glaucous, and the cones have reflexed cone scales.

It is a strong-growing, large tree, 70 to 90 ft. (21 to 27 m) tall and 25 to 40 ft. (8 to 12 m) wide with a straight trunk. It can be narrow and conical or wide-spreading with long horizontal branches and slender pendulous branchlets. The pale green ½ to 1¾ in. (1.2 to 4.5 cm) long needles are in tufts of 40 to 50. The pollen-bearing cones are dark red-brown in clusters. The seed-bearing cones are egg-shaped on short stalks, ¾ to 1¼ in. (2 to 3 cm) long. The upper edges of the cone scales are rolled back, giving a rosette-like appearance. The fall foliage color is golden (not just yellow). It has

*Larix kaempferi*

*Larix kaempferi* mature seed-bearing cones

*Larix kaempferi* foliage

*Larix kaempferi* pollen- and seed-bearing cones

*Larix kaempferi* fall color

### *Larix kaempferi* (continued)

reddish exfoliating bark, and the twigs appear reddish in the winter landscape. These twigs help differentiate *Larix decidua* from the European larch; it also has more widely spaced branches on a more massive trunk, giving it a more open form.

This is a tree for large, sunny landscapes. It is adaptable to lowland and wet areas, tolerates clay soils, and is disease-resistant.

'Blue Dwarf': low and slow-growing with short blue-green needles on red shoots, reaches 12 × 24 in. (30 × 60 cm) in ten years.

'Blue Rabbit': narrow and conical with blue foliage, reaches 70 ft. (21 m) in height and 15 ft. (4.5 m) wide, often grown on a standard ('Blue Rabbit Weeping').

'Diana': small upright tree with graceful branching, curled and twisted branches, needles are also twisted, can be pruned to desired size or tub-planted, also listed as 'Diane', reaches 12 × 8 ft. (3.6 × 2.5 m) in ten years.

'Haverbeck': low, spreading, with dense foliage, to 2 ft. (0.6 m) tall and wide in ten years.

*Larix kaempferi* 'Blue Rabbit'

*Larix kaempferi* bark

*Larix kaempferi* 'Blue Dwarf'

*Larix kaempferi* 'Diana'

*Larix kaempferi* 'Haverbeck'

'Nana': globose, slow-growing, dense soft green foliage in season, golden yellow in fall.

'Pendula': weeping habit or prostrate unless grafted onto a stake and permitted to drape to the ground. Often sold as *Larix decidua* 'Pendula' or *L. d.* 'Julian's Weeper'.

'Stiff Weeping': similar to 'Pendula' except foliage is compact and close to trunk.

'Wolterdingen': dwarf, slow-growing, irregular conical growth reaches 20 × 24 in. (50 × 60 cm) in ten years, blue-green.

*Larix kaempferi* 'Nana'

*Larix kaempferi* 'Stiff Weeping'

*Larix kaempferi* 'Pendula'

*Larix kaempferi* 'Wolterdingen'

### *Larix laricina*  American larch
Zones (1)2 to 5

This species is the most extensive of the three species found in North America. The American larch, or tamarack, grows further north than any other tree on the continent. It is native from eastern Canada (it is a major species in Labrador) to the Yukon River and south into the northern central United States and eastward into Ohio, Pennsylvania, New Jersey, and New York. It will grow to the high timberline, but in more southern locations it is usually found growing in areas where its roots are constantly wet. It is one of the widest-ranging conifers on the continent. It seldom forms pure stands but tends to grow where few other trees will survive. It seldom grows over 60 ft. (18 m) in height. The crown is narrowly conical and open, with horizontal branches and drooping branchlets. The root system is shallow. The trunk is straight, but the tree often becomes asymmetrical at maturity. Even a grove of these trees does not produce heavy

shade. *Larix laricina* will live 150 years. The pale green, soft and flexible, ½ to 1¼ in. (1.2 to 3 cm) needles emerge early in the spring. They are in clusters of 10 to 30 on short spur-like shoots, or solitary and spiraling around the stem on new shoots. The leaves turn golden yellow in fall and are shed. The pollen-bearing cones are bright yellow and round, hanging onto the twig. The seed-bearing cones are oblong with scarlet-colored scales that have long green tips. The mature chestnut-brown cones are ½ to ¾ in. (1.2 to 2 cm) long on short stalks. They

open in late summer to release their seeds. They are held erect on the stem and persist for several seasons. This larch begins bearing cones at age 12 to 15 and produces a good crop every three to six years. The bark is thin, scaly, and bright reddish brown.

This fast-growing, shallow-rooted species tolerates a wide range of (low) temperatures, rainfall, and amounts of daylight. It does not like heat; however, it should be given full sun. *Larix laricina* is not usually considered an attractive ornamental; the winter habit is some-

*Larix laricina* fall foliage

*Larix laricina* mature seed-bearing cones

*Larix laricina* in winter

*Larix laricina* bonsai 165 years old

what cheerless. It will not only survive but grow well in conditions that are far too wet for most woody plants.

The wood is heavy, very strong, close-grained, and durable. Its traditional use was for railroad ties and utility poles. Native Americans used the roots for stitching their birch-bark canoes together. Even today boatbuilders bend and steam larch for frames of wooden boats. The resinous wood is susceptible to forest fires. It is not a plant one would choose for the benefit of wildlife, although porcupines love to climb these trees and eat the inner bark, which sometimes kills the tree. Grouse will eat the needles and buds, and crossbills will harvest the seeds. It is seldom planted in England.

'Blue Sparkler': vigorous grower with excellent blue foliage, reaches 5 ft. (1.5 m) at maturity, sometimes listed as selection of *Larix kaempferi*.

'Craftsbury Flats': dwarf round ball of pale green foliage, matures at 4 ft. (1.2 m).

'Girard's Dwarf': broadly conical form, 5 ft. (1.5 m) tall and wide in ten years, also listed as a selection of *Larix decidua*.

### *Larix occidentalis*   western larch
Zones 5 to 7

The western larch is native to British Columbia south to Oregon, Montana, and Idaho, where it typically grows on north-facing slopes and other moist sites. It is intolerant of shade. This is one of the major lumber trees of western North America, and before they were harvested, specimens 200 ft. (60 m) high were not uncommon. It can live 500 years or more. The tall straight trunks of this fast-growing tree display rather short branches on mature specimens. In youth the fine-textured soft green foliage covers branches that adorn the tree to the ground. The pale grass-green needles are 14 to 30 in a cluster, 1 to 1¾ in. (2.5 to 4.5 cm) long. The foliage turns bright yellow in autumn. Many consider this the most fire-resistant tree in the forests it inhabits, which are subject to periodic fires. The mature trees have red-brown, 3 to 6 in. (7.5 to 15 cm) thick bark with low resin, the lack of which protects the tree. The cones are 1 to 1½ in. (2.5 to 3.5 cm) long with protruding bracts, deep purple-brown on a short stalk. The cones of burned trees open after being exposed to fire, and the dispersed seeds germinate readily in the resulting sunlight.

The wood is hard and rather heavy for a conifer. It is milled for general construction. It is durable in the ground and is used for railroad ties, utility poles, and in boat construction. It is also considered a very fine fuel wood because of its high heating value and easy splitting. Many species of birds and small rodents make homes in the cavities of snags. The needles are a food source for grouse. Bears have been noted to strip the bark from young trees to reach the sap, which is high in sugar.

*Larix laricina* 'Blue Sparkler'

*Larix laricina* 'Girard's Dwarf'

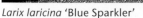
*Larix laricina* 'Craftsbury Flats'

### *Metasequoia glyptostroboides*
### dawn redwood    Zones 4 to 8

This deciduous conifer was known only by fossil records and was thought to be extinct until 1941, when a few trees were found in central China. It was known to be a wide-ranging species from 50-million-year-old preserved specimens in the Arctic areas of Canada, as well as other places in the northern hemisphere. The seeds were distributed by the Arnold Arboretum in 1948 to many arboretums and public gardens, and the species is now widely planted in North America and Europe and available at most nurseries. This is a vigorous, strong-growing tree. It can reach 100 ft. (30 m) in its native habitat, a small area in the provinces of Hubei and Sichuan. Under cultivation it will reach 40 to 50 ft. (12 to 15 m) in fewer than 20 years. It grows quickly, often 3 to 4 ft. (0.9 to 1.2 m) a year early on. It becomes broad and conical, very orderly and uniform, with a sharply pointed top on a central single stem. It has a very distinctive winter habit. The ferny leaves are deciduous, two-ranked, in an opposite arrangement. They are about ¾ in. (2 cm) long on the deciduous shoots. The leaves are bright green when they first emerge and become a shade darker during the growing season. The autumn color changes from a yellow-brown to pink, even apricot, then a copper-brown. The leaves fall attached to the twiglet. The pollen-bearing cones are in the axils of the deciduous shoots and open in early spring; they are borne in dangling racemes or panicles. The solitary seed-bearing cones are ¾ to 1 in. (2 to 2.5 cm) round on the ends of short side twigs. They ripen from green to brown in the first year. The orange to russet-brown bark becomes fissured with age and peels in long strips. The trunk becomes buttressed and irregularly fluted. Children call this the "armpit tree."

Dawn redwood will tolerate very wet, even boggy soil for part of the year. It will grow best in moist, deep soil but will grow on dry sites once established. It will accept pollution and urban conditions. Although commonly known as dawn redwood, it is more cold-hardy than the evergreen redwoods. Give it room and pull up a chair and watch it grow. It is an excellent tree to grow in groves where space is available. Although the foliage looks similar, the way to tell the difference between this and another deciduous conifer, *Taxodium distichum* (bald-cypress), is that the latter has alternately arranged foliage and a completely different bark and trunk.

*Metasequoia glyptostroboides*

*Metasequoia glyptostroboides* foliage (note the opposite leaf arrangement)

*Metasequoia glyptostroboides* pollen-bearing cones

*Metasequoia glyptostroboides* seed-bearing cones

*Metasequoia glyptostroboides* in fall

*Metasequoia glyptostroboides* fall foliage

*Metasequoia glyptostroboides* buttressed trunk

*Metasequoia glyptostroboides* distinctive winter look

*Metasequoia glyptostroboides* outlined in front of *Picea abies*

A closely planted grove of *Metasequoia glyptostroboides*

*Metasequoia glyptostroboides* 'Ogon' newly planted

*Metasequoia glyptostroboides* 'Ogon' in a mixed border

### *Metasequoia glyptostroboides*
(continued)

'Jack Frost': green and white variegated leaves.

'National': a more narrow form with upright branching.

'Ogon': slower growing with bright gold-yellow foliage, needs some protection from scorching summer sun, also known as 'Gold Rush'.

'Sheridan Spire': narrow compact form with ascending limbs, bright green foliage, handsome orange-brown fall color, reaches 60 × 20 ft. (18 × 6 m), possibly narrower than 'National'.

*Metasequoia glyptostroboides* 'Ogon' foliage

*Metasequoia glyptostroboides* 'Ogon' allée

*Metasequoia glyptostroboides* 'Sheridan Spire'

### *Microbiota decussata* Siberian cypress Zones 2 to 8

The Siberian cypress is native to eastern Siberia, where it is found above the tree line in the mountains. It is the only species in its genus. It is a very cold hardy, dense, prostrate, juniper-like plant. It prefers cool conditions and demands good drainage but will tolerate a wide range of soils. Unusually for a conifer, it prefers to grow in high shade, although it will do well in full sun with adequate moisture. *Microbiota decussata* is only about 12 in. (30 cm) high but is very wide-spreading, to 6 to 12 ft. (1.8 to 3.6 m). The soft, fine-textured, lacy leaves are in flat sprays that arch over with drooping tips. The foliage is pale green in summer and bronze to purple in winter. It is reported to be dioecious, but most plants in cultivation are male clones and have inconspicuous cones. The slender stems are reddish brown. This species does not appreciate heat or heavy soils and is probably not a good choice for southern gardens. Under good growing conditions (again, that means good drainage and cool), it forms a wide-spreading carpet and is excellent as a foundation plant or on slopes. It accepts open wind-exposed sites. It combines well with upright plants. It is worthy of much wider use.

*Microbiota decussata*

*Microbiota decussata* on a slope

*Microbiota decussata* foliage with ceratostigma

*Microbiota decussata* winter color

## *Picea* spruce

The spruces are a genus of about 50 species. Seven are native to North America: *Picea glauca*, *P. mariana*, and *P. rubens* in the east and *P. breweriana*, *P. engelmannii*, *P. pungens*, and *P. sitchensis* in the west. Identifying individual spruces is often difficult. Wide-ranging species will vary from one part of their range to another. Often one needs the cones as the most accurate guide to identification. Many members of this genus are very tall and beautiful. They usually have a pyramidal form but often lose lower branches and become less attractive as

they age. Sometimes they look a bit shabby low down because they retain small dead branchlets for a long time. Most prefer cooler, moister climates and often do not do well in hot, dry conditions. They are prone to pests and diseases when grown in less than ideal circumstances. They do not like alkaline soils and will not abide salt spray and atmospheric pollution.

Spruce leaves are evergreen and needle-like. They can be all shades of green as well as the much-loved forms of "blue" spruce. The needles are borne separately, not in bundles, and often crowd densely on the twig and spiral around in all direc-

tions. They are quadrangular in cross section. The needles are attached to the twig by a small brown peg, and when the needle is carefully pulled off a piece of the twig epidermis pulls off with it. This is one way of distinguishing a spruce from a fir. Another distinctive ID feature is that the twig is bumpy after the needles drop naturally because this peg remains on the stem. These needles have a barbed tip that will poke your skin if you play rough with them. The needles remain on the tree for seven to ten years. The pollen-bearing cones are cylindrical, fleshy, catkin-like, and held erect. They are usually positioned in the middle and

Spruces have a pyramidal form

*Picea* (continued)

lower part of the crown on terminal and lateral positions on the previous year's twig. The seed-bearing cones are in the upper part of the crown laterally and at the tips of the previous year's twigs. The mature cones of spruces hang down. They mature during the first season and drop as a unit, intact, to the ground either the first winter or persist on the branches for one or more years (remember the cones of firs, *Abies*, are held upright on the branch and disintegrate on

Spruce cones hang down, the needles are held singly

the tree). The pollen- and seed-bearing cones are borne on the same plant (monoecious). Pollination takes place in the spring as new leafy shoots emerge from their buds. The pollen-bearing cones then wither and fall away. At pollination the conelets are less than 1 in. (2.5 cm) long, soft, fleshy, green or purplish red, and held erect. The scales spread apart to permit entry of pollen. After a few days the scales come together and the cone bends downward. It reaches full size by mid-July and matures in late summer or early autumn. These mature cones are pendulous. The seeds are released over several months. The cones remain on the tree until the next growing season when they fall intact from the tree. Spruces often begin to form cones by the tenth year of growth. Spruce seeds are said to be among the easiest to store and remain viable for many years when kept dry in airtight containers below freezing.

Spruces prefer full sun and good drainage. They are rugged and adaptable and are widely planted in the northern half of the United States, in England, and across Europe. In their native habitat many spruces are tall and narrow, but in cultivation they are often shorter and broader at the base. Size varies from the mammoth Sitka spruce in the Pacific

Northwest to the stunted Engelmann spruce in higher elevations and the undersized black spruce in bogs. Very little pruning is needed on spruces. One can prune new growth while it is still soft or prune off whole branches or cut off laterals. Spruces produce abundant amounts of pitch in their bark, wood, needles, and cones. There are hundreds of cultivars from seed, sports, or mutations and dwarf varieties. Many are propagated by grafting. The root system of spruces is shallow and fibrous; they do not perform as well grown in a container and are usually field dug. They are best transplanted balled-and-burlapped in the spring.

Spruces are important timber trees. Their soft, white wood furnishes construction lumber and pulp. The wood is light, strong, and easy to work with. It is easy on carpentry tools, holds nails, glues well, and doesn't split or warp. But it does tend to be knot-ridden. Its long fibers and low resin content make it ideal for pulp and paper. It is used for newsprint, facial tissues, toilet paper, and other paper products. Spruce roots were soaked and split to form the thread that bound the birch-bark canoes, baskets, and snowshoes of Native Americans. The light but strong wood formed part

Spruce twigs are bumpy

Spruce cones fall to the ground intact

of the inner structure of the canoes; boiled spruce gum was used to caulk the seams. The gum was chewed to prevent toothaches. A beer can be brewed from the foliage; it is an acquired taste.

The highly resonant wood of white and red spruce is prized for its quality of transmitting vibrations, and is often the wood of choice for crafting musical instrument components. Carefully selected for uniformity of structure and seasoned under exacting conditions, spruce wood is used for organ pipes, the sounding boards of pianos, violins, guitars, and other stringed instruments.

The wildlife value of spruce is confined to northern animals. Grouses, especially the spruce grouse, Franklin grouse, and blue grouse, obtain much of their food from spruce needles. The foliage and twigs are also browsed extensively by rabbits and deer in winter. Porcupines eat the bark. The small, winged seeds of spruce are a valuable food of the white-winged crossbill and several other kinds of birds, and are eaten by squirrels and chipmunks as well.

Spruces can be infested with adelgids, aphid-like insects that produce disfiguring 1 in. (2.5 cm) galls, which protect the nymphs while they feed on tender shoots. These growths are sometime mistaken for cones. They distort and can eventually kill the branches. Most susceptible are the Norway (*Picea abies*) and white (*P. glauca*) spruces, but red (*P. rubens*), black (*P. mariana*), and Engelmann (*P. engelmannii*) spruces are also hosts. Galls can be removed by hand or affected branches pruned. Dormant-oil treatments can be applied spring or fall. Some adelgids overwinter on another host, the Douglas-fir (*Pseudotsuga menziesii*); any trees nearby will also have to be treated.

A common disease of Norway (*Picea abies*) and Colorado (*P. pungens*) spruces is cytospora canker caused by a fungal organism, *Cytospora kunzei*. Older trees growing under stressful conditions are more likely to be infected. The disease causes needles to turn brown and drop and branches to turn brittle, starting at the bottom of the tree. The dead tissue on the bark will be covered with a noticeable white resin. The fungal spores are spread by splashing rain, insects, and gardening tools. The disease is prevented by growing spruces under favorable conditions and avoiding mechanical injury to the bark and roots. Chemical control is not effective.

Another fungus that causes foliar disease in numerous spruces is a needle cast disorder caused by *Rhizosphaera kalkhoffii*. Colorado spruces are said to be especially susceptible. Needles turn brown and drop, starting with the lower branches.

Spruces bear snow well

### *Picea abies*  Norway spruce
Zones 3 to 7

Norway spruce is native to central and northern Europe, where it is the most common *Picea* species found and a very important timber tree. It has become the most widely used horticultural spruce in North America and the major introduced spruce used in reforestation in eastern Canada and the northeastern United States. It is a huge spruce, up to 100 ft. (30 m) tall and 40 ft. (12 m) wide. It can reach 200 ft. (60 m) in Europe. It is a wide pyramidal tree; the primary branches are upturned, but the secondary side branchlets usually become pen-dulous with age. It is popular in large part because it grows fast, up to 2 ft. (0.6 m) a year; that it is widely available adds to its popularity as an ornamental. Unfortunately, gardeners often forget that it gets really big.

The dark green foliage often appears shiny, ½ to 1 in. (1.2 to 2.5 cm) long, pointing forward on the twigs. The stems are very rough after needle drop. The pollen-bearing cones are reddish, ½ to ¾ in. (1.2 to 2 cm) long. The mature seed-bearing cones are cylindrical up to 9 in. (23 cm) long, light brown becoming reddish brown. They are pendulous and mature the first autumn but persist throughout the first winter. The cone scales are thin and round. The bark on older trunks becomes roughened with thick, flaky, reddish brown scales. This spruce can be ugly when old, as the lower branches are shaded out and die.

*Picea abies* is easily transplanted. It prefers full sun but is very adaptable to a wide variety of soil conditions. It will tolerate dry sites and wind. Often used as windbreak or screen, it can be sheared in the spring into a hedge. It tends to be healthier in cooler climates. It is widely employed (some would say overplanted) in the cultivated landscape for its fast growth, tolerance, and deep green color. The dark green foliage of this large tree makes a wonderful backdrop for smaller

*Picea abies*

*Picea abies* pendulous secondary branchlets and seed-bearing cone

*Picea abies* pollen-bearing cones

*Picea abies* shedding pollen in spring

*Picea abies* bark

*Picea abies* makes a dark backdrop for other plants

*Picea abies* 'Acrocona'

*Picea abies* 'Acrocona' cones in spring

trees with interesting bark, flowers, or fall color. It is best known in Britain as a choice holiday tree. The light strong wood is widely used for lumber and pulp.

There is an enormous natural variation in this species, and it has over 160 cultivars, which includes many dwarfs effective for the home garden. It is often difficult to tell what distinguishes one from the other.

'Acrocona': produces long red cones at the tips of its shoots even as a young plant, irregular bush that eventually forms a leader, slow-growing and broad-spreading to 15 ft. (4.5 m) tall and wide.

*Picea abies* 'Arnold Dwarf'

*Picea abies* 'Brevifolia'

*Picea abies* 'Barryi'

## *Picea abies* (continued)

'Acrocona Push': a slow-growing dwarf form that displays small red cones.

'Argenteospica': creamy white new growth.

'Arnold Dwarf': broadly conical dwarf, pale green foliage.

'Aurea': needles brushed with gold when grown in sun, fast-growing.

'Barryi': vigorous and compact, conical, rich dark green needles.

'Brevifolia': slow-growing, conical, short dark green needles, likely to reach 8 × 10 ft. (2.5 × 3 m).

'Capitata': dense, small round shrub with dark green needles.

'Cincinnata': a small tree with bright green needles on pendulous branches, a "snake branch" form.

*Picea abies* 'Cincinnata'

*Picea abies* 'Clanbrassiliana'

*Picea abies* 'Cranstonii'

*Picea abies* 'Clanbrassiliana Stricta'

*Picea abies* 'Compacta Asselyn'

'Clanbrassiliana': dense flat-topped bush, wider than tall, only 3 ft. (0.9 m) tall after decades. Choice.

'Clanbrassiliana Stricta': formal cone shape with ascending branches, dense dark green foliage, reaches 3 ft. (0.9 m) high and wide in ten years.

'Columnaris': narrower than the species.

'Compacta Asselyn': compact with dense dark green foliage, reaches 15 × 10 ft. (4.5 × 3 m).

'Cranstonii': irregular in growth with open habit and long loose branches, spare and snake-like, reaches 40 × 20 ft. (12 × 6 m), this and 'Virgata' for those who like freaky conifers.

## *Picea abies* (continued)

'Crippsii': horizontal branching, broad and conical to 10 ft. (3 m), turns yellow-green in winter.

'Cruenta': slow-growing upright small tree with red-purple new growth, reaches 15 ft. (4.5 m).

'Cupressina': narrower than the species, vigorous and columnar with upward-sweeping branches, subject to snow damage, popular in Europe.

'Dicksonii': similar to 'Cranstonii' but foliage denser and new growth red.

'Echiniformis': slow-growing compact shrub with prickly congested foliage above a wide-spreading skirt, 5 × 11 ft. (1.5 × 3.4 m) after decades.

*Picea abies* 'Cupressina'

*Picea abies* 'Crippsii'

*Picea abies* 'Cruenta'

*Picea abies* 'Echiniformis'

'Elegans': similar to 'Nidiformis' with more dome-shaped center.

'Elegantissima': pendulous, growing 1 ft. (0.3 m) a year with gold-yellow foliage early in season, turning green by autumn.

'Ellwangeriana': conical to upright dwarf.

'Formanek': prostrate form, eventually a dense-spreading mat, useful in a rock garden.

'Frohburg': slow-growing, prostrate with weeping branches, can be trained into sculptural forms, short medium green needles, often narrow, strict weeping habit with full spreading skirt.

*Picea abies* 'Elegantissima'

*Picea abies* 'Ellwangeriana'

*Picea abies* 'Formanek'

*Picea abies* 'Frohburg'

### Picea abies (continued)

'Gold Drift': yellow foliage that burns in full sun, weeping form, can be staked to desired height.

'Gregoryana': dwarf, tight flat-topped bun 18 in. (46 cm) tall and wide, reaches 4 ft. (1.2 m) after many years.

'Gregoryana Parsonii': uneven mounded dwarf, more open than 'Gregoryana'.

'Hauerstein': a dwarf cone.

'Hillside Upright': slow-growing, small conical tree, almost black-green needles.

'Hornibrookii': low-spreading, egg-shaped dwarf with dark green needles, reaches 10 ft. (3 m) after three decades.

'Humilis': globose to broadly conical habit with dense gray-green foliage, benefits from corrective pruning, slow-growing, useful in rock gardens.

*Picea abies* 'Gold Drift'

*Picea abies* 'Hillside Upright'

*Picea abies* 'Gregoryana'

*Picea abies* 'Hornibrookii'

'Inversa': vigorous weeping tree, needs to be trained on a stake to the desired height and then allowed to drape, often has unusual shapes, if not staked will be 20 ft. (6 m) wide and only 4 ft. (1.2 m) tall, often called 'Pendula', 'Reflexa' is similar but coarser, with larger needles.

'Kamon': broadly conical dwarf.

'Kellerman's Blue': dense low bun to 3 ft. (0.9 m) tall and wide but grows only 3 to 4 in. (7.5 to 10 cm) a year, gray-blue-green needles on thick stems give a bottlebrush effect, also listed as 'Kellerman's Blue Cameo'.

'Kirkpatrick': slow-growing, upright and compact, reaches 18 ft. (5.5 m) in 30 years.

'Lavoucy': a globose bluish dwarf that grows 1 in. (2.5 cm) a year.

*Picea abies* 'Inversa'

*Picea abies* 'Kamon'

*Picea abies* 'Kellerman's Blue'

*Picea abies* 'Lavoucy'

*Picea abies* 'Little Gem'

*Picea abies* 'Loreley'

*Picea abies* 'Magnifica'

### *Picea abies* (continued)

'Little Gem': tight flat dome of dense branches with small light green soft needles, grows 1 to 2 in. (2.5 to 5 cm) a year.

'Loreley': a slow-growing weeping form with fine needles.

'Magnifica': golden foliage.

'Maxwellii': a very slow-growing tight bun similar to 'Gregoryana' but larger with sharp light green needles, matures into a flat-topped mound.

*Picea abies* 'Maxwellii'

*Picea abies* 'Microsperma'

*Picea abies* 'Minima'

*Picea abies* 'Nana'

*Picea abies* 'Mucronata'

'Microsperma': a spreading conical habit with symmetrical branches at various angles from trunk, dark green needles, slow-growing.

'Minima': dwarf and compact.

'Mucronata': dense bright blue-green foliage on a broad pyramidal form, irregular when young, 15 to 30 ft. (4.5 to 9 m) tall.

'Nana': dense slow-growing cone with sharp needles.

**Picea abies** (continued)

'Nidiformis': dwarf shrub reaching 3 ft. (0.9 m) high and 5 ft. (1.5 m) wide in 10 to 15 years with a depression in the center of its flat top, widely available and planted in gardens as a foundation plant, also known as bird's nest spruce.

'Ohlendorffii': small, conical, densely foliaged with yellow-green needles.

'Pachyphylla': dwarf and slow-growing with very thick rigid needles.

'Parsonsii': open irregular shrub, also called 'Gregoryana Parsonsii'.

'Pendula': weeping habit that tends to stay low unless trained upright on a post, may be the same as 'Inversa' in the trade, dark green needles, some specimens grow in all directions with a carpet at the base. A collective name and sometimes listed as f. *pendula*.

*Picea abies* 'Nidiformis'

*Picea abies* 'Ohlendorffii'

*Picea abies* 'Pendula'

*Picea abies* 'Pendula' (left) trained upright

'Procumbens': wide-spreading plant with stiff sprays of foliage and a flat top, slow-growing, similar to 'Repens'.

'Prostrata': ground-hugging and wide-spreading, mounds a bit with age, light green in summer, darker with cool weather.

'Pseudo-Maxwellii': upright plant with medium green needles.

'Pumila': slow-growing, dense, flat-topped and spreading, sometimes irregular, dark green shiny foliage, similar to 'Nidiformis' and 'Repens' but better for cold climates because it breaks bud later in the spring.

*Picea abies* 'Procumbens'

*Picea abies* 'Prostrata'

*Picea abies* 'Pumila'

*Picea abies* 'Pseudo-Maxwellii'

**Picea abies** (continued)

'Pumila Glauca': wide-spreading and low with gray-green foliage.

'Pygmaea': extremely slow-growing, compact shrub becoming broad and dome-shaped, reaches 18 in. (46 cm) after many years. Outstanding selection.

'Pyramidalis': vigorous, fastigiate, with pointed apex, also listed as 'Pyramidata'.

'Reflexa': dense, rigid, irregular creeping groundcover form unless trained on a pole.

'Remontii': slow-growing, cone-shaped with congested bright green needles.

*Picea abies* 'Pumila Glauca'

*Picea abies* 'Pygmaea'

*Picea abies* 'Pyramidalis'

*Picea abies* 'Remontii'

*Picea abies* 'Repens'

*Picea abies* 'Rothenhaus'

*Picea abies* 'Repens Gold'

'Repens': slow-growing, flat-topped, center builds up in time, dark green foliage, shorter and more spreading than 'Nidiformis'.

'Repens Gold': gold form.

'Rothenhaus': upright branches that weep.

*Picea abies* 'Saint James'

*Picea abies* 'Sherwoodii'

### *Picea abies* (continued)

'Saint James': very small, bun-shaped with olive-green leaves, red buds in spring.

'Sherwoodii': rapid-growing with a wide-spreading, craggy, striking habit, probably same as 'Sherwood Gem'.

'Tabuliformis': slow-growing, spreading prostrate form with a flat top, grows in irregular layered mounds.

'Vassar Broom': compact form with small needles.

*Picea abies* 'Tabuliformis'

*Picea abies* 'Vassar Broom'

*Picea abies* 'Virgata'

*Picea abies* 'Virgata' "snake" branches

*Picea abies* 'Wagner'

*Picea abies* 'Wilson'

'Virgata': long, whorled, sparsely produced undivided long and thick branches with few secondary branchlets, grows 3 ft. (0.9 m) a year, sometimes listed as f. *virgata*, also known as snake branch spruce.

'Wagner': dwarf, dense, and rounded.

'Wilson': dwarf bun, lime-green in spring darkening through season, reaches 5 ft. (1.5 m) tall and wide.

### *Picea bicolor* alcock spruce Zone 5

This relatively rare spruce is native to Japan. It is a medium to large tree with a broad pyramidal habit and ascending branches. It can reach 80 × 15 ft. (24 × 4.5 m), growing under 12 in. (30 cm) a year. It is also known as *Picea alcoquiana*.

'Howell's Dwarf': a broad-spreading form that is flat-topped but matures to a pyramidal tree, with silver-blue undersides, the needles appear blue-green.

'Prostrata': a ground-hugging form with gray-blue needles that can be used in a container.

*Picea bicolor*

*Picea bicolor* 'Prostrata'

*Picea bicolor* 'Howell's Dwarf'

*Picea breweriana* in maturity

### *Picea breweriana*   Brewer spruce   Zone 5

The Brewer spruce is a rare tree that grows in some of the least accessible areas of the west, in the mountains of California and Oregon, where it can reach 100 ft. (30 m) and live for many centuries. It is considered a really beautiful plant, slow-growing, with wide-spreading side branches that eventually produce the weeping branchlets suggested by its other common name, Brewer's weeping spruce. From a distance it looks dusty gray. It grows best in the cool high-moisture habitat where it is found in nature. It does not seem to have commercial value and is difficult to find in nurseries.

A choice young specimen of *Picea breweriana*

### *Picea engelmannii* Engelmann spruce Zones 2 to 5

The Engelmann spruce is found at higher elevations in moist mountain forests of the Canadian Rockies in British Columbia and southward through the Rockies to the southern parts of New Mexico and Arizona. It grows 50 to 100 ft. (15 to 30 m) tall and can live more than 300 years. It is a slender tree with a relatively dense crown and short, dense, downward-sweeping boughs. In its highest habitats it is dwarfed; however, it is a hardy and adaptable tree in cool climates. The dark prickly needles are flexible, 1 in. (2.5 cm) long, blue-green, with white bands underneath. They are pungent when crushed. The violet cones are 1 to 2½ in. (2.5 to 6 cm) long. It hybridizes readily with *Picea glauca*. It is the most common spruce in the Rockies and is an important western timber tree. It is commonly used for telephone poles.

'Hoodie': conical with pendulous branches and blue-green fragrant needles, used in the garden like Colorado spruce.

*Picea engelmannii*

*Picea engelmannii* 'Hoodie'

*Picea glauca*

*Picea glauca* dwarf collection

## *Picea glauca*   white spruce
### Zones 2 to 6

This is the most widespread native conifer in North America. It is found throughout Canada and the northern United States. The vast forests of this tree look almost black. In Canada it is valued as an important source of timber and pulpwood. The pliable roots are used by Native Peoples to lace birch-bark canoes. It is found on the banks of streams and lakes and other wet areas as well as on ocean cliffs. It can reach 150 ft. (46 m) in the Canadian Rockies but is usually half that size in cultivation. It can live 200 years. It is conical in outline with dense foliage and downward-sweeping boughs. In open areas it keeps its branches to the ground.

The blue-green or pale green needles are crowded and twisted on the upper side of the twig, ¼ to ¾ in. (0.6 to 2 cm) long, with a sharp tip. They tend to curl and look combed. The needles emit a pungent odor when crushed, leading to the common name of skunk spruce. The needles persist on the tree for seven to ten years. The cones are 2 in. (5 cm) long. They turn pale brown and are somewhat shiny. The mature bark is gray, tinged with brown, with thin scales and a cinnamon-brown inner bark. This rather variable species is seldom placed in gardens, but a number of notable and hardy cultivars are available. It could be a useful large-scale spruce for cold climates. The wood is light, straight-grained, and resilient. It is used for general construction and pulpwood. It is the state tree of South Dakota and the provincial tree of Manitoba.

## *Picea glauca* (continued)

'Alberta Blue': similar to 'Conica' but with blue foliage.

'Alberta Globe': slow-growing, neat and rounded, dense ¼ in. (0.6 cm) needles, reaches 24 × 20 in. (60 × 50 cm) in ten years.

'Blue Planet': a dense flat globe.

'Blue Wonder': conical, blue-green needles, good for trough and rock gardens.

'Cecilia': compact with short glossy dense silver-blue needles, slow-growing, flat and spreading.

*Picea glauca* 'Alberta Blue'

*Picea glauca* 'Alberta Globe'

*Picea glauca* 'Blue Planet'

*Picea glauca* 'Blue Wonder'

*Picea glauca* 'Cecilia'

*Picea glauca* 'Conica'

*Picea glauca* 'Conica' in a border

*Picea glauca* 'Conica' foliage

'Conica': a dense, conical shrub with light green foliage, widely available and planted but too often poorly grown. Dwarf Alberta spruce becomes 3 to 4 ft. (0.9 to 1.2 m) tall by 18 in. (46 cm) wide in 10 to 15 years. Does best in a cool location with some shade and good air circulation; needs protection from hot and cold winds, reflected sunlight, and heat from walls. With maturity it is a glorious plant and wonderful accent in a mixed border, often used as a container plant. By nature it has a very neat conical and compact shape, looking like it has been devotedly trained. It never seems to lose this shape. It is a retreat for spider mites because of its tight foliage. Deer do not usually browse on it. It is often labeled 'Albertiana Conica'. Many of the other cultivars in this listing are simply bud sports of 'Conica'. Zones 3 to 7.

## *Picea glauca* (continued)

'Cy's Wonder': dense and compact with tiny light green needles, reaches 8 × 4 ft. (2.5 × 1.2 m).

'Daisy's White': flushes white new foliage in spring, grows 2 in. (5 cm) a year.

'Delp's Dwarf': dwarf and conical with soft, dense, blue foliage, reaches 5 ft. (1.5 m).

'Del Val': grows only 2 in. (5 cm) a year but can reach 15 ft. (4.5 m).

var. *densata*: Black Hills white spruce, very hardy, dense, symmetrical tree slow-growing to 30 ft. (9 m) in 50 years, with variable foliage from green to blue-green, the state tree of South Dakota.

*Picea glauca* 'Delp's Dwarf'

*Picea glauca* 'Del Val'

*Picea glauca* 'Daisy's White'

*Picea glauca* 'Cy's Wonder'

*Picea glauca* var. *densata*

*Picea glauca* 'Eagle Rock'

*Picea glauca* 'Echiniformis'

*Picea glauca* 'Elf'

*Picea glauca* 'Fort Ann'

*Picea glauca* 'Gnome'

'Eagle Rock': upright and rounded, blue-green foliage, reaches 15 ft. (4.5 m).

'Echiniformis': low pillow shape with short, thin, gray-green needles, good for trough gardens because of its extremely slow growth, becomes bluer with age.

'Elf': extremely slow-growing, dark green, reaches 18 in. (46 cm) in ten years.

'Fort Ann': rapid growth with irregular habit, sparse branches, and gray-blue foliage.

'Gnome': very slow-growing columnar form.

*Picea glauca* 'Itty Bitty'

*Picea glauca* 'Jean's Dilly' with *P. abies* 'Little Gem'

*Picea glauca* 'Laurin'

## *Picea glauca* (continued)

'Itty Bitty': slow-growing, similar to 'Pixie'.

'Jean's Dilly': slower growing than 'Conica', even more tailored and darker green.

'Laurin': slow-growing cone, reaches only 10 in. (25 cm).

'Lilliput': very slow-growing, more dwarf than 'Conica'.

'Little Globe': rounded dense habit, grows only 1 in. (2.5 cm) a year, good for rock gardens.

'Pendula': formal narrow cone with weeping branches, soft blue-green foliage, grows slowly to 30 × 15 ft. (9 × 4.5 m), does not need staking.

*Picea glauca* 'Lilliput'

*Picea glauca* 'Little Globe'

*Picea glauca* 'Pendula'

*Picea glauca* 'Pixie'

*Picea glauca* 'Pixie Dust'

'Pixie': slow-growing, upright narrow cone with dark green needles, reaches 12 in. (30 cm) in ten years.

'Pixie Dust': dense and compact, emerging bud growth is yellow, reaches 16 in. (40 cm) in ten years.

'Rainbow's End': similar to 'Conica' but has creamy yellow new growth, benefits from light shade to avoid burning.

'Sander's Blue': tight conical growth, soft slate-blue foliage but unfortunate tendency to revert to green.

'Tiny': very compact, slow-growing, similar to 'Pixie'.

'Wild Acres': flat-topped, compact, spreading, short gray-green needles.

'Zuckerhut': another dwarf with green foliage.

*Picea glauca* 'Rainbow's End'

*Picea glauca* 'Sander's Blue'

*Picea glauca* 'Wild Acres'

*Picea glauca* 'Zuckerhut'

### *Picea glehnii*  Sakhalin spruce
Zones 4 to 7

In its native habitat on Russia's Sakhalin Island *Picea glehnii* is a tall, narrow tree: it reaches 80 to 100 ft. (24 to 30 m) with a 30 ft. (9 m) spread. It grows in full sun where there are moist conditions. It differs from other spruces with its flaky dark chocolate-brown bark and conspicuous red-orange spring growth. The sharp ⅝ in. (1.5 cm) needles are blue-green and densely arranged. The pollen-bearing cones are 3½ in. (9 cm) long. It is a plant suitable only for large-scale plantings in parks, recreational areas, or near large buildings, places where one might think of planting a Norway spruce. The timber is used for construction and pulp.

*Picea glehnii*

*Picea jezoensis*

*Picea jezoensis* 'Yatsubusa'

### *Picea jezoensis*  Yezo spruce  Zones 4 to 8

This native to moist areas of Japan, North Korea, China, and Russia reaches 125 ft. (38 m) tall in the wild. It has glossy dark green needles that are ¾ in. (2 cm) and seed-bearing cones that are 2 to 3 in. (5 to 7.5 cm) long. Its fissured and peeling bark is gray-brown. It is a valuable timber tree and is occasionally found in gardens.

'Yatsubusa': slow-growing, irregularly rounded dwarf with needles smaller than the species, grows 2 in. (5 cm) a year, ultimately to 6 ft. (1.8 m), useful for bonsai, often listed as a selection of *Picea glehnii*.

### *Picea mariana*  black spruce  Zones 2 to 5

It is often difficult to distinguish the black spruce from the red spruce, *Picea rubens*, since they often hybridize. Some authorities claim they are variations of the same species. *Picea mariana* is the second most widely distributed conifer tree in North America. It ranges from eastern Canada across to the interior of Alaska, south to the northern midwest United States, and along the Appalachian Mountains to Virginia. It is also found in the coastal swamps of New Jersey. It extends as far north as any tree, growing on barren and stony slopes. In more southern areas it is found near wet areas. It frequently grows where no other tree will survive. Although it has reached 100 ft. (30 m) in Saskatchewan, it typically grows slowly only to 30 ft. (9 m) and is often stunted and shorter. Some call it the bog spruce since it is found in acidic bogs and cold swamps. It is hard to say what its normal form is. It is usually narrowly conical. The pale green needles are ¼ to ¾ in. (0.6 to 2 cm) long and appear brushed forward with a sharp tip. They are arranged radially around the twig. The cones are ½ to 1½ in. (1.2 to 3.5 cm) long on strongly recurved stalks. They remain on the tree for many years, often massed at the top of the tree and with viable seeds. The mature bark is grayish brown, thin, and flaky. The inner bark is yellow-green.

*Picea mariana* has little value as a timber tree because of its small stature and is used only for the manufacture of boxes, lathing, paper pulp, and chopsticks. It reproduces well after fires, which open the cones and release the seeds. It is the provincial tree of Newfoundland.

## *Picea mariana* (continued)

'Doumetii': a large bush with dense, compact, irregular habit with thin and sharp blue-gray needles, reaches 20 ft. (6 m).

'Ericoides': low-spreading uniform habit with dense, soft, blue-green needles, tolerates moist soil.

'Fastigiata': upright and columnar with blue-green foliage.

'Golden': broadly upright habit, blue-gray needles, creamy yellow on top.

'Nana': dense and compact, very slow-growing, small deep blue-green needles, useful in troughs.

*Picea mariana* 'Doumetii'

*Picea mariana* 'Fastigiata'

*Picea mariana* 'Ericoides'

*Picea mariana* 'Nana'

*Picea omorika*

*Picea omorika* upturned branch tips

### *Picea omorika*   Serbian spruce
Zones 4 to 7

The Serbian spruce is native to Bosnia and Serbia. Although it has a very narrow natural range (it escaped extinction during the Ice Age because its habitat was so elevated), it is very adaptable and has broad ornamental potential. It generally grows with one trunk and reaches a height of 60 ft. (18 m). It is a tall, very stylish tree. It is narrow with short drooping branches that curve upward at the tips. Since this species tends to remain rather narrow, it is great for suburban gardens. The ½ to 1 in. (1.2 to 2.5 cm) needles are rather flat, glossy dark green on one side and glaucous on the other. The whitish undersides of the flat needles makes the tree look flushed with silver. It is a very graceful two-toned spruce. The pollen-bearing cones are light red. The violet, 1½ to 2½ in. (3.5 to 6 cm) seed-bearing

*Picea omorika*, depending on origin, will be narrower

## *Picea omorika* (continued)

cones appear in clusters. *Picea omorika* should be planted in full sun on well-drained soil. It tolerates heat, humidity, and wind, and is not damaged by snow. Many consider it a good choice for urban landscapes because it will tolerate atmosphere pollution better than most spruces and is also forbearing of limestone soil. It is resistant to the pests and diseases that plague many other spruces. Serbian spruces are usually seedling grown, but some are grafted on Norway spruce rootstock. It is easy to transplant but should not be allowed to dry out until established. It will usually grow 12 to 18 in. (30 to 46 cm) a year. Plants from lower elevations seem to achieve larger sizes and are wider than those originating from higher habitats. It has always been widely planted in Germany. It is magnificent either as a specimen or in a grouping. It is very flammable.

'Aurea': usual habit but with yellow foliage.

'Berliner's Weeper': narrowly upright with strongly pendulous branches.

*Picea omorika* 'Aurea'

*Picea omorika* pollen-bearing cones

*Picea omorika* seed-bearing cones

*Picea omorika* 'Berliner's Weeper'

*Picea omorika* 'Expansa'

*Picea omorika* 'Frohnleiten'

*Picea omorika* 'Fröndenberg'

*Picea omorika* 'Gunter'

*Picea omorika* 'Gnom'

'Expansa': low-spreading form, will become a broad irregular mass 4 ft. (1.2 m) tall, develops a leader if grafted.

'Frohnleiten': irregular dwarf.

'Fröndenberg': dwarf bun, tiny blue-green needles with silver undersides, grows 1 in. (2.5 cm) a year.

'Gnom': small and irregular with rounded habit, short blue-green needles on dense branches, reaches 30 in. (75 cm).

'Gunter': dwarf mounding plant with blue-green foliage, grows 2 in. (5 cm) a year.

## *Picea omorika* (continued)

'Nana': broadly conical shrub with two-toned needles eventually becomes pyramidal, reaches 3 ft. (0.9 m) in ten years, ideal for small gardens.

'Pendula': central leader is upright with very vertical pendulous branches and a trailing skirt, slower growing.

'Pendula Bruns': very narrow selection with strongly pendulous side branches. Stunning!

*Picea omorika* 'Nana'

*Picea omorika* 'Pendula'

*Picea omorika* 'Pendula Bruns'

'Pimoko': broad-growing bun, short blue-green needles with silver undersides on short branches, smaller than 'Nana', good for rock gardens.

'Pimpf': slow-growing, dense and rounded.

'Schneverdingen': very slow-growing, globose, 8 × 10 in. (20 × 25 cm) after eight years, two-toned needles, useful for trough gardens.

'Treblitzsch': compact cushion, coarse foliage.

'Tremonia': bun-shaped with silver-blue needles, grows less than 1 in. (2.5 cm) a year.

'Tijn': dwarf globose form, bright yellow foliage, grows 2 in. (5 cm) a year.

'Virgata': less columnar and dense than the species with random, undivided, jutting, snake-like branches, slow-growing, rare.

*Picea omorika* 'Pimoko'

*Picea omorika* 'Pimpf'

*Picea omorika* 'Treblitzsch'

*Picea omorika* 'Tremonia'

*Picea omorika* 'Virgata'

### *Picea orientalis*   oriental spruce
Zones 4 to 7

The oriental spruce is native to south-eastern Europe and southwestern Asia. It is a beautifully shaped pyramidal tree reaching 60 ft. (18 m) tall by 20 ft. (6 m) wide, densely branched with graceful, very dark green foliage that is maintained to the ground. It does not tend to get as wide as *Picea abies* and does not grow quite as fast, 8 to 12 in. (20 to 30 cm) a year. The soft, glossy, dark green needles are shorter than any other spruce, only ¼ to ½ in. (0.6 to 1.2 cm) long, thick, and close to the twig. They stay on the branch for up to four years. The new growth is regularly a lighter green. The pollen-bearing cones are often bright red before shedding pollen. The pendulous seed-bearing cones are 2 to 4 in. (5 to 10 cm) long. Purple when young, they brown with age. *Picea orientalis* does best in full sun but will tolerate light shade. The bark is brown with some exfoliation. The oriental spruce is relatively tolerant of drought and wind, but it would be prudent to protect it from excessive winter dryness and cruel winds. Few would dispute that this spruce is far superior to the ubiquitous Norway spruce and deserves to be planted more often. Many selections for smaller gardens are available.

*Picea orientalis*

*Picea orientalis* foliage and pollen-bearing cones

*Picea orientalis* seed-bearing cones

*Picea orientalis* mature seed-bearing cone

'Atrovirens': more open than species with exceptionally shiny dark green needles, reaches 60 ft. (18 m).

'Aurea': most authorities equate with 'Aureospicata'.

'Aureospicata': new growth comes out butter-yellow in the spring, eye-catching for about six weeks above the previous year's waxy rich dark green foliage.

'Barnes': nest-like bush with depression in top, slow-growing, shiny dark green needles, will reach 3 × 6 ft. (0.9 × 1.8 m).

'Bergman's Gem': cushion-shaped in youth, becoming a flat globe, dense shiny dark green needles.

*Picea orientalis* 'Atrovirens'

*Picea orientalis* 'Aureospicata' spring foliage

*Picea orientalis* 'Aureospicata'

*Picea orientalis* 'Barnes'

*Picea orientalis* 'Bergman's Gem'

## *Picea orientalis* (continued)

'Compacta': broadly conical.

'Connecticut Turnpike': dense, compact, and very dark green.

'Gowdy': a dense, narrow tree with recurved sweeping branches, pale green new growth in spring becoming dark glossy green.

*Picea orientalis* 'Compacta'

*Picea orientalis* 'Gowdy'

*Picea orientalis* 'Connecticut Turnpike'

'Gracilis': slow-growing, becoming a dense small conical tree, reaches 20 ft. (6 m).

'Mount Vernon': slow-growing, dense and mounding.

'Nana': dense globose form usually not more than 3 ft. (0.9 m) high.

'Nutans': slow-growing irregular cone, bright pollen-bearing cones in spring.

'Shadow's Broom': spreading habit with depression in center, rich green foliage.

*Picea orientalis* 'Gracilis'

*Picea orientalis* 'Mount Vernon'

*Picea orientalis* 'Nana'

*Picea orientalis* 'Nutans'

*Picea orientalis* 'Shadow's Broom'

### *Picea orientalis* (continued)

'Skylands': grows slowly for several years, then 12 to 18 in. (30 to 46 cm) a year, tall and conical, foliage bright yellow year-round with dark green inner needles, give midday summer shade protection. Elegant.

'Tom Thumb': dwarf and globose with golden new foliage.

*Picea orientalis* 'Skylands'

*Picea orientalis* 'Skylands' in youth

*Picea orientalis* 'Skylands' foliage

*Picea orientalis* 'Tom Thumb'

### *Picea pungens*  Colorado spruce
Zones 2 to 6

The Colorado spruce is found in western Montana, Idaho, and the mountains of Colorado south to New Mexico and Arizona. In its native stands it is predominantly green. It is the most planted of the western conifers in the eastern United States. It is a dense, pyramidal tree to 60 ft. (18 m) tall by 25 ft. (8 m) wide, growing 6 to 12 in. (15 to 30 cm) a year. The needles are sharp and stiff, 1½ in. (3.5 cm) long. They are sharply acid when chewed. All specimens display a blue cast or bloom on the foliage, especially on the tips of the new growth of older trees. The seed-bearing cones are tan, pendulous, and 3 to 4 in. (7.5 to 10 cm) long. Old plants tend to lose lower branches and become unattractive. Grow in full sun. It is tolerant of dry sites, wind, air pollution, and salt. It does not thrive in warm, humid areas. It is very prone to pests, especially red spider mites, and is also subject to galls. The species is not commonly planted because there are many cultivars chosen for bluer foliage; selections of this species are some of the bluest of conifers. The intensity of the silvery blue foliage of a few cultivars can be discordant in some plant combinations but is especially attractive when combined with purple or pink flowers. There are sizes and habits for every purpose. It is often sold as a holiday tree.

This spruce is readily used as a nest site, especially by robins, mockingbirds, sparrows, purple finches, and mourning doves. In the fall, the seed eaters—crossbills, evening grosbeaks, nuthatches, and goldfinches—congregate for the cone-ripening season. It is the state tree of Colorado and Utah.

*Picea pungens*

### *Picea pungens* (continued)

'Argentea': silvery blue selection, grows relatively large, possibly no different from f. *glauca*.

'Aurea': golden new growth, changing to blue-green in summer.

'Baby Blueyes': slow-growing, dense, symmetrical, pyramidal with bright blue foliage, slower growing than 'Hoopsii', faster than 'Montgomery'. Stunning.

'Bakeri': long blue needles.

'Blue Mist': a ground-hugging selection.

'Blue Pearl': compact globe, grows under 1 in. (2.5 cm) a year, good for troughs and miniature railroads.

*Picea pungens* 'Aurea'

*Picea pungens* 'Bakeri'

*Picea pungens* 'Baby Blueyes'

*Picea pungens* 'Blue Pearl'

'Blue Totem': upright and narrow, not exceptionally blue.

'Compacta': dense with horizontal branching and flat top, with age forms a graceful spreading skirt, blue-green.

'Corbet': similar to 'Montgomery', coarse needles, blue-gray.

'Dietz Prostrate': prostrate form unless staked, silver-blue needles.

'Egyptian Pyramid': dense and broadly pyramidal, to 6 ft. (1.8 m) tall and wide, cones are blue.

*Picea pungens* 'Blue Totem'

*Picea pungens* 'Compacta'

*Picea pungens* 'Dietz Prostrate'

*Picea pungens* 'Egyptian Pyramid'

### *Picea pungens* (continued)

'Erich Frahm': conical with blue foliage.

'Fat Albert': densely compact, symmetrical with a broad base, soft silvery blue, reaches 15 ft. (4.5 m).

'Girard Dwarf': mounded with short rich blue needles.

f. *glauca*: the common name, blue Colorado spruce, explains a lot. This conifer would rather be growing in the Rocky Mountains, where it is native, than in locations with hot, humid summers. In its native habitat there are specimens that are 700 years old. It usually grows with one trunk. The needles are sharp and stiff. It is usually a bluish green, and the needles are four-sided. Often the new growth will be bluest, and the tree will darken by winter. The cones are 4 in. (10 cm) long and hang down. *Picea pungens* f. *glauca* does not age well. It will tolerate dryness, wind, air pollution, and salt. It tolerates clay fairly well. Great variation can occur

*Picea pungens* 'Erich Frahm'

*Picea pungens* 'Fat Albert'

*Picea pungens* 'Girard Dwarf'

*Picea pungens* f. *glauca*

among the specimens offered by the trade, which are often seedling grown. Zones 2 to 6.

'Glauca Compacta': similar to 'Montgomery'.

'Glauca Pendula': will spread along the ground or drape if trained as a standard to desired height, irregular form, very sculptural, sometimes difficult to place.

'Glauca Procumbens', 'Glauca Prostrata': similar ground-creeping plants.

*Picea pungens* f. *glauca* foliage

*Picea pungens* 'Glauca Compacta'

*Picea pungens* 'Glauca Pendula'

*Picea pungens* 'Glauca Procumbens'

## *Picea pungens* (continued)

'Globe': slow-growing, compact, rounded in youth, more mounding with age.

'Globosa': see 'Montgomery'.

'Hillside': compact with gray-green needles.

'Hoopsii': silvery blue selection, sometimes almost white, with long sharp needles, irregular early on but grows into elegance.

*Picea pungens* 'Globe'

*Picea pungens* 'Globosa'

*Picea pungens* 'Hillside'

*Picea pungens* 'Hoopsii'

*Picea pungens* 'Hoopsii' foliage

'Hunnewelliana': slow-growing, conical but eventually tall, silver-blue foliage.

'Iseli Fastigiate': narrowly upright, blue foliage, subject to snow damage.

'Iseli Foxtail': upright, dense, pyramidal, reaches 15 ft. (4.5 m), new growth is blue, bushy and twisted, tapered needle length, longer at the base of the shoot than at the tip, also listed as 'Foxtail'.

'Koster': irregular shape in youth, becomes pyramidal, silvery blue, adaptable, small to medium-sized, also listed as 'Kosteri'.

*Picea pungens* 'Hunnewelliana'

*Picea pungens* 'Koster'

*Picea pungens* 'Iseli Fastigiate'

*Picea pungens* (continued)

'Maigold': new growth pale yellow turning blue-green.

'Mesa Verde': spreading and uniform, green needles, tough.

'Millburn': dense and shrub-like, reaches 8 ft. (2.5 m) tall and wide, blue.

'Mission Blue': fast-growing, bright blue, matures into dense broad pyramidal habit, reaches 40 ft. (12 m).

'Moerheim': dense conical habit, needles bright blue all seasons, may need staking, can reach 30 ft. (9 m), also listed as 'Moerheimii'.

*Picea pungens* 'Maigold'

*Picea pungens* 'Mesa Verde'

*Picea pungens* 'Millburn'

*Picea pungens* 'Moerheim'

*Picea pungens* 'Mission Blue'

*Picea pungens* 'Montgomery'

*Picea pungens* 'Mrs. Cesarini'

*Picea pungens* 'Pendens'

*Picea pungens* 'Pendula'

*Picea pungens* 'Porcupine'

*Picea pungens* 'Prostrata'

'Montgomery': compact, broadly pyramidal, silvery blue shrub that grows 3 to 6 in. (7.5 to 15 cm) a year, one of the most commonly grown dwarf Colorado spruces, this and 'Globosa' are completely mixed up in the trade.

'Mrs. Cesarini': flat globe with shiny blue-green foliage, grows 1 in. (2.5 cm) a year.

'Pendens': a prostrate form.

'Pendula': variable in cultivation, can be grown as a ground-cover or developed into sculptural shapes by staking and training, the growing shoots cascade downward, also known as 'Glauca Pendula'.

'Porcupine': irregular upright dwarf with congested blue foliage, grows 1 in. (2.5 cm) a year.

'Prostrata': grows as a groundcover, nice draped over wall or rocks.

*Picea pungens* 'Sester's Dwarf'

### *Picea pungens* (continued)

'Royal Knight': uniform compact pyramid, develops a well-filled outline without pruning or staking.

'Sester's Dwarf': reaches 16 × 10 in. (40 × 25 cm) in ten years.

'Split Rock': spreading to 3 × 5 ft. (0.9 × 1.5 m) with soft blue needles.

'Spring Ghost': conical, creamy white new growth becoming blue-green, reaches 4 ft. (1.2 m) in ten years.

*Picea pungens* 'Royal Knight'

*Picea pungens* 'Split Rock'

*Picea pungens* 'Spring Ghost'

*Picea pungens* 'St. Mary'

*Picea pungens* 'Sunshine'

*Picea pungens* 'Thuem'

*Picea pungens* 'Thomsen'

*Picea pungens* 'Walnut Glen'

*Picea pungens* 'Walnut Glen' foliage

'St. Mary': rounded mound that does not develop a leader, long blue needles, also listed as 'Saint Mary's Broom'.

'Sunshine': spring growth lemon-yellow, reaches 4 ft. (1.2 m) in ten years.

'Thomsen': bright silver-blue with thick needles.

'Thuem': compact and mounding, grows slowly to 4 × 3 ft. (1.2 × 0.9 m), powder-blue, also listed as 'Thume'.

'Walnut Glen': compact conical upright habit, gold-tinged gray-blue needles, grows 3 in. (7.5 cm) a year.

### *Picea rubens*   red spruce
Zones 3 to 5

The red spruce is native to eastern Canada southward to Pennsylvania and following the Appalachian Mountains through West Virginia as far south as Georgia. It is described as the only native spruce that lives on the southern mountains. It reaches 40 to 80 ft. (12 to 24 m) with a dense pyramidal crown. The twisted needles are ½ to ¾ in. (1.2 to 2 cm) long, dark green, and surround the stem. The cones are 2 in. (5 cm) long on a very small stalk, reddish brown, and persist on the tree until autumn or up to a year. The mature bark is reddish brown, flaky, and thin. *Picea rubens* can live 300 years. It prefers cold and moist situations with well-drained soils. It is often found in rocky sites and on the borders of wet areas. It is frequently in groves with balsam firs. It grows very slowly and seldom does well under cultivation. Red spruce is used in all areas of house construction. Its soft, light wood has resonant qualities and is unsurpassed for the sounding boards of musical instruments. It is commonly used for pulp. The seeds are devoured by pine siskins, crossbills, and rodents. It is the provincial tree of Nova Scotia.

'Pocono': cushion-shaped plant with short gray-green needles, grows 2 in. (5 cm) a year.

*Picea rubens*

*Picea rubens* 'Pocono'

## *Picea sitchensis*  Sitka spruce
### Zone 7

The Sitka spruce is found from Alaska south through British Columbia and Washington, Oregon, and northern California. It seldom grows more than 30 miles (48 km) inland from the Pacific. There are trees that are more than 200 ft. (60 m) high and 10 ft. (3 m) in diameter. Some have lived 800 years. It is the largest spruce in the world. It is a straight tree with a narrow, conical crown. The branches of this fast-growing tree are upward-sweeping with downward-hanging branchlets. The needles are ½ to 1 in. (1.2 to 2.5 cm) long, flat, stiff, sharply pointed, and held on all sides at right angles to the stem. They are glossy dark green above and powder-blue beneath. The 2½ to 4 in. (6 to 10 cm) cones hang down on short stalks. The trunks above the buttressed bases are often bare unless it is growing in the open. It is named after Sitka, Alaska, which has an annual rainfall of over 80 in. (203 cm); no surprise, then, that this species will tolerate rainforest conditions. Although it is a very important timber tree, no selections have been widely planted in gardens. It has been extensively planted in reforestation projects in the British Isles and western North America. This spruce is a favorite roosting place for bald eagles.

The wood is soft but strong with a uniform texture and is considered excellent for trim, paneling, and furniture. It has a high strength-to-weight ratio. It has little tendency to warp and is useful for piano sounding boards, the backs of violins, and organ pipes. It is also well known for its use in the building of airplanes for allied forces in World Wars I and II, when the Sitka forests were heavily logged. It is also used for mundane pulp manufacture. It is the state tree of Alaska.

'Aurea': the legendary one.

'Röm': a dwarf with bright silver-blue foliage.

'Silberzwerg': conical dwarf.

'Tenas': slow-growing flat-topped dwarf with blue-gray foliage, also known as 'Papoose'.

*Picea sitchensis* 'Aurea'

*Picea sitchensis* 'Röm'

*Picea sitchensis* 'Silberzwerg'

*Picea sitchensis* 'Tenas'

### *Pinus*   pine

Pines are perhaps the most famous of the conifers—nearly everyone calls any conifer a pine and any cone a pinecone. The pines consist of over 100 species of trees and shrubs that are distributed throughout the northern hemisphere. Three dozen are native to North America, one to Great Britain. There are few places in the United States or southern Canada where you won't find some species of pine. One could argue that *Pinus* is the most wideranging and successful genus of trees on the continent, rivaled only by *Quercus* (oak) in its ability to grow in a diversity of climates. Pines date back 130 million years; other members of the 12-genera pine family (Pinaceae)—*Abies* (fir), *Picea* (spruce), *Tsuga* (hemlock), and *Pseudotsuga* (Douglas-fir), to name a few—are later offshoots. Pines put down deep roots and can grow in hotter and drier areas than other fashionable garden conifers like spruces, firs, or falsecypresses (*Chamaecyparis*). All pines prefer to grow in full sun, and very few will tolerate urban pollution. Pines are usually conical and more or less symmetrical in habit in their youth; left on their own, however, pines usually become tall and more openbranching and picturesque with age.

A vast number and diversity of pine cultivars have been selected from seedlings and plants in the wild, and propagated from witches' brooms. They vary from dense, compact, slow-growing types to large landscape trees. All are monoecious and evergreen.

The principal species of pines are planted extensively in large landscape settings, estates, cemeteries, public areas, and recreational sites. The dwarf selections and those with interesting foliage or branching habits are employed in home settings, mixed borders, and collections.

Pines have clustered needles. The number of needles per cluster varies from species to species but is usually two, three, or five. This is one of the main ways one can distinguish among the pines. Their foliage color ranges from green to bluegreen, and there are even variegated needles. The needles are usually long and soft. The new needle growth on pines is one of their most striking features, emerging like erect candles of very soft tissue, sometimes a different color from the rest of the foliage and in time expanding to normal size and rigidity. Pines make this flush of growth only once a year; when it is over, the tips of the new shoots develop a terminal bud in preparation for the following year's growth. Each year's needles

build on the framework set down by the previous. Gardeners often snap off part of the candle before it stretches to create a more compact plant or to shape it into a cloud-like habit. This is commonly referred to as candling.

Pines retain their needles for periods varying from one year to decades, but each year some interior needles will turn brown and fall off. This normal occurrence often causes alarm among homeowners and prompts calls to horticultural hot lines.

The cones vary in size from narrow and cylindrical to broad and rounded and often hang on the branches for several years. They usually open at maturity, but some remain closed for many years, storing the seeds until the parent tree is hit by a forest fire, which causes the cones to open. The pollen- and seed-bearing cones are generally easy to distinguish. The bark of pines is typically fissured and scaly with age.

The seeds of numerous species of pines are suitable for food; in fact, they rank near the very top of conifers in importance to wildlife. There is even a bird named after this conifer, the pine siskin. "Pine nuts" constitute more than 50 percent of the diet of three birds—the red crossbill, Clark's nutcracker, and the

Clustered needles of pines

Spring "candles" on pines

white-headed woodpecker—an unusual wildlife record. Many other birds and mammals feed on these nutritious, oily seeds to a lesser degree. The annual crop of pine seeds varies considerably; some years bring a heavy yield, and in others the crop is light. Several small rodents use the bark as food, and pines are valuable as cover and nesting sites for wildlife.

Pine wood is an important construction and lumber product. It has a uniform texture, is finely grained and easy to work with, and is used for lots of everyday furniture and household products. Pines also provide turpentine, lacquer, paints, rosin, and other resin products. Pine branches are popular holiday decorations.

A common pest on red (*Pinus resinosa*), Scots (*P. sylvestris*), mugo (*P. mugo*), Japanese red (*P. densiflora*), and jack (*P. banksiana*) pines is the so-called pine sawfly (*Neodiprion sertifer* and many others). It is not actually a fly at all, but a cousin of ants, wasps, and bees. The adult sawfly does no harm but creates a slit in foliage to insert its eggs, and the emerging larval-stage caterpillar will feed for weeks on pine needles. Entire branches can be defoliated. The pest is easy to spot: it has a black head and gray-green body with several light and dark green stripes.

They can be removed by hand or hosed off. Chemical sprays are effective when the larvae are small, in early spring. This pest is particularly fond of mugo pines.

Several small moths can infest pines; their larvae feed on the growth tips. The European and the Zimmerman pine shoot moths afflict two- and three-needled pines, especially red, Scots, mugo, and Austrian (*Pinus nigra*) pines. It can be a special problem in nurseries. Terminal branches will be killed, causing distortions and the production of multiple stems. The injured tips, where the larvae overwinter, should be pruned. Chemicals could be applied as the larvae hatch in the early spring.

Diplodia blight (*Sphaeropsis sapinea*, formerly *Diplodia pinea*) causes stunted new shoots with short, brown needles. It attacks pines growing under cultivation, beginning by killing the current year's growth but eventually destroying entire trees. Sometimes one notices small black fruiting bodies, which contain the spores that spread the disease, particularly in very moist conditions. Control is difficult. Fallen debris should be removed. Repeated fungicide treatments are sometimes necessary. Diplodia blight is perhaps most commonly found on mature Austrian and Scots pines; a possible sub-

stitute for these would be Bosnian pine (*Pinus leucodermis*), with its bold, dark green foliage.

Pine needle scale (*Chionaspis pinifoliae*) is a common armored scale on pines. The white scale is oystershell-shaped and can completely cover needles to protect the eggs, which hatch in spring to feed on the foliage. Dormant oils and insecticidal soaps can be effective against scale insects. Timing of systemic insecticide applications is critical and should only be applied by licensed persons. This scale especially troubles Scots and mugo pines.

Pine wilt can affect Scots, Austrian, and Japanese red pines. It is caused by a nematode, *Bursaphelenchus xylophilus*. It is carried from tree to tree by a beetle and enters the bark as the beetle feeds. The nematode infects and clogs the vascular system of the tree, often causing a rapid decline and death. Infected trees cannot be successfully treated and should be removed and burned. Replace the tree with something other than a *Pinus* species.

Air pollutants like sulfur dioxide and ozone can damage the needles of pines. Highway salt is particularly harmful to *Pinus strobus*, *P. banksiana*, *P. cembra*, and *P. densiflora*. *Pinus thunbergii*, *P. nigra*, and *P. ponderosa* are relatively salt-tolerant.

Normal loss of pine needles

Typical pine seed-bearing cone

### *Pinus aristata*   Rocky Mountain bristlecone pine   Zones 4 to 7

This pine is native to the southwestern United States from Nevada, east to Colorado and south to Arizona. It originates in alpine and subalpine forests on dry rocky sites, often in pure stands at higher elevations of 7,500 to 10,000 ft. (2,290 to 3,050 m). Some living specimens are said to be over 2,000 years old. It is a dwarf, shrubby plant with an irregular habit, growing very slowly to 8 to 20 ft. (2.5 to 6 m). The needles are rather stiff, 1 to 1¾ in. (2.5 to 4.5 cm) long, in fascicles of five. The needles are often covered with flecks of sticky dried white resin, which could easily be mistaken for a woolly scale insect infestation. In the first year of growth the densely placed needles point forward along the shoot but become more spreading in the second year. They persist for 5 to 40 years. The seed-bearing cone is stalkless, 2 to 4 in. (5 to 10 cm) long, and 1½ in. (3.5 cm) wide. There is a sharp, slender bristle on the tip of the seed scales, which gives the pine its common name. The developing cones are deep purple. The bark is red-brown and becomes shallowly fissured into long irregular ridges. Like other pines it requires full sun. It is very tolerant of poor, rocky, and dry soils but grows poorly in hot, humid summers. It is not tolerant of air pollution. *Pinus aristata* is grown for its picturesque habit in small gardens. It is often difficult to cultivate.

'Sherwood Compact': a dense dwarf upright selection with upswept branches and shorter needles with fewer resin spots, unlikely to reach 4 ft. (1.2 m) after 15 years.

*Pinus aristata*

*Pinus aristata* needles showing flecks of resin

*Pinus aristata* cone

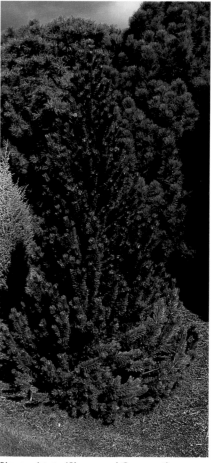

*Pinus aristata* 'Sherwood Compact'

*Pinus banksiana* foliage and cones

### *Pinus banksiana*   jack pine   Zones 2 to 6

A member of Captain Cook's expedition, Sir Joseph Banks found a conifer on the east coast of Canada which was subsequently named after him. It is the most widely distributed of the pine species of North America, and the most northerly as well, reaching far into the tundra. It grows from northern New England and Newfoundland west to Alaska and south into New York, Michigan, Illinois, and Minnesota. It displays great variability in height and habit as it adapts to different sites. It is usually a small pyramidal tree, ranging from 15 to 40 ft. (4.5 to 12 m), but can be up to 80 ft. (24 m) when growing on fertile, sandy locations. More often it develops into a scrubby, stunted tree only 25 ft. (8 m) tall with a crooked trunk, lacking its lower branches and with an irregular crown. It is often a pioneer species, seeding into dry, sandy soils and rocky ridges. It can live more than 100 years. It often interbreeds with its cousin, the lodgepole pine.

The needles of the jack pine are in groups of two, thick, stiff, curved and twisted, dull dark green, and short, ¾ to 1¼ in. (2 to 3 cm) long, persisting for two to three years. The stemless seed-bearing cones are found in forward-pointing clusters of two to four, 1 to 2½ in. (2.5 to 6 cm) long, dark purple at first, becoming contorted and remaining closed. The cone scales are armed with small, incurved, deciduous prickles. On some trees the mature gray cones remain closed on the tree for up to 20 years, still containing viable seeds. The cones are sealed with resin, which melts only when temperatures are above 120°F (50°C), releasing the seeds. There is a good seed crop every three to four years. Stands of jack pine are reported to burn every 40 to 80 years. The bark is dark brown to black with red tones, ridged and flaky, maturing to a dark grayish brown and furrowed with plates or scales.

Jack pine is not often used as a timber tree because the

*Pinus banksiana*

*Pinus banksiana* bonsai 90 years old

## *Pinus banksiana* (continued)

wood is light, soft, weak, and closely grained. It is used in the pulp industry and to some extent for construction. It was once valued for making frames for the First Nations peoples' canoes. Although *Pinus banksiana* is a very important reforestation species, it cannot be recommended as an ornamental conifer. It often has a short, irregular, and gnarly habit. It appears rumpled. On the other hand, it is a hardy and tough tree, grows rapidly in its youth, and is adaptable to tough sites that are dry or sandy and could be used for windbreaks or mass plantings in those situations. It is the provincial tree of the Northwest Territories.

'Chippewa': an irregular compact globe with short dark green stiff and twisted needles, grows ⅓ to ¾ in. (0.8 to 2 cm) a year, often used for bonsai or troughs.

'Pendula': weeping form.

'Schoodic': very slow-growing, dense ground-hugging form with short emerald-green needles.

'Uncle Fogy': weeping form that will be prostrate and sprawl in all directions unless trained, can be grafted to an upright standard, 2 × 15 ft. (0.6 × 4.5 m) tall and wide.

'Wisconsin': dense globular flat-topped bush, reaches 7 in. (18 cm) in ten years.

*Pinus banksiana* 'Chippewa'

*Pinus banksiana* 'Pendula'

*Pinus banksiana* 'Schoodic'

*Pinus banksiana* 'Uncle Fogy'

*Pinus banksiana* 'Wisconsin'

*Pinus bungeana* mature

## *Pinus bungeana*  lacebark pine
Zones 5 to 8

The lacebark pine is native to east and central China and has long been a favorite planting in temple gardens. It is pyramidal when young and often multistemmed. It has a sparse branching habit and becomes open, flat-topped, and rounded with age. It grows 6 to 12 in. (15 to 30 cm) a year, eventually reaching 50 ft. (15 m) tall by 30 ft. (9 m) wide. It is extremely slow-growing when young. This species tolerates wind and drought, but good drainage and full sun are essential. The foliage is 2 to 4 in. (5 to 10 cm) long. The stiff dark green needles are grouped in threes and appear rather sparse in distribution. They remain on the tree two to four growing seasons. The ferociously spiny seed-bearing cones are oval, 2 to 3 in. (5 to 7.5 cm) long by 1½ in. (3.5 cm) wide. They appear terminally or laterally on the stem and have very short stalks. *Pinus bungeana* is grown for its open habit and showy bark. The bark exfoliates in patches of brown, gray, green, and white after the tree is five to eight years old. One could contend that it has the most beautiful bark of any conifer. Place it where it can be viewed throughout the year. The open multistemmed habit will allow filtered

*Pinus bungeana* cones

*Pinus bungeana* bark

*Pinus bungeana* is often multistemmed

### *Pinus bungeana* (continued)

light to underplantings, but this characteristic also causes it to break apart under heavy snow loads.

'Compacta', 'Diamant': both are good dwarf forms with short pale green needles.

'Silver Ghost': striking silver-gray tones in the bark at an early age.

'Temple Gem': a very slow-growing selection appropriate for rock gardens.

*Pinus bungeana* 'Diamant'

*Pinus bungeana* a young specimen

*Pinus bungeana* can break apart in snow

## *Pinus cembra*  Swiss stone pine
Zones 3 to 7

This formal-looking tree is an ideal pine for smaller landscapes. It is very slow-growing and after 25 years will reach 30 ft. (9 m) high but be only 10 ft. (3 m) wide. It should be grown in full sun with good drainage. It is very wind- and salt-tolerant. *Pinus cembra* is handy for its dense, conical form with branches to the ground. It makes an excellent ornamental with its dark green foliage and uniform growth. Its formal bearing suggests distinct landscape design possibilities. It is very upright early on, spreading slightly with maturity (like humans). The blue-green needles are 2 to 3 in. (5 to 7.5 cm) long, rather stiff and straight, and densely set with blue-white lines beneath. They remain on the tree up to five years. The stems are thick and covered with dense orange-colored downy hairs. The foliage is flammable. It is native to the central European Alps, northeast Russia, and northern Asia. The short-stalked, 2 to 3½ in. (5 to 9 cm) long cones are terminal, green and globe-shaped in the first year and becoming

*Pinus cembra*

*Pinus cembra* is a good choice for narrow area

*Pinus cembra* densely set blue-green needles

*Pinus cembra* thick orange stems

*Pinus cembra* bark

### *Pinus cembra* (continued)

egg-shaped and purple-brown the second year with incurved scales. The cone does not release its seeds until it falls to the ground in the third year. The bark is dark gray and smooth on young trees, eventually developing fissures that expose red-brown and scaly ridges.

'Blue Mound': slower growing than the species, low and mounding reaching 3 × 2 ft. (0.9 × 0.6 m) in 16 years, useful for the rock garden.

'Chalet': a dense, rounded column of soft bluish green foliage reaching 5 to 10 ft. (1.5 to 3 m) in ten years.

'Chamolet': an upright column with dense blue foliage, slowly matures at 6 ft. (1.8 m).

'Compacta': grows slowly to 15 × 5 ft. (4.5 × 1.5 m).

*Pinus cembra* 'Blue Mound'

*Pinus cembra* 'Chamolet'

*Pinus cembra* 'Chalet'

*Pinus cembra* 'Compacta'

'Compacta Glauca': denser than species, blue foliage.

'Egli': faster growing selection, 1 ft. (0.3 m) a year, maturing to 35 × 12 ft. (10.5 × 3.6 m).

'Matterhorn': said to be the first true dwarf form.

'Nana': slow-growing pyramidal dwarf for small gardens, reaches 24 in. (60 cm) in ten years.

*Pinus cembra* 'Compacta Glauca'

*Pinus cembra* 'Egli'

*Pinus cembra* 'Matterhorn'

*Pinus cembra* 'Nana'

## *Pinus cembra* (continued)

'Pygmaea': an irregular, flat-topped form to 4 × 2 ft. (1.2 × 0.6 m) tall and wide, short blue-green needles grow in congested tufts, some authorities regard this as a selection of *Pinus pumila*.

'Silver Sheen': reaches 4 ft. (1.2 m) in ten years, cone-shaped with silver-blue, slightly twisted needles.

'Stoderzinken': extremely slow-growing, reaching 8 in. (20 cm) in 20 years.

'Stricta': a slow-growing, dense, narrowly upright form with closely ascending branches.

*Pinus cembra* 'Pygmaea'

*Pinus cembra* 'Silver Sheen'

*Pinus cembra* 'Silver Sheen' foliage

*Pinus cembra* 'Stoderzinken'

*Pinus cembra* 'Stricta'

## *Pinus contorta*   lodgepole pine
### Zone 5

The lodgepole pine, or shore pine, is native from the Yukon Territory and Alaska south to California and east to South Dakota. It is found exposed to salt spray on the coast and at dryer elevations of 10,000 ft. (3,050 m). It is variable throughout its wide range and is often said to have three distinct geographic subspecies. Some have a straight trunk and narrow crown up to 75 ft. (23 m) tall; those near the coast are often shorter, 25 ft. (8 m), and crooked. Its branches are twisted (the epithet *contorta* is appropriate). The needles are in bundles of two, 2 in. (5 cm) long, spreading around the stem. They are straight, tapering to a point, bluish to deep green but turning yellow-green in winter. These pines are often loaded with cones, which hang on the trees for decades. Cones are 1 to 2 in. (2.5 to 5 cm) long and are covered with prickles. The seeds remain viable locked inside the cones for many years. In many areas the cones remained sealed with resin until the heat of a fire releases the small seeds into the ashes (similar to the jack pine, *Pinus banksiana*). The bark is red-brown or yellow-brown on young trees, developing deep fissures and dark scales or plates on old trees. This species is the provincial tree of Alberta.

The common name derives from the First Nations peoples' use of this straight, slender tree for poles to support lodges and tepees; it is still a source of posts and house logs.

'Frisian Gold': golden yellow needles.

var. *latifolia* 'Chief Joseph': very slow-growing, compact, bright golden-yellow form, named to honor the leader of the Nez Perce nation, who led his people across the Snake River into the wilderness of Idaho and Montana ahead of the U.S. Cavalry.

var. *latifolia* 'Taylor's Sunburst': displays golden yellow candles that become yellow-green, slow-growing to 20 ft. (6 m) with an upright to rounded habit and twisted branches.

'Spaan's Dwarf': slow-growing coarse dwarf, produces upright and irregular spreading branches that are densely clothed with short dark green needles.

*Pinus contorta* 'Frisian Gold'

*Pinus contorta* var. *latifolia* 'Chief Joseph' foliage

*Pinus contorta* var. *latifolia* 'Taylor's Sunburst'

*Pinus contorta* var. *latifolia* 'Chief Joseph'

*Pinus contorta* 'Spaan's Dwarf'

### *Pinus densiflora* Japanese red pine Zones 3 to 7

This hardy native of Japan, Korea, and northeastern China is widely planted as a specimen tree in gardens for its interesting habit and attractive bark. It is drought-tolerant and will tolerate salt. The Japanese red pine can reach 75 ft. (23 m) in its native habitat but is much shorter in cultivation. It is usually narrow and conical when young but spreads out in old age with a curved trunk and irregular habit with rather horizontal branches and forming a flat or domed top. *Pinus densiflora* is a two-needled pine; the needles remain three years, twisted and soft, 3 to 5 in. (7.5 to 12 cm) long, bright to dark green, displayed upright on the stem. The buds are small and red. The short-stalked cones are small, up to 2 in. (5 cm), and often clustered in groups of three to five. They remain two to three years. The bark is orangish to orange-red and flaking, hence the common name. *Pinus densiflora* is particularly popular as a bonsai specimen and is often used in Asian gardens.

*Pinus densiflora* pollen-bearing cones

*Pinus densiflora* bud

*Pinus densiflora* immature seed-bearing cones

*Pinus densiflora* mature seed-bearing cones

*Pinus densiflora* bark

*Pinus densiflora* 'Aurea'

*Pinus densiflora* 'Glitzer's Weeping'

*Pinus densiflora* 'Green Diamond'

*Pinus densiflora* 'Jane Kluis'

*Pinus densiflora* 'Jim Cross'

'Alice Verkade': a wide-spreading, bun-shaped, multi-stemmed plant with dense foliage, grows only 3 in. (7.5 cm) a year.

'Aurea': upright, foliage turns bright gold in winter.

'Glitzer's Weeping': weeping form with pendulous branches.

'Green Diamond': exhibits an upright diamond-shaped habit, reaches 20 ft. (6 m) in 20 years, long green needles.

'Jane Kluis': low mounding flat-topped selection, sometimes thought to be a cross with either *Pinus nigra* or *P. thunbergii* (authorities differ), straight stiff needles are held radially around the stem and the buds are prominent, reaches 5 ft. (1.5 m) tall in 20 years.

'Jim Cross': dwarf, dense and flat-topped, reaches 3 ft. (0.9 m) in 15 years.

### Pinus densiflora (continued)

'Low Glow', a flat, dense dwarf globe with vibrant green needles, will reach 6 ft. (1.8 m).

'Oculus-draconis': needles marked with two yellow bands, reaches 15 × 25 ft. (4.5 × 8 m).

'Pendula': a weeping form, needs to be staked over a standard to display its pendulous character, can be grown as a groundcover and is very effective planted at the top of a wall, down which its branches can cascade.

*Pinus densiflora* 'Low Glow'

*Pinus densiflora* 'Oculus-draconis'

*Pinus densiflora* 'Oculus-draconis' foliage

*Pinus densiflora* 'Pendula' as a groundcover

*Pinus densiflora* 'Pendula' cascading over a wall

*Pinus densiflora* 'Pumila'

*Pinus densiflora* 'Umbraculifera'

*Pinus densiflora* 'Soft Green'

*Pinus densiflora* 'Umbraculifera Compacta'

*Pinus densiflora* 'Vibrant'

'Pumila': a dwarf plant growing eventually to 12 ft. (3.6 m).

'Soft Green': smaller than 'Umbraculifera' with thin bright green needles, the name questionably legitimate.

'Umbraculifera': an upright branching habit with an umbrella-like head, called 'Tanyosho' in Japan, slow-growing, reaches 12 × 20 ft. (3.6 × 6 m) in 30 years, older bark exfoliates exposing patterns of red-brown, often grown as a standard.

'Umbraculifera Compacta': grows slowly to 6 ft. (1.8 m).

'Vibrant': a dwarf dense rounded plant with bright green needles, reaches 5 ft. (1.5 m) tall and wide.

*Pinus echinata*

### *Pinus echinata*   shortleaf pine
#### Zones 6 to 9

The shortleaf pine is found in New York, Pennsylvania, south to Georgia, and west to Missouri, Oklahoma, and Texas. It is one of the most widely distributed pines in the United States. It thrives on poor, clayey and sandy soils and is typically found colonizing on ridges and on sandy loams, or on floodplains, often in pure stands or with oaks and loblolly pines. *Pinus echinata* matures at a height of 80 to 100 ft. (24 to 30 m), with a broad crown and slender, pendulous, brittle branches. It will be smaller in cultivation. It often loses its lower branches, displaying a tall, clean, straight trunk. The crown opens with age with a twisting branching outline. This species grows fast and forms a deep taproot. It will adapt to dry soils and will resprout after fire injury.

The needles are in groups of two or three, pointed, soft and flexible, a dark bluish green, 3 to 5 in. (7.5 to 12 cm) long. They persist for two to five years. The seed-bearing cones are chestnut-brown, 1½ to 2 in. (3.5 to 5 cm) long, short-stalked, sometimes dangling, maturing in two years. They are usually in pairs or even clusters of four. They persist on the tree for several years even after opening to release their seeds. There is a prickle on the tip of each scale (*echinata* means "hedgehog-like"). The mature bark is dark brown tinged with red, with irregular, scaly plates.

This is an important timber species in the South. The wood is heavy, hard, and strong and is used for general carpentry. This species is only occasionally used in urban plantings and then because of its character, good looks, and platy bark.

*Pinus echinata* bark

*Pinus edulis*

*Pinus edulis* foliage

### *Pinus edulis*   piñon pine
Zones 6 to 8

The piñon pine is native to dry slopes in the mountains of California east to Texas and south to Mexico. This slow-growing, shrubby tree is usually 15 to 35 ft. (4.5 to 10.5 m) tall. It is irregularly rounded with a spreading crown. It can live 500 years. The blue-green, curved, sharp-pointed needles are in twos and set radially around the shoot. They are ¾ to 1½ in. (2 to 3.5 cm) long and persist up to six years. The undersides have lines of white dots. The resinous seed-bearing cones are 1½ in. (3.5 cm) long on short stalks. The bark is red-brown with scaly ridges. *Pinus edulis* is characterized by slow growth and small cones, which contain large seeds. It is uncommon in cultivation. This is a predominant pine in the Southwest, and the oily, tasty seeds were much eaten and traded by Native Americans. Most of the nuts are eaten by wildlife—jays, turkeys, and bears. The tree's abundant pitch was used to caulk boats and make baskets watertight. The wood was used as firewood. It is the state tree of New Mexico.

### *Pinus flexilis* limber pine
Zones 4 to 7

The limber pine is a small to medium-sized tree, usually growing 30 to 45 ft. (9 to 14 m), with an open habit. In its native habitat from Alberta, Canada, to the Rocky Mountains in Colorado and as far south as Arizona, it can reach 70 ft. (21 m). It is a timberline tree, growing at 4,000 to 10,000 feet (1,220 to 3,050 m). In cultivation the limber pine will likely eventually reach 50 ft. (15 m) with a 35 ft. (10.5 m) spread. It often is multi-stemmed with straight, vertical trunks and forked, upswept branches. With maturity it becomes broad and flat-topped. The gray-barked branches are frequently long, somewhat twisted, sparsely foliated, and very flexible. The twigs are so flexible that they can be tied into a knot. The blue-green needles are in sheathless bundles of five, 2½ to 3½ in. (6 to 9 cm) long. They are stiff, twisted, and bunched, clasping the tip of the branches, and persist up to six years. The cones have short stalks; they are egg-shaped, 3 to 6 in. (7.5 to 15 cm) long and 1½ in. (3.5 cm) wide. They are bright green and ripen to yellow-brown. The basal scales are reflexed and lack bristles. They contain almost wingless edible seeds. The bark of old trunks is thick, dark gray-brown or almost black and covered with thin, irregular, abun-

*Pinus flexilis*

*Pinus flexilis* cones

*Pinus flexilis* foliage

*Pinus flexilis* bark

*Pinus flexilis* 'Extra Blue'

*Pinus flexilis* 'Glauca' foliage and cones

*Pinus flexilis* 'Glauca Pendula'

*Pinus flexilis* 'Vanderwolf's Pyramid'

*Pinus flexilis* 'Watnong'

dant little scales; younger stems are whitish gray and smooth.

*Pinus flexilis* should be grown in full sun in well-drained, moist soil. It tolerates wind. It was an important source of construction lumber in earlier times. Most of the cultivars are grafted. This species has a symbiotic relationship with the pine white butterfly, *Neophasia menapia*, which feeds upon and spends its entire life span on or near the limber pine.

'Extra Blue': needles are a gray powdery blue, 8 ft. (2.5 m) high in ten years.

'Glauca': open branched, wide pyramidal form with silvery blue foliage, also known as 'Firmament'.

'Glauca Pendula': a fast-growing weeping, groundcover form unless staked.

'Vanderwolf's Pyramid': some say the best of the blue foliage forms with a dense, uniform habit, 30 to 50 ft. (9 to 15 m) high with a 20 to 30 ft. (6 to 9 m) spread, grows 2 ft. (0.6 m) a year and is adaptable to heat and a wide range of soil conditions.

'Watnong': an upright vigorous blue form to 50 ft. (15 m) tall and 35 ft. (10.5 m) wide.

### *Pinus jeffreyi*   Jeffrey pine
### Zone 5

The Jeffrey pine is native to mountain ranges from southern Oregon to lower California. It is closely related to the ponderosa pine but is seldom cultivated. A large, commanding tree, it can reach 100 ft. (30 m) with a conical crown. The twisted, blue-green, 7 to 9 in. (18 to 23 cm) long needles are in threes, crowded toward the ends of the branches. The seed-bearing cones are 6 to 9 in. (15 to 23 cm) long. The seeds are heavy and are carried and dispersed by chipmunks. The dark red-brown bark has a sweet odor, an identifying feature. This pine is particularly sensitive to air pollution.

*Pinus jeffreyi*

*Pinus koraiensis*

### *Pinus koraiensis*   Korean pine
Zones 4 to 7

This hardy, adaptable, and underused pine is native to Korea and the Amur region of China and Japan. Although pyramidal in youth, it becomes oval to rounded with maturity. The structure is often forked and somewhat open with graceful branching to the ground. In the garden it can be expected to be 30 to 60 ft. (9 to 18 m) in height with a 10 to 15 ft. (3 to 4.5 m) spread, but in the wild it can reach 90 ft. (27 m). The serrated needles are in fascicles of five, 3½ to 4½ in. (9 to 11 cm) long. They are somewhat loosely arranged and appear stiff with a bluish cast. They persist for three years. The cones are stalkless 3½ to 6 in. (9 to 15 cm) long and 2 in. (5 cm) wide. They are resinous and solitary (or sometimes several together). They often appear even on very young plants. The seeds are edible. The bark is gray-brown in color. *Pinus koraiensis* grows in most garden soils but prefers moist, well-drained conditions. This is a fine species to plant as a specimen or to use in groups. It produces top-quality timber. The cultivars are usually grafted.

*Pinus koraiensis* foliage

*Pinus koraiensis* cones

*Pinus koraiensis* (continued)

'Compacta Glauca': strong-growing, soft-textured, extremely graceful compact selection with very blue foliage on upright branches, reaches 15 to 20 ft. (4.5 to 6 m).

'Jack Corbit': blue-green needles tinged with yellow at the base, an adaptable plant that will reach 12 ft. (3.6 m) tall in ten years.

'Morris Blue': two-toned blue needles and resinous cones, grows rapidly to 40 ft. (12 m) tall.

'Rowe Arboretum': a cone-shaped slow-growing dwarf.

'Silveray': slow-growing selection with long silvery green needles and a pyramidal form, also known as 'Glauca'.

*Pinus koraiensis* 'Compacta Glauca'

*Pinus koraiensis* 'Jack Corbit'

*Pinus koraiensis* 'Rowe Arboretum'

*Pinus koraiensis* 'Compacta Glauca' foliage

*Pinus koraiensis* 'Morris Blue'

*Pinus koraiensis* 'Silveray'

### *Pinus leucodermis*   Bosnian pine
Zones 6 to 8

The Bosnian pine is native to Albania, Yugoslavia, Greece, and Italy. It is a slow-growing, medium-sized tree that reaches 30 ft. (9 m) in the garden and 60 to 90 ft. (18 to 27 m) in its native habitat. In its native areas the soils are dry and limey, but it adapts well to landscape culture in well-drained soil. It takes on a neat, conical outline as a young tree and exhibits medium dense foliage on densely packed and ascending branches. This habit is maintained for many years. Its erect, rich dark green needles are 2½ in. (6 cm) long and joined in bundles of two. They persist five to six years. They are quite stiff, sharply pointed, and often appear densely tufted at the ends of the branches. The spring buds are silvery white. The 2 to

*Pinus leucodermis*

*Pinus leucodermis* foliage

*Pinus leucodermis* bark

*Pinus leucodermis* pollen-bearing cones and immature seed-bearing cones

*Pinus leucodermis* seed-bearing cone

*Pinus leucodermis* (continued)

3 in. (5 to 7.5 cm) long, egg-shaped seed-bearing cones are blue for one year then turn purplish brown. The lower scale often has an incurved prickle. They are in groups of one to three. The bark on young branches is whitish in color, thus the epithet *leucodermis*. The very handsome mature bark is greenish gray in color, sometimes with a little exfoliation.

Grow in full sun as a specimen tree in a medium to large garden. It is excellent on dry or shallow chalk soils. *Pinus leucodermis* is said to be salt-tolerant.

'Aureospicata Nana': slow-growing with yellow-tipped leaves.

'Compact Gem': slow-growing dwarf with a slender, dense, compact, conical shape, nice drought- and salt-tolerant selection.

'Emerald Arrow': a compact spire form with rich dark green foliage on silver branches.

'Green Bun': a slow-growing compact dwarf.

'Irish Bell': grows as wide as tall with short, stiff deep green needles.

'Iseli Fastigiate': in ten years reaches 15 ft. (4.5 m) tall but only 3 ft. (0.9 m) wide, useful for screening.

*Pinus leucodermis* 'Aureospicata Nana'

*Pinus leucodermis* 'Compact Gem'

*Pinus leucodermis* 'Emerald Arrow'

*Pinus leucodermis* 'Green Bun'

*Pinus leucodermis* 'Irish Bell'

Pinus leucodermis 'Malinik'

Pinus leucodermis 'Mint Truffle'

Pinus leucodermis 'Shira'

Pinus leucodermis 'Schneverdingen'

Pinus leucodermis 'Smidtii'

Pinus leucodermis 'Satellite'

'Malinik': an upright-growing plant that will tolerate tough exposed situations.

'Mint Truffle': develops a dense upright broad teardrop shape with mint-green foliage, 5 to 10 ft. (1.5 to 3 m) in ten years.

'Satellite': a narrow dark green selection that grows slower than the species and with needles that are more erect, also known as 'Satellit'.

'Schneverdingen': a compact spherical form with short rich green needles.

'Shira': very slow-growing and compact, taking 25 years to reach 6 ft. (1.8 m) tall, new growth is creamy yellow.

'Smidtii': grows 1 in. (2.5 cm) a year into a dense, compact mound, also known as 'Schmidtii'.

### *Pinus longaeva*   Great Basin bristlecone pine
Zones 4 to 8

This species is famous for some specimens that are over 4,000 years old, making them the oldest living plants. One tree felled in Nevada in 1964 was documented at 4,844 years. They grow in the White Mountains of eastern California and into Nevada and Utah at elevations between 10,000 and 11,500 ft. (3,050 to 3,500 m), where they experience below-freezing temperatures half the year and annual rainfall of little more than 12 in. (30 cm). They inhabit steep slopes with poor soil. It is said that these trees comprised forests that once covered large areas of western United States. Today, few specimens are more than 30 ft. (9 m) tall with spreading crowns and large branches. The trees are narrow and conical. The branches are covered thickly with needles, which are short, deep green, shiny, and in sheathless clusters of five. These needles can live up to four decades. Many branches can be long and undivided. The bark is a deep red-brown. The seed-bearing cones are dark purple, about 3 in. (7.5 cm) long, and, of course, have prominent prickles on the scales. They mature in two years.

*Pinus longaeva* is closely related to *P. aristata* and was formerly grouped with it, but it differs in its leaves, which lack the white resin specks of *P. aristata*. Both these bristlecone pines are nearly always dwarf when grown in garden situations.

'Sherwood Compact': a slow-growing dense conical form reaching 4 ft. (1.2 m) after 15 years (sometimes confused in the trade with *Pinus aristata* 'Sherwood Compact', which see).

### *Pinus monticola*   western white pine   Zone 5

Some call this the mountain pine since this western relative of the eastern white pine (*Pinus strobus*) prefers to grow in elevations where the air is fresh and the surroundings are not crowded. In the wild it is found at 7,500 to 10,000 ft. (2,290 to 3,050 m), where the season without snow is brief. It is found in western Canada, Washington, Oregon, Idaho, Montana, and California. David Douglas, the great Scottish explorer-botanist, found this species in 1825. This is typically a straight-trunked tree, similar to *P. strobus* except it is usually denser and narrower. Only the upper branches arch upward; the lower branches are horizontally tiered, giving the tree a layered look. The species is even larger than its eastern kin, towering 150 to 200 ft. (46 to 60 m) above the forest floor. The slender, twisted, blue-green needles are in groups of five, 2 to 4 in. (5 to 10 cm) long, with a slight frosty appearance imparted by the rows of white stomata on all sides. They remain on the tree for about

*Pinus longaeva*

*Pinus longaeva* 'Sherwood Compact'

*Pinus monticola* foliage and cone

*Pinus monticola*

four years. The bark is a smooth gray until maturity when it is black with purple highlights and checkered—divided by narrow furrows and cross-checks into small, oblong scaly plates. The stalked seed-bearing cones are similar to the cones of its eastern cousin but larger, 6 to 10 in. (15 to 25 cm), and woodier. They appear in clusters and are covered with pitch. There are no spines. It is not a prolific tree: 40 cones on a single tree are considered a good crop, and the tree seldom produces fertile cones before it is 50 years old. *Pinus monticola* is rare in cultivation. It is the state tree of Idaho.

The tall, clear trunk of a mature western white pine produces very valuable wood. It is light and strong with a straight grain useful for framing and outstanding for wood carving. It is the wood from which matches are made.

'Pendula': drooping branches with dark green needles, best to stake when young.

'Rigby's Weeping': strongly pendulous with light green needles.

*Pinus monticola* 'Pendula'

*Pinus monticola* 'Rigby's Weeping'

### *Pinus mugo*   mugo pine
#### Zones 2 to 8

Mugo pine, or Swiss mountain pine, is widely planted and typically shrubby in habit; however, it is a very variable species. It can be a rambling prostrate shrub 2 to 6 ft. (0.6 to 1.8 m) or occasionally a small tree to 15 ft. (4.5 m) in the garden. It can reach 30 ft. (9 m) or even higher in its natural habitat in the mountains of central and southern Europe, from Spain to the Balkans. It succeeds in almost all soils. The needles are 1 to 2 in. (2.5 to 5 cm) long, typically curved or twisted, and in bundles of two, persisting five or more years. The needles are a rich green in well-grown plants but can turn yellowish green in the winter. The seed-bearing cones are stalkless, egg-shaped, 1 to 2½ in. (2.5 to 6 cm) long, in groups of one to four. The buds are resinous and red-brown in color. The bark is gray-brown and scaly. With age there are irregular plates. Mugo pines prefer growing in full sun with good air circulation in moist to dry, well-drained soil. This species can become unattractive in the garden if grown with poor drainage and no air circulation. It is also subject to pine needle scale and sawfly damage. It will tolerate high pH soils. Mugos usually do not produce a tap root and are easy to move.

*Pinus mugo*

*Pinus mugo* cone

*Pinus mugo* a mature specimen

*Pinus mugo* bonsai 28 years old

*Pinus mugo* 'Allen's'

*Pinus mugo* 'Aurea'

*Pinus mugo* 'Aurea' foliage

*Pinus mugo* 'Benjamin'

*Pinus mugo* is a very important landscape crop species in the United States and is commonly grown as a small specimen plant, often for use in groups in sunny mixed borders or as a foundation planting (remember that nursery specimens can sometimes lack uniformity). It is popular because of its hardiness (zone 2), its adaptability to low fertility in either acid or alkaline soil, and its wind, drought, and heat tolerance. It is best to select a cultivar; many of the more than 130 are very similar to one another. Mugos can be dwarf, upright, or ground-hugging, and have green, gold, or even variegated needles.

'Allen's': a dwarf slow-growing globose selection sometimes listed as 'Allen's Seedling'.

'Aurea': light green needles that turn bright gold in a sunny winter, a semi-dwarf, usually about 3 ft. (0.9 m) tall and wide, but sometimes up to 8 ft. (2.5 m) tall.

'Benjamin': a dwarf cushion to globular bush with medium green needles.

### *Pinus mugo* (continued)

'Big Tuna': a dense and compact but broad and upright tree with emerald-green needles, grows 3 to 5 in. (7.5 to 12 cm) a year.

'Bubikopf': short-needled dwarf.

'Compacta': dense, compact, globose, and slow-growing to 20 ft. (6 m) tall and wide.

'Corley's Mat': a dwarf, wide-spreading carpeting form with long twisted green needles.

*Pinus mugo* 'Big Tuna'

*Pinus mugo* 'Bubikopf'

*Pinus mugo* 'Compacta'

*Pinus mugo* 'Corley's Mat'

*Pinus mugo* 'Dolly's Choice'

*Pinus mugo* 'Fastigiata'

'Dolly's Choice': a dense upright dark green dwarf that grows less than 1 in. (2.5 cm) a year.

'ENCI': selected for superior and uniform mounding habit, reaches 5 to 6 ft. (1.5 to 1.8 m) with equal spread, attractive spring candles are light green.

'Fastigiata': compact, columnar, 6 × 2 ft. (1.8 × 0.6 m) in ten years.

'Gnom': a compact selection with deep jade-green foliage that grows in a dense, dark green globular mound.

'Goldspire': dwarf, 2 ft. (0.6 m) high by 4 ft. (1.2 m) wide with bright yellow spring shoots that mature to green, plant in a sunny site.

*Pinus mugo* 'ENCI'

*Pinus mugo* 'Gnom'

*Pinus mugo* 'Gnom' grown as a standard

*Pinus mugo* 'Goldspire'

### *Pinus mugo* (continued)

'Green Alps': a very slow-growing dense form that reaches 15 ft. (4.5 m) tall and wide at maturity.

'Green Candle': provides a spreading mound with dark green leaves, grows 2½ in. (6 cm) a year.

'Honeycomb': squat and globe-shaped, lime-green in summer changing to yellow in winter.

'Humpy': slow-growing with short dark green foliage.

'Jakobsen': a flat and spreading selection with thick, somewhat contorted dark green needles, grows 3 in. (7.5 cm) a year.

*Pinus mugo* 'Green Alps'

*Pinus mugo* 'Green Candle'

*Pinus mugo* 'Honeycomb'

*Pinus mugo* 'Humpy'

*Pinus mugo* 'Jakobsen'

*Pinus mugo* 'Krauskopf'

'Krauskopf': ground-hugging and irregular with bright green needles.

'Lilliput': broadly conical with short needles.

'Mayfair Dwarf': dark green and globe-shaped to 2 ft. (0.6 m).

'Mini Mops': a dwarf form derived from 'Mops', also known as 'Minimops'.

'Mitsch Mini': one of the best bun-shaped mugos but very slow-growing at 1 in. (2.5 cm) a year, short dark green twisted needles all seasons and very salt-tolerant.

*Pinus mugo* 'Lilliput'

*Pinus mugo* 'Mayfair Dwarf'

*Pinus mugo* 'Mini Mops'

*Pinus mugo* 'Mitsch Mini'

**Pinus mugo** (continued)

'Mops': a formal compact and globose form that reaches 3 ft. (0.9 m), growing about 2 in. (5 cm) a year, resinous bright green needles yellow a bit in winter.

var. *mugo*: various typical low-growers, size varies depending on seed source but wider than tall, sometimes spelled *mughus* and listed as a subspecies.

'Ophir': green during the growing season, turning golden in winter, com-pact and flat-topped, reaching 2 ft. (0.6 m) in ten years.

'Oregon Jade': tight, low bun, grow-ing 2 to 4 in. (5 to 10 cm) a year with ex-cellent jade-green foliage.

'Paul's Dwarf': an upright irregular miniature with very short needles, ¼ to ½ in. (0.6 to 1.2 cm), grows 2 to 3 in. (5 to 7.5 cm) a year but can be candled in spring and kept tiny for use in a trough or rock garden, good for bonsai.

*Pinus mugo* 'Mops' in November

*Pinus mugo* var. *mugo*

*Pinus mugo* 'Ophir'

*Pinus mugo* 'Oregon Jade'

*Pinus mugo* 'Paul's Dwarf'

*Pinus mugo* 'Picobello'

*Pinus mugo* 'Pot o' Gold'

*Pinus mugo* 'Prostrata'

*Pinus mugo* 'Pudgy'

*Pinus mugo* var. *pumilo*

'Picobello': a dwarf with short dark green needles.

'Pot o' Gold': slow-growing, mounding and compact, orange-yellow foliage in cold season, green in summer.

'Prostrata': deep dark green 6 in. (15 cm) tall and 24 in. (60 cm) wide, the name questionably legitimate.

'Pudgy': dark green with short twisted needles, grows 2 to 4 in. (5 to 10 cm) a year to 3 ft. (0.9 m) tall by 5 ft. (1.5 m) wide.

var. *pumilo*: potentially prostrate, sometimes with erect branching, but very variable, can be 10 ft. (3 m) wide,

*Pinus mugo* var. *pumilo* in a trough

*Pinus mugo* var. *pumilo* 'Kissen'

*Pinus mugo* 'Sherwood Compact'

### *Pinus mugo* (continued)

seed grown and inexpensive, unlikely to maintain a compact mound, making it inappropriate for limited-space plantings, turns yellow-green in winter, sometimes listed as a subspecies.

var. *pumilo* 'Kissen': slow-growing, 2 in. (5 cm) a year, short-needled, globe-shaped selection, formerly distributed as 'Brevifolia'.

'Sherwood Compact': dwarf, compact, and globe-shaped, growing only 1 to 2 in. (2.5 to 5 cm) a year, a superb choice for rock or trough gardens, dark green all seasons with showy buds.

'Slowmound': a dwarf uniform flat carpet of upward-facing shoots, slow-growing.

*Pinus mugo* 'Slowmound'

Pinus mugo 'Spaan'

Pinus mugo 'Sunshine'

Pinus mugo 'Tannenbaum'

Pinus mugo 'Tyrol'

Pinus mugo 'Teeny'

'Spaan': a low, slowly spreading plant with extremely short curved needles.

'Sunshine': new growth creamy yellow, turning green.

'Tannenbaum': a tough, nicely shaped conical plant that grows slowly to 10 ft. (3 m) by 6 ft. (1.8 m) wide.

'Teeny': a very tight, dense, rounded, short-needled plant with dark green winter color.

'Trompenburg': a slow-growing, spreading bush form.

'Tyrol': upright and open to 6 ft. (1.8 m) tall with dark green foliage.

## *Pinus mugo* (continued)

'Valley Cushion': a slow-growing flat bun with short dark green needles and informal habit.

'Varella': rounded form, deep green needles, grows 2½ in. (6 cm) a year, eventually reaching 20 in. (50 cm).

'Winter Gold': an open shrub with light green twisted needles that turn bright yellow in cold weather, reaches 3 to 5 ft. (0.9 to 1.5 m) in ten years.

'Winzig': tiny and cushion-shaped with small needles.

*Pinus mugo* 'Valley Cushion'

*Pinus mugo* 'Varella'

*Pinus mugo* 'Winter Gold'

*Pinus mugo* 'Winzig'

## *Pinus nigra*  Austrian pine
### Zones 4 to 7

The Austrian pine is native to eastern and southern Europe, France and Spain to Turkey, Cyprus, and the Ukraine; it is also seen in Morocco and Algeria. It is well adapted to the harsh Mediterranean climate, and in the United States it has naturalized in parts of Illinois. It grows to 120 ft. (36.5 m) tall in its native stands and will reach 60 to 80 ft. (18 to 24 m) in cultivation. Typically broad and conical when young, it becomes flat-topped with a short trunk and low-spreading branches as it gets older. The pointed and very stiff needles are 3 to 6 in. (7.5 to 15 cm) long in bundles of two. They are dark green with silvery lines of dots on both surfaces. They persist four years or more. The leaf sheath is ½ in. (1.2 cm) long and also persists. The needles do not break cleanly when bent, unlike another two-needled pine, *Pinus resinosa*. The 2 to 4 in. (5 to 10 cm) long, yellow-brown to light brown seed-bearing cones appear in groups of two to four and are stalkless or very short-stalked. The cone scales have thickened tips terminated by a short, blunt spine. They open over the winter and fall in the third spring. The very attractive mature bark of *P. nigra* is fissured with broad flat ridges that are light gray in color with dark brown, nearly black, crevices.

*Pinus nigra* is a large tree but has little value as a timber tree because the wood is coarse and knotty. It is best grown in full sun in moist, well-drained soils, although in the wild it appears in poor, rocky soils. It is tolerant of most soils (including alkaline soils), wind, salt (all forms are excellent for maritime areas), and urban pollution. It thrives better than any other pine in chalky soils and

*Pinus nigra*

*Pinus nigra* cone

*Pinus nigra* bark

### *Pinus nigra* (continued)

in bleak exposures and makes an excellent windbreak. In cultivation it is planted as an ornamental and in hedges; it is grown commercially for as a holiday tree. It is commonly planted in parks and other urban settings because of its dark green, salt- and pollution-tolerant leaves. Note that there are many subspecies with a great variation in different locations.

'Arnold Sentinel': upright, narrow and conical to 30 ft. (9 m) tall and 6 to 10 ft. (1.8 to 3 m) wide.

'Aurea': pale yellow needles.

'Bright Eyes': cone-shaped with pale green needles and white buds.

'Compacta': a broadly conical semidwarf 12 to 15 ft. (3.6 to 4.5 m) by 6 to 8 ft. (1.8 to 2.5 m) wide. The 6 in. (15 cm) long needles stay dark green all year and in spring display long white buds.

*Pinus nigra* 'Arnold Sentinel'

*Pinus nigra* 'Aurea'

*Pinus nigra* 'Bright Eyes'

*Pinus nigra* 'Compacta'

Pinus nigra 'Crapo'

Pinus nigra 'Fastigiata'

Pinus nigra 'Frank'

Pinus nigra 'Globosa'

Pinus nigra 'Helga'

'Crapo': low, rounded, and compact with dark green foliage, slow-growing and tough.

'Fastigiata': tall and narrow, eventually reaching 40 × 12 ft. (12 × 3.6 m).

'Frank': slow-growing, 2 to 3 in. (5 to 7.5 cm) a year, eventually more wide than tall.

'Globosa': a dense plant that will reach 8 ft. (2.5 m) high and wide, often multitrunked with long dark green needles, bark is almost black.

'Helga': a slow-growing, rounded, upright form with bright green needles and white buds.

## *Pinus nigra* (continued)

'Hornibrookiana': a slow-growing dwarf compact shrub form with long glossy dark green needles on stout branches, has cream-colored candles in spring, reaches 3 ft. (0.9 m) tall by 6 ft. (1.8 m) wide in 30 years.

'Obelisk': narrow and columnar, growing 6 to 8 in. (15 to 20 cm) a year, good accent plant.

'Oregon Green': reaches 40 to 60 ft. (12 to 18 m) by 30 to 40 ft. (9 to 12 m) wide with long coarse dark green needles, becomes flat-topped in time and is very tolerant of salt.

'Pygmaea': low-growing and globose to 6 ft. (1.8 m) tall, cones are smaller than the species.

'Wurstle': similar to 'Pygmaea' but faster growing.

*Pinus nigra* 'Hornibrookiana'

*Pinus nigra* 'Hornibrookiana' tailored

*Pinus nigra* 'Pygmaea'

*Pinus nigra* 'Obelisk'

*Pinus nigra* 'Oregon Green'

*Pinus nigra* 'Wurstle'

## *Pinus palustris* longleaf pine
### Zones 7 to 9

Pinus palustris

The longleaf pine is native to Virginia and south to Florida along the coastal plain. This fast-growing tree has an unusual growth habit. For the first six years it is a rosette, a cluster of long needles with a central bud at ground level. During this "grass" stage the plant is putting down deep roots, and the top growth starts only when the roots reach a sufficient supply of water. It is not tolerant of shade; the seedlings need open, sunny locations to establish. Plants grown in containers do not develop these deep roots and will often topple in the wind after a few year's growth. Longleaf pine becomes a loose, pyramidal to irregularly rounded tree reaching 40 to 60 ft. (12 to 18 m) in the garden, and up to 90 ft. (27 m) in the wild. Majestic stands of this pine prospered in the southeastern coastal plains of the United States in colonial times and were harvested for shipbuilding. This species is considered relatively fire-resistant.

The soft and flexible needles are extremely long, 10 to 16 in. (25 to 40 cm), and arranged in fascicles of three. They often occur in tufts on the ends of branches and persist for two years. The seed-bearing cones, 6 to 8 in. (15 to 20 cm) long and 2 in. (5 cm) wide, are often held at the end of branches. The cone scales are tipped by a small prickle. The bark is reddish brown and deeply furrowed. *Pinus palustris* should be grown in full sun in well-drained soil. It will tolerate hot, dry conditions. This is a useful pine for coastal conditions. The wood has commercial value because it is sturdy and strong. It is the state tree of Alabama and North Carolina.

Pinus palustris in youth

Pinus palustris foliage

Pinus palustris bark

### *Pinus parviflora* Japanese white pine Zones 5 to 8

Although pyramidal when young, this native of Japan and Korea becomes open and flat-topped with age. The trunk is often crooked, producing a picturesque plant in maturity. Growing 8 to 18 in. (20 to 46 cm) a year, it can reach 50 ft. (15 m) tall by 35 ft. (10.5 m) wide. The five-to-a-group needles are 1 to 3 in. (2.5 to 7.5 cm) long. They are crowded, curved, twisted, and finely toothed, with white bands that give the needle a glaucous appearance. The needles are held for three or four growing seasons. The species produces cones freely on young trees. They are 2 to 4 in. (5 to 10 cm) long and very conspicuous on the tree. They open wide when ripe and persist up to six years. The cones are solitary or in clusters, and nearly stalkless, with scales that are larger than those of other five-needled pines. The bark is charcoal-gray with flecks of red and exfoliates with age.

*Pinus parviflora* is an attractive, slow-growing tree, less than 1 ft. (0.3 m) a year. It is tolerant of most soils but demands good drainage. Japanese white pine should be grown in full sun or partial shade. It will tolerate salt spray but has trouble accepting heat. It is useful as a street tree and in containers. This species, very popular for its dwarf and slow-growing cultivars and commonly trained as a bonsai, has been the cause of numerous arguments among botanists; many bonsai trees have been produced on a multitude of different graft understocks, producing dissimilar results, and given invalid cultivar names.

*Pinus parviflora* foliage

*Pinus parviflora* cone

*Pinus parviflora* bark

*Pinus parviflora* bonsai 45 years old

*Pinus parviflora* bonsai 350 years old

*Pinus parviflora* 'Adcock's Dwarf'

*Pinus parviflora* 'Aoba-jo' foliage

*Pinus parviflora* 'Aoba-jo'

*Pinus parviflora* 'Aoi'

'Adcock's Dwarf': a dense, slow-growing, globose form with short gray-green needles clustered at the branch tips, sometimes varies depending on the understock, reaches 3 to 4 ft. (0.9 to 1.2 m) after 25 years.

'Aoba-jo': a narrow fastigiate tree with short curly blue needles.

'Aoi': displays tight bunches of silver-blue needles on an irregular upright habit, popular for bonsai because of its good trunk formation, grows 1 to 1½ in. (2.5 to 3.5 cm) a year.

### Pinus parviflora (continued)

'Ara-kawa': also popular for bonsai, corky bark with only 3 in. (7.5 cm) annual growth, reaching 4 ft. (1.2 m) in time.

'Bergman': grows 2 in. (5 cm) a year to produce a broadly conical plant with twisted blue-green needles, pollen-bearing cones are bright red in the spring.

'Blue Wave': semi-upright form, blue foliage, "wavy" branch structure, reaches 4 ft. (1.2 m) in ten years.

'Brevifolia': a small tree with sparse open branching and tight bundles of short blue-green needles.

'Disetsu': a conical pine with attractive tiered branching and green needles, reaches 36 × 24 in. (90 × 60 cm) in ten years.

'Doctor Landis Gold': a low-growing, spreading plant with golden needles.

*Pinus parviflora* 'Ara-kawa'

*Pinus parviflora* 'Bergman'

*Pinus parviflora* 'Blue Wave'

*Pinus parviflora* 'Brevifolia'

*Pinus parviflora* 'Disetsu'

*Pinus parviflora* 'Ei-ko-nishiki'

*Pinus parviflora* 'Fuku-zu-mi'

*Pinus parviflora* 'Gimborn's Ideal'

*Pinus parviflora* 'Glauca'

*Pinus parviflora* 'Glauca' foliage and cones

'Ei-ko-nishiki': artistic irregular branching with an almost prostrate form, deep green foliage, corky bark developing with age.

'Fuku-zu-mi': a low-spreading dwarf that usually looks windswept if not staked, twisted silver-blue needles, grows 6 in. (15 cm) a year to 8 ft. (2.5 m), said not to produce cones.

'Gimborn's Ideal': makes a large shrub to 25 ft. (8 m) with upright-reaching branches in an irregular outline and congested, curved, strikingly blue-green needles, reaches 6 to 8 ft. (1.8 to 2.5 m) in ten years.

'Glauca': popular and available, an irregular pyramidal small tree with long twisted silver-blue needles, persistent cones (some would say they outstay their welcome), reaches 6 to 8 ft. (1.8 to 2.5 m) in ten years. 'Pentaphylla Glauca' is the same as 'Glauca'.

## *Pinus parviflora* (continued)

'Glauca Brevifolia': needles are shorter and more upcurved than 'Glauca'.

'Glauca Nana': extremely slow-growing with an open habit, eventually becomes a flat-topped globe with short, twisted, blue needles.

'Goldilocks': a small cushion with bright gold leaves that will burn in full sun.

'Goykuri': very slow-growing and upright with gray-green needles and lots of cones.

'Kokonoe': a good choice for Asian-style gardens or bonsai because it grows slowly into a miniature tree-shaped plant.

*Pinus parviflora* 'Goldilocks'

*Pinus parviflora* 'Goykuri'

*Pinus parviflora* 'Glauca Brevifolia'

*Pinus parviflora* 'Kokonoe'

*Pinus parviflora* 'Ogon Janome'

*Pinus parviflora* 'Peterson'

*Pinus parviflora* 'Tani-mano-uki'

*Pinus parviflora* 'Watnong'

*Pinus parviflora* 'Watnong' foliage

'Ogon Janome': a dragon's-eye pine with bands of distinctive bright golden yellow bands on green needles.

'Peterson': more columnar than others, reaches 10 ft. (3 m) in 20 years, blue-green in all seasons, densely branched with no cones.

'Tani-mano-uki': slow-growing, its creamy white needles benefit from some protection.

'Watnong': very slow-growing into a regular pyramidal form, often rather full with incurving gray-blue needles.

### *Pinus peuce* Macedonian pine
Zones 4 to 7

This excellent specimen tree is native to Yugoslavia, Albania, and Greece. It grows slowly and keeps its dense, pyramidal habit. Although adaptable, it prefers full sun and moist, well-drained soil. It reaches 30 to 60 ft. (9 to 18 m). The foliage is dark blue-green; the cones, 3 to 6 in. (7.5 to 15 cm) long. The wood is light and durable and used in building. The resin is used in optical instruments. It is widely planted in Scandinavian parks and gardens.

'Cesarini': a very slow-growing upright pine with silver-gray needles.

*Pinus peuce*

*Pinus peuce* 'Cesarini'

*Pinus peuce* foliage and seed-bearing cone

*Pinus peuce* bark

*Pinus ponderosa*

### *Pinus ponderosa*   ponderosa pine   Zones 3 to 6(7)

This tall and stately tree grows on sunny mountain slopes and valleys from British Columbia south into Mexico and east as far as Nebraska. Stands occur from sea level up to 8,000 ft. (2,500 m). They can live 400 to 500 years. Lewis and Clark camped under them along their voyage of discovery; they wrote about this species, too, but it was named "ponderosa" by another botanical explorer, David Douglas, who noted the impressive size of the average specimen, up to 125 feet (38 m) in height. No doubt because of their deep and extensive root system, ponderosa pines are able to grow in locations that have as little as 12 in. (30 cm) of annual rainfall.

The ponderosa pine is widely appreciated not only as a very beautiful conifer but also for a long history of notable use as a timber tree. The species is intolerant of shade; it depends on fires to keep its stands open and to remove plants that compete with its seedlings for light. The bark of ponderosa pines helps them survive fires; in mature trees the bark can be more than 3 in. (7.5 cm) thick.

Ponderosa pines are straight-trunked

*Pinus ponderosa* needles and immature seed-bearing cones

*Pinus ponderosa* mature seed-bearing cone

*Pinus ponderosa* bark

***Pinus ponderosa*** (continued)

with short branches and as tall as 60 to 100 ft. (18 to 30 m) in cultivation. The needles are up to 10 in. (25 cm) long and are three to the bundle with a persistent sheath and arranged radially around the stout shoots. They are gray-green, stiff, and linear with a sharp point. The foliage is aromatic when crushed. The purple-brown seed-bearing cones are 3 to 5 in. (7.5 to 12 cm) long and covered with reflexed prickles. They appear solitary or in groups of three to five together. The cones fall after opening. The long needles and armed cones make *Pinus ponderosa* easy to identify. The edible seeds are relished by squirrels and chipmunks that disperse them. The bark is dark brown or purple-gray on young trees; with maturity the bark is orange-brown or purple-gray in broad flat scaly plates. The tree is a major timber species producing a high-grade lumber used for framing and finishing work. The stumps provide pitch-filled kindling for trouble-free fire-starting. It is the state tree of Montana.

***Pinus pumila*** dwarf stone pine Zones 3 to 8

This low, shrubby plant is native to east Asia—eastern Siberia, northeast China, Korea, and Japan. Very hardy, it grows at high elevations and is tolerant of winter winds. Although highly variable, it often grows rather prostrate. It can be 1 to 9 ft. (0.3 to 2.7 m) tall at maturity and grows very slowly. The blue-green needles are 1½ to 3 in. (3.5 to 7.5 cm) long in groups of five. They are densely arranged on the stem and somewhat appressed to the stem. The 1 to 2 in. (2.5 to 5 cm) long seed-bearing cones are held in terminal groups. Immature purple-violet cones mature to reddish to yellow-brown. The new stem growth is green and becomes gray-brown. *Pinus pumila* should be grown in full sun in well-drained soils. This species is popular in rock gardens or where a dwarf conifer is appropriate. It is closely related to *P. cembra*, and it is often difficult to tell the dwarf forms of the two species apart.

'Barmstedt': long twisted silver leaves.

*Pinus ponderosa* bonsai 150 years old

*Pinus pumila*

*Pinus pumila* 'Barmstedt'

*Pinus pumila* 'Blue Mops'

*Pinus pumila* 'Dwarf Blue'

*Pinus pumila* 'Glauca'

*Pinus pumila* 'Globe'

*Pinus pumila* 'Nana'

*Pinus pumila* 'Yes-Alpina'

'Blue Mops': dense and ground-hugging with short gray-blue needles.

'Dwarf Blue': a spreading, dense, horizontal form with outstanding blue color, grows 4 to 6 in. (10 to 15 cm) a year and can reach 6 ft. (1.8 m) tall, also listed as 'Blue Dwarf'.

'Glauca': a medium-sized shrub with bright gray-blue needles, this and 'Dwarf Blue' are confused in the trade or might be the same.

'Globe': dwarf and spherical with blue-gray needles.

'Nana': a globose semi-dwarf.

'Yes-Alpina': a horizontal-growing selection, 3 ft. (0.9 m) high with a spread of 6 to 8 ft. (1.8 to 2.5 m), and silver-blue winter color. It does not produce cones.

### *Pinus pungens*   Table Mountain pine   Zone 7

The Table Mountain pine is a small to medium-sized tree that is typically 20 to 40 ft. (6 to 12 m) tall and has an irregular crown with sparse, large, heavy branches. It is a two-needled pine with twisted yellow-green needles that are 1½ to 3½ in. (3.5 to 9 cm) long and persist for three years. The stalkless seed-bearing cones are egg-shaped, 3 in. (7.5 cm) long, dark red-brown, and armed with large, stout, curved, hooked spines. *Pungens* means "sharp-pointed" and refers to the cone prickles. The branches are often covered with many persistent whorls of closed cones. The bark is dark brown to gray-brown with scaly plates. Although Table Mountain is in the state of Tennessee, this pine is native to the Appalachian Mountains on rocky, dry ridges and slopes from Pennsylvania to Georgia. It is used for fuel, pulpwood, and low-grade timber.

*Pinus pungens* foliage and cone

*Pinus pungens*

## *Pinus resinosa*   red pine
### Zones 2 to 5

The red pine is so named because of the reddish appearance of the bark. This extremely cold hardy pine is native in Newfoundland and Manitoba, south to the mountains of Pennsylvania and west to Michigan. The trunk is typically short, and the tree develops a heavily branched crown while young. With age the crown takes on a symmetrical, oval to rounded shape. It reaches 50 to 80 ft. (15 to 24 m) high but can grow to 125 ft. (38 m) or more. They can exist 200 to 300 years. The foliage is tufted. The needles are in twos, 4 to 6 in. (10 to 15 cm) long, and densely arranged on the branches in tufts near the end of branches; they persist four to five years. The medium to dark green sharply pointed needles are slender, straight, and shiny, and snap easily when bent. Liquid resinous sap exudes from the broken foliage, making the stems sticky and strongly scented. The leaf sheaths are ⅝ to ⅞ in. (1.5 to 2.1 cm) long and are shed the second year. The seed-bearing cones are small; they are borne near the end of the branch singly (or in pairs) and stalkless (or with a short stalk). They turn from green to purple to chestnut-brown in color and remain on the tree two years. They are held at right angles to the branches. There are no prickles on the cone scales. Red pine begins to bear cones at 15 to 25 years of age and produces a good seed crop every three to seven years. The bark is orange-red and scaly on young trees and with age forms large, flat, reddish brown scaly plates; these are often diamond-shaped with flat ridges.

*Pinus resinosa* should be grown in full sun, protected from high winds. It will tolerate dry, acid, sandy, or gravelly soils but is rarely found on wet ground and will not tolerate sea or road salt, or urban pollution. It tends to lose its lower

*Pinus resinosa*

*Pinus resinosa* foliage and seed-bearing cones

*Pinus resinosa* bark

### *Pinus resinosa* (continued)

branches. Its seeds germinate immediately upon sowing. It is a beautiful tree with its dark green tufts of foliage and attractive, broadly pyramidal, dome-shaped crown. Countless seedlings have been planted in abandoned fields to prevent erosion. With its height, straightness, and lack of taper, this adaptable pine provided ideal logs for posts and cabins, and in the 19th century was prized for ships' masts. The light, hard, closely grained wood is used today for construction and pulp. It is among the most extensively planted species in the northern United States and Canada for wood production, snow breaks, windbreaks, and holiday trees. It is the state tree of Minnesota, where it is called the Norway pine, for the homeland of the men who logged it.

'Don Smith': a mounding form broader than high with ascending branches, growing 6 in. (15 cm) a year, striking tiny red pollen-bearing cones at the tip of spring candles.

'Morel': a globose and compact but informal shrub form.

'Quinobequin': a dwarf, globe-shaped form, 10 × 15 ft. (3 × 4.5 m), with coarse 6 in. (15 cm) needles and brown branches.

'Ruby's Upright': narrow and oval-shaped, 30 × 10 ft. (9 × 3 m).

'Wissota': a dwarf form that can reach 6 ft. (1.8 m).

*Pinus resinosa* 'Don Smith'

*Pinus resinosa* 'Morel'

*Pinus resinosa* 'Quinobequin'

*Pinus resinosa* 'Ruby's Upright'

*Pinus resinosa* 'Wissota'

## *Pinus rigida*   pitch pine
### Zones 4 to 7

Found in New Brunswick to Lake Ontario, south to Georgia and west to West Virginia, Tennessee, and Kentucky, *Pinus rigida* grows both in upland areas and on the coastal plain. This is the species that dominates Cape Cod, eastern Long Island, and the New Jersey Pine Barrens. Pitch pine thrives on poor soil: shallow, sandy, and acidic. It tolerates drought but is also found in swamps. It often helps to stabilize the land and will survive forest fires, making new sprouts from the roots or trunk. It is often the only tree that is able to survive on repeatedly burned-over areas. It can be 70 to 80 ft. (21 to 24 m) tall but is more commonly 30 to 60 ft. (9 to 18 m). With maturity the crown is often irregular and gnarly. In southern locations it tends to have a straighter form. The tree is extremely variable and is often described as picturesque. It can live 150 to 200 years.

The grouped-in-three needles are stiff, twisted, and sharply toothed with blunt points. They are 3 to 5 in. (7.5 to 12 cm) long, yellow-green, and set radially around the shoot, persisting for two years. The seed-bearing cones are prickly, egg-shaped, 1 to 3 in. (2.5 to 7.5 cm) long, unstalked, and displayed at right angles to the branch, often in clusters of two or three. A short, rigid, recurved prickle makes the cone difficult to handle. Cones can remain on the tree for ten years or more. They open irregularly or remain closed until opened by fire. This species begins cone-bearing as early as age three to five years and produces a good seed crop every four to nine years. The bark is dark reddish brown and thick with deep furrows. The trunks are often fire-scarred.

Pitch pine is not often cultivated as an ornamental or used as a lumber tree; however, its scraggly, scenic appearance and tolerance of poor soils make it a worthwhile choice for wasteland locations. The wood is fairly decay resistant. It is heavy and strong and can be used for construction, mine supports, and railroad ties, though it is usually not available in large sizes. It is often used as a fuel wood and in the manufacture of charcoal. In earlier times the wood was appreciated for its abundant resin, which was used to make turpentine and tar. Pitch pine seeds are important to nuthatches, pine grosbeaks, and black-capped chickadees.

*Pinus rigida*

Pinus rigida foliage and immature seed-bearing cone

Pinus rigida mature seed-bearing cone

Pinus rigida bark

Pinus rigida bonsai 100 years old

## Pinus rigida (continued)

'Sherman Eddy': dwarf and upright with dense deep green whorled foliage.

Pinus rigida 'Sherman Eddy'

## *Pinus strobiformis*
### southwestern white pine
#### Zones 6 to 9

The southwestern white pine is native to Arizona, New Mexico, and south into Mexico. It grows 30 to 50 ft. (9 to 15 m) in the garden but can reach 80 ft. (24 m) in the wild. It has a broad, rounded crown and sometimes looks untidy. The soft needles are 1½ to 3½ in. (3.5 to 9 cm) long in groups of five. They are often twisted and somewhat bluer than eastern white pine. The cylindrical seed-bearing cones are short-stalked or stalkless, 6 to 10 in. (15 to 25 cm) long. The bark is dark brown and deeply furrowed. Southwestern white pine grows best in full sun in moist, well-drained soils. It is no surprise that it is somewhat more heat- and drought-tolerant than the eastern white pine, but otherwise the trees are very similar. It is sometimes grown as a holiday tree.

*Pinus strobiformis* is part of a "continuum of pine," so to speak, beginning with *P. monticola* in the Pacific Northwest, intergrading into *P. flexilis* in the Rocky Mountains (Colorado), south to *P. strobiformis* in the southwestern United States, and ending up as *P. ayacahuite* in Mexico. Understandably, these pines are all very similar and have similar uses in the landscape. They have, however, subtle differences both as immature and mature specimens.

*Pinus strobiformis* foliage

*Pinus strobiformis*

### *Pinus strobus*   eastern white pine   Zones 3 to 7

Without disturbance, an eastern white pine can grow as long as 400 years. It is the tallest tree native to eastern North America, the state tree of Maine and Michigan, and the provincial tree of Ontario. Legend claims that when settlers first came from Europe, the eastern white pine forests were so vast that a squirrel could travel all its life without ever coming down from the trees. The trees, marvelously straight and thick, were 150 ft. (46 m) tall; 80 ft. (24 m) or more of the trunk might be free of branches. No other tree has played so great a role in the life and history of the people of North America. It spawned the forest industry: navy fleets were built with it (the British Crown needed the tall, straight white pines for Royal Navy masts), settlements grew up around the sawmills, and railroads and canals were constructed to move the pine from the forests. Native peoples used the bark, needles, and gum of *Pinus strobus* to treat lung problems, and even modern cough syrups contain ingredients derived from it.

Eastern white pine is found from New-

*Pinus strobus*

*Pinus strobus* foliage

*Pinus strobus* cone

*Pinus strobus* bark

foundland west to southeastern Manitoba and south into northern Georgia. It often is found growing in pure stands on well-drained sandy soils. In cultivation, *Pinus strobus* grows best in a rich moist soil in full sun. It is not tolerant of salt, air pollution, ozone or sulfur dioxide and should not be planted close to highways. This species is not tolerant of clay soil. It is easily transplanted because of its wide-spreading root system. Eastern white pine will grow 1 to 3 ft. (0.3 to 0.9 m) a year. It is pyramidal when young and open and spreading with age, often becoming flat-topped and irregular. It typically grows with one trunk and seldom needs any pruning. One should provide plenty of open space for adequate root development. Pines are very flammable.

*Pinus strobus* often sheds part of its canopy from the weight of snow

*Pinus strobus* is a very handsome and ornamental species, a valuable plant for parks, estates, and other large properties. It is one of the most beautiful pines native to North America. In England it is known as the Weymouth pine (after Lord Weymouth, who planted it in Wiltshire in the early 18th century), but it does not do as well in that climate. A well-grown mature white pine is without equal. Unfortunately this imposing tree is often placed in spaces too small for it to achieve its potential.

The bluish green needles are in groups of five, up to 5 in. (12 cm) long. They are soft, thin, straight, and flexible. The needles are held for two seasons. The buds are small, pointed, and resinous. The late summer and autumn browning and shedding of the older needles always leads to concern about the tree's health and calls to arboretum hot lines. This is entirely natural. Needles develop only toward the ends of the twigs. The cones are cylindrical, 4 to 6 in. (10 to 15 cm) long; they take two years to mature and hang from a thick, short, round stem. Trees begin bearing cones at age five to ten and produce heavily every three to five years. The cones are aromatic and often ooze white resin. The bark on older trees is dark gray-brown, rough, and furrowed, 1 to 2 in. (2.5 to 5 cm) thick. The smooth, thin bark of young trees is damaged easily by fire or by careless use of string trimmers.

White pine blister rust is a fungus (*Cronartium ribicola*) that attacks *Pinus strobus* and other five-needled pines, including western white pine (*P. monticola*) and limber pine (*P. flexilis*). The pathogen has a complicated life cycle with an alternate host genus, *Ribes* (currants and gooseberries); it does not spread pine to pine. The rust eventually invades the tree's bark and spreads until the stem is girdled, killing the tree. White pine blister rust has invaded most white pine areas in North America. This is an im-

**Pinus strobus** (continued)

portant and troublesome forest pathogen. Many states have quarantines to prevent cultivation of *Ribes* species.

A destructive native insect that attacks *Pinus strobus* is the white pine weevil (*Pissodes strobi*). This pest kills the terminal leader. It sometimes affects other pines, especially the Scots (*Pinus sylvestris*), Japanese (*P. densiflora*), limber (*P. flexilis*), and jack (*P. banksiana*) pines. Occasionally the Norway spruce (*Picea abies*), Colorado spruce (*P. pungens*), and Douglas-fir (*Pseudotsuga menziesii*) are targeted. Typically trees over 3 ft. (0.9 m) tall in full sun will be susceptible. The adult beetles emerge from their winter stay in leaf litter and lay eggs in the terminal leaders. The emerging larvae feed on the inner bark of the leader. Gardeners will usually first notice curling, wilting, and dying of the previous year's terminal leader in mid-summer. Side branches will often bend upward to take over as terminal leaders, making the tree permanently forked. Application of insecticide effective against adult weevils can be done by a licensed person in early spring. Only the terminal leader needs to be sprayed.

Dwarf forms of *Pinus strobus* can be very confusing. The same plant often appears under several names (for instance, 'Nana' is frequently labeled 'Umbraculifera'). The cultivars 'Radiata', 'Blue Shag', 'Pumila', 'Compacta', and 'Umbraculifera' can be differentiated only by an expert. The same is true of the faster growing 'Pygmaea' and 'UConn' as well as the dwarfs 'Horsford', 'Minuta', and 'Sea Urchin'.

'Bennett Contorted': a small tree with contorted foliage and strongly weeping side branches, reaching 15 to 20 ft. (4.5 to 6 m) if trained, does not produce cones.

'Bennett Dragon's Eye': a small dragon's-eye selection, growing less than 6 in. (15 cm) a year.

'Billaw': a compact globose dwarf.

'Bloomer's Dark Globe': broadly oval dwarf to 6 ft. (1.8 m) tall with dark blue needles, does not produce cones.

'Blue Shag': slow-growing, 4 in. (10 cm) a year with a dense, rounded habit and silver-blue needles.

*Pinus strobus* 'Bennett Contorted'

*Pinus strobus* 'Bennett Dragon's Eye'

*Pinus strobus* 'Billaw'

*Pinus strobus* 'Bloomer's Dark Globe'

*Pinus strobus* 'Blue Shag'

*Pinus strobus* 'Brevifolia'

*Pinus strobus* 'Cesarini'

*Pinus strobus* 'Colson's Nest'

*Pinus strobus* 'Compacta'

*Pinus strobus* 'Coney Island'

*Pinus strobus* 'Contorta'

*Pinus strobus* 'Curtis Dwarf'

'Brevifolia': a slow-growing, compact, pyramidal form with dark blue-green needles that are silvery beneath.

'Cesarini': a globular bush with long dark gray-green needles.

'Colson's Nest': slow-growing, dwarf, and mounding.

'Compacta': a name applied to any dwarf cultivar.

'Coney Island': dense foliage that is tufted at the ends of the branches with a cloud-like form wider than tall, growing 3 in. (7.5 cm) a year to 3 × 5 ft. (0.9 × 1.5 m) tall and wide, producing many small cones.

'Contorta': densely set twisted branches and leaves.

'Curtis Dwarf': compact and dense.

**Pinus strobus** (continued)

'Diggy': a dwarf reaching 5 to 8 ft. (1.5 to 2.5 m) over 12 years with a conical habit and short needles.

'Elf': narrowly conical and very slow-growing, eventually reaching 12 ft. (3.6 m).

'Fastigiata': branches ascend at a 45° angle from the trunk, beautiful fast-growing, narrowly upright cultivar, less likely to lose branches from ice and snow. An excellent choice.

'Golden Candles': an upright, densely branched, shrubby plant reaching 7 × 5 ft. (2 × 1.5 m) in eight years, candles and the early year's growth display a bright golden color.

Pinus strobus 'Fastigiata'

Pinus strobus 'Diggy'

Pinus strobus 'Elf'

Pinus strobus 'Fastigiata' branching structure

Pinus strobus 'Golden Candles'

*Pinus strobus* 'Green Shadow'

*Pinus strobus* 'Hillside Gem'

*Pinus strobus* 'Hillside Winter Gold'

*Pinus strobus* 'Horsford'

*Pinus strobus* 'Louie'

*Pinus strobus* 'Hershey'

'Green Shadow': a dense multi-trunked form that has a remarkable dark green needle color, reaching 10 ft. (3 m) in 20 years.

'Hershey': dwarf and bun-shaped, stiff-looking blue needles, grows 4 in. (10 cm) a year to 2 to 3 ft. (0.6 to 0.9 m) tall and 5 ft. (1.5 m) wide.

'Hillside Gem': grows to 6 ft. (1.8 m) tall with dense, upright tufts of short, dark green foliage.

'Hillside Winter Gold': a vigorous large tree 50 to 80 ft. (15 to 24 m) tall and 20 to 40 ft. (6 to 12 m) wide, needles are blue-green in summer turning bright golden in winter.

'Horsford': one of the best bun-shaped dwarf pines, seldom reaches 5 ft. (1.5 m) tall and wide, growing 2 in. (5 cm) a year, thin, medium green needles, cones early.

'Louie': golden needles all seasons.

*Pinus strobus* 'Merrimack'

*Pinus strobus* 'Minima'

*Pinus strobus* 'Minuta'

*Pinus strobus* 'Nana'

### *Pinus strobus* (continued)

'Merrimack': a dense, compact, rounded globe of silver-blue foliage growing 4 in. (10 cm) a year to 8 ft. (2.5 m).

'Minima': rich green needles.

'Minuta': a low-growing compact bun with short blue-green needles, reaching 5 ft. (1.5 m) after 20 years, does not produce cones, questionably legitimate name.

'Nana': dense, spreading, irregular mound, slow-growing with puffy mounds of blue-green foliage, some of the numerous variations of this form become larger.

*Pinus strobus* 'Nana' a mature plant

*Pinus strobus* 'Oliver Dwarf'

'Oliver Dwarf': dense, broad, and flat-topped.

'Ontario': an irregular dwarf with a layered, spreading habit and short needles; it sometimes puts out coarse growth and loses its dwarfness.

'Ottawa': a pendulous meandering form unless staked, graceful weeping branches.

*Pinus strobus* 'Fastigiata' and *P. s.* 'Nana' side by side

*Pinus strobus* 'Ottawa'

*Pinus strobus* 'Pendula' foliage

*Pinus strobus* 'Pendula'

### *Pinus strobus* (continued)

'Pendula': often multistemmed and irregular in form, the branches are horizontal with the branchlets pendulous, reaches 10 ft. (3 m) tall and wide, can be a living sculpture with its large clusters of long, twisting, graceful blue-green needles. Old specimens are wonders to behold.

'Prostrata': a procumbent plant, with a sprawling open habit without a leader.

'Pumila': a globose dwarf with twisted needles, growing 2 in. (5 cm) a year.

'Pygmaea': a globose dwarf with bright green needles.

*Pinus strobus* 'Pendula' a mature plant

*Pinus strobus* 'Pygmaea'

*Pinus strobus* 'Radiata'

*Pinus strobus* 'Raraflora'

*Pinus strobus* 'Sea Urchin'

*Pinus strobus* 'Shaggy Dog'

*Pinus strobus* 'Soft Touch'

'Radiata': a garden white pine, slow-growing and globose, to 4 ft. (1.2 m) tall after 25 years, often labeled 'Nana'.

'Raraflora': often found but possibly an illegitimate name.

'Sea Urchin': thin but dense blue needles on a low mounded plant that grows only 2 in. (5 cm) a year to 3 to 4 ft. (0.9 to 1.2 m) tall and wide.

'Shaggy Dog': the name says it all.

'Soft Touch': a dense, flat-topped cushion with short, twisting needles.

*Pinus strobus* 'Torulosa'

*Pinus strobus* 'Torulosa' foliage

*Pinus strobus* 'UConn'

## *Pinus strobus* (continued)

'Torulosa': a weird, open, upright form with twisted branches and densely set, twisted needles.

'UConn': an upright, broad, dense, compact, flat-topped selection that reaches 18 ft. (5.5 m) in 15 years, a nice form without shearing.

'Umbraculifera': similar to 'Nana'.

'Vanderwolf's Green Globe': dark green foliage, similar to 'Nana' but faster growing and denser.

'Verkade's Broom': rounded and wider than tall with light green foliage. Popular.

*Pinus strobus* 'Umbraculifera'

*Pinus strobus* 'Vanderwolf's Green Globe'

*Pinus strobus* 'Verkade's Broom'

### *Pinus sylvestris*   Scots pine
#### Zones 2 to 8

The Scots pine, or Scotch pine, is the only pine native to the British Isles. Once common throughout England and Wales, the species is still encountered in wild stands in northern Scotland; and it is established in most of Europe and Asia, across northern Europe from Spain north and east as far as Siberia and south into Turkey, making it one of the most widely distributed and hardiest pines in the world. It is one of the most important timber trees in those regions. Since its introduction in 1752, it has naturalized in North America from southeastern Canada and New England west to Iowa. It is striking with its bright orange-red peeling bark when young and its cones that point backward along the branches. With age the bark becomes rugged, gray, and fissured. The Scots pine grows 30 to 60 ft. (9 to 18 m) typically but can be up to 90 ft. (27 m) tall. Young plants are conical, but with age the species becomes high-branched, flat-topped, or umbrella-shaped. Some plants develop a gnarled, interesting shape. It grows rapidly during youth and is very tolerant of moisture and climatic extremes; still, it should be placed in a well-drained situation. The needles are 1½ to 3 in. (3.5 to 7.5 cm) long, twisted, rigid, and in twos. The foliage is a glaucous blue-green with waxy white lines on both surfaces, persisting for three years. The pollen-bearing cones are yellow, clustered at the base of the current season's shots. Dark red seed-bearing cones develop at the tips of the current season's shoots. Cones appear singly or in groups of two or three. They are only 1 to 3 in. (2.5 to 7.5 cm) long, short-stalked, and usually point backward on

*Pinus sylvestris*

*Pinus sylvestris* foliage and pollen-bearing cones

*Pinus sylvestris* seed-bearing cones

*Pinus sylvestris* bark

*Pinus sylvestris* bonsai

## *Pinus sylvestris* (continued)

the branch. The cone scales are often flat and quite thick at the tip. There are no prickles on the back of the cone. This helps distinguish it from *Pinus virginiana* (scrub pine), which has prickles. The mature bark is gray or red-brown with long fissures. Stems up to 12 in. (30 cm) in diameter have a thin orange bark (light to dark brown, reddish, or cinnamon) that exfoliates in small, irregular papery plates. It is very attractive and noticeable, since the trees so often are high branched.

Grow this pine in full sun on acidic, well-drained soils. It will tolerate a wide range of soil conditions, including poor soil. It will seed into poor sandy soils

*Pinus sylvestris* tailored

where it can outgrow other species. This is an important holiday tree because of its rapid growth and blue-green color. With its resistance to urban smog, its hardiness, and its adaptability, it is also useful for windbreaks and screens. Intolerant of heat and drought, it is not a good choice for zones 7 or 8.

*Pinus sylvestris* 'Albyns'

*Pinus sylvestris* 'Argentea Compacta'

*Pinus sylvestris* 'Aurea'

*Pinus sylvestris* 'Beacon Hill'

*Pinus sylvestris* 'Bergman'

'Albyns': a slow-growing, prostrate form 8 ft. (2.5 m) across by only 16 in. (40 cm) high, displays thick shiny needles all seasons.

'Argentea Compacta': a dense form with silvery foliage that can reach 10 ft. (3 m).

'Aurea': foliage that turns golden yellow in early winter and is blue-green with a hint of yellow during the warm seasons, growing slowly to 30 to 50 ft. (9 to 15 m).

'Beacon Hill': dwarf rounded globe with blue-green porcupine needles, grows 4 in. (10 cm) a year, reaches 4 ft. (1.2 m) tall and wide in ten years.

'Bergman': dense and solid, 20 × 36 in. (51 × 91 cm) tall and wide.

*Pinus sylvestris* 'Beuvronensis'

*Pinus sylvestris* 'Compressa'

*Pinus sylvestris* 'Fastigiata'

### *Pinus sylvestris* (continued)

'Beuvronensis': a broad, low, bushy, dome-shaped form with blue-green needles, grows very slowly to 4 ft. (1.2 m) after decades. Ideal for rock gardens.

'Compressa': strongly ascending branches are tightly pressed around the central leader, producing a columnar tree to about 6 ft. (1.8 m).

'Fastigiata': a narrow columnar form to 25 ft. (8 m), long blue-green needles and orange papery bark. A great accent plant, but the branches should be tied in winter to prevent snow and wind damage.

'Frensham': slow-growing with congested blue-green foliage.

*Pinus sylvestris* 'Frensham

*Pinus sylvestris* 'Gold Coin' foliage

*Pinus sylvestris* 'Greg's Variegated'

*Pinus sylvestris* 'Globosa Viridis'

*Pinus sylvestris* 'Helms'

*Pinus sylvestris* 'Gold Coin'

'Globosa Viridis': an ovoid shrub that is densely clothed to the ground with long, shaggy, mid-green foliage, a knobby appearance, sometimes listed as *Pinus nigra*.

'Gold Coin': slow-growing, good yellow foliage in winter.

'Greg's Variegated': creamy yellow foliage.

'Helms': medium green with short, tufted needles.

*Pinus sylvestris* 'Hillside Creeper'

*Pinus sylvestris* 'Mitsch Weeping'

*Pinus sylvestris* 'Nana'

### Pinus sylvestris (continued)

'Hillside Creeper': grows 12 in. (30 cm) a year to form a large mat of undulating branches with medium green needles. A strong grower.

'Mitsch Weeping': a prostrate form that can be trained on a standard.

'Nana': very slow-growing small bush, with blue-gray needles, reaches 18 in. (46 cm).

'Nana Compacta': a compact rounded shrub reaching 4 ft. (1.2 m) tall by 6 ft. (1.8 m) wide in ten years, blue-green all seasons.

*Pinus sylvestris* 'Nana Compacta'

*Pinus sylvestris* 'Repens'

*Pinus sylvestris* 'Riverside Gem'

*Pinus sylvestris* 'Sentinel'

*Pinus sylvestris* 'Sherwood'

'Repens': forms a slow-growing low mat that is never over 8 in. (20 cm) high in an irregular outline with dull green needles and large resinous buds.

'Riverside Gem': a slow-growing, conical, dense, upright tree that can become large with time.

'Saxatilis': a dense, irregular, dwarf prostrate bush without a leader, becomes flat-topped with maturity.

'Sentinel': a relatively slow-growing selection with a dense, neat, narrow, columnar habit and good blue color.

'Sherwood': a dense, upright dwarf.

*Pinus sylvestris* 'Spaan's Slow Column'

*Pinus sylvestris* 'Tabuliformis'

*Pinus sylvestris* 'Viridis Compacta'

### *Pinus sylvestris* (continued)

'Spaan's Slow Column': a slow-growing, narrow columnar form with coarse, thick, blue needles, holds snow well.

'Tabuliformis': a table-forming clone.

'Viridis Compacta': dwarf with rich green twisted needles.

'Watereri': usually considered a dwarf plant with globose form only 8 to 12 in. (20 to 30 cm) tall and wide, will grow 4 to 6 in. (10 to 15 cm) a year to 12 ft. (3.6 m) high, appears blue.

*Pinus sylvestris* 'Watereri'

*Pinus taeda*

### *Pinus taeda*   loblolly pine
Zones 6 to 9

The loblolly pine is native to New Jersey, south to Florida and west to Oklahoma and Texas. It grows in the Piedmont and to a lesser extent in the coastal plain. Loblolly means "mud puddle," and in olden times it was apparently much commoner in poorly drained sites. It has now expanded onto richer locations and often regenerates abandoned fields. It is fast-growing. Although pyramidal in youth, it develops a high, thin canopy with maturity. It provides light shade and permits underplanting. It reaches 40 to 50 ft. (12 to 15 m) in cultivation and 90 ft. (27 m) in its native habitat. The needles, which stay on the branch for two years, are 6 to 10 in. (15 to 25 cm) long in groups of three (occasionally two) set radially around the shoot. They are slender, relatively stiff, and often twisted. They are gray-green with dots of white stomata (breathing pores). The fascicle sheath is up to 1 in. (2.5 cm) long and persistent. The stalkless cone is 3 to 6 in. (7.5 to 15 cm) long and 2 in. (5 cm) wide. Cones open as soon as they are mature, but remain attached. The back of each scale is armed with a prominent short, stout prickle. They are grouped two to five together. The bark is very dark brown and scaly in young trees but turns charcoal-

*Pinus taeda* foliage

**Pinus taeda** (continued)

gray and scaly with deep fissures, revealing red-brown inner bark with age.

*Pinus taeda* should be grown in full sun in moist, even poorly drained soils. It will grow in sandy soils and is very tolerant of hot climates. It is easily transplanted and, although admittedly not a refined tree, it is adaptable to a variety of soil conditions. Often grown in the southern states as a quick screen, it is one of the largest and commercially most important of southern pines. The tree produces fairly good timber and also resins for the rosin blocks used by stringed-instrument players on their bows. It is the state tree of Arkansas.

'Nana': compact, dense and rounded, slow-growing, tiered branching, reaches 20 ft. (6 m).

*Pinus taeda* seed-bearing cones

*Pinus taeda* bark

*Pinus taeda* 'Nana

### *Pinus thunbergii*  Japanese black pine  Zones 5 to 10

The Japanese black pine is native to Japan and Korea, where it is often found growing along the seacoasts. The habit is often fairly symmetrical but with a curved trunk. It will grow 8 to 12 in. (20 to 30 cm) a year to a height of 50 ft. (15 m) and half as wide. The dark green, sharply pointed needles are stiff, 4 to 6 in. (10 to 15 cm) long, in bundles of two. They persist for three to five years. The buds of *Pinus thunbergii* are covered with silky white hairs, a simple way to identify this species. The fissured bark is charcoal-gray. The cones are 1½ to 2½ in. (3.5 to 6 cm) long and short-stalked with prickly scales. The cones are solitary or carried in clusters. This pine will grow in any well-drained soil; it tolerates salt spray and salt in soil. It has great heat and drought tolerance but demands full sun. It commonly breaks apart in ice and snow storms. This species is very popular in Asian gardens, where it is typically trained to create the appearance of ancient wild trees. Of course, it is also a popular subject for bonsai. It is one of the most important timber trees in Japan. It has been planted to stabilize sand dunes.

*Pinus thunbergii*

*Pinus thunbergii* foliage

*Pinus thunbergii* bark

### *Pinus thunbergii* (continued)

'Banshosho': becomes dense and globose with rich green foliage.

'Globosa': a dense-growing small tree with branching to the ground.

'Green Elf': pyramidal, dark green with little white buds, reaches 2 ft. (0.6 m).

*Pinus thunbergii* pollen-bearing cones

*Pinus thunbergii* seed-bearing cones

*Pinus thunbergii* bonsai

*Pinus thunbergii* 'Banshosho'

*Pinus thunbergii* tailored

*Pinus thunbergii* 'Green Elf'

*Pinus thunbergii* 'Oculus-draconis'

'Oculus-draconis': irregularly shaped dragon's-eye black pine has yellow-white stripes on its needles, most apparent in the fall.

'Pygmaea': slow-growing.

'Shirome Janome': two bright yellow bands on the needles.

'Thunderhead': a broadly spreading, irregularly branched dwarf that reaches 8 ft. (2.5 m) tall by 10 ft. (3 m) wide after ten years, displays clusters of distinctive silver-white buds and candles against rich dark green, densely packed needles in early spring.

*Pinus thunbergii* 'Pygmaea'

*Pinus thunbergii* 'Shirome Janome'

*Pinus thunbergii* 'Thunderhead'

*Pinus thunbergii* 'Thunderhead' buds

### *Pinus virginiana* scrub pine
Zones 4 to 8

The scrub pine grows in the Piedmont and coastal plain of the eastern United States from New York south to Alabama. It is particularly common in the New Jersey Pine Barrens. This is a small to medium-sized, 15 to 40 ft. (4.5 to 12 m) tall, irregularly shaped tree. It becomes broad and flat-topped with maturity. The lower lateral branches often die yet remain on the tree for years, giving the tree a scrubby look. The needles are usually clustered in twos but can be one to four together. They are 1½ to 3 in. (3.5 to 7.5 cm) long, and are twisted and divergent. They sometimes are bright green but are characteristically yellowish green in color. They persist for two to three years and are fragrant. The numerous seed-bearing cones are 1½ to 3 in. (3.5 to 7.5 cm) long and 1 to 1½ in. (2.5 to 3.5 cm) wide. They are shiny and dark red-brown and often bend backward on the twig. A sharp, hooked barb is present on the back of each cone scale. These short-stalked or stalkless cones persist on branches for three to four years. The thin bark is red-brown with shallow fissures.

Scrub pine should be grown in full sun. Unlike most pines, this species tolerates poor, dry, rocky places and will grow in sandy as well as clay soil. It has not been very useful as a lumber tree because of its small size and knottiness, but is used for fuel and pulpwood and is very important for reforestation. It will spread rapidly over abandoned fields and clear cuts. This is a species for tough situations, including heavy clay and impoverished soil, although with the variability of its form it is not particularly ornamental. It is grown as a holiday tree in southern states.

'Wate's Golden': slow-growing with golden yellow foliage in winter.

*Pinus virginiana* bark

*Pinus virginiana*

*Pinus virginiana* foliage and cone

*Pinus virginiana* 'Wate's Golden'

### *Pinus wallichiana* Himalayan pine Zones 5 to 7

This handsome pine is used in much the same way as *Pinus strobus* and has the same cultural requirements; however, it grows a tad slower and can be a bit more broad. It is native to the Himalayas, from Afghanistan to Nepal. Danish surgeon Nathaniel Wallich (1786–1854), who is commemorated in the epithet, was a botanist with the East India Company and superintendent of the Calcutta Botanic Garden. He introduced this plant from his travels into England in 1823. It has also been known as *P. griffithii*. It can reach 80 ft. (24 m) in cultivation and tends to be wide-spreading. Older specimens usually retain their lower branches; however, it can become tattered and shabby in old age. It benefits from a sheltered position.

The Himalayan pine exhibits great grace, owing to the feathery effect of the 6 to 8 in. (15 to 20 cm) long needles; these are in fascicles of five and persist for three to four years. They appear bent, and most of the needle is pendulous. The grayish green to blue-green foliage has a soft appearance. The solitary seed-bearing cones are up to 10 in. (25 cm) long and hang on a long 1 to 2 in. (2.5 to 5 cm) stalk. They are very resinous.

*Pinus wallichiana*

*Pinus wallichiana* bark

*Pinus wallichiana* foliage

*Pinus wallichiana* cone

Pinus wallichiana 'Densa'

Pinus wallichiana 'Nana'

Pinus wallichiana 'Zebrina' foliage

### Pinus wallichiana (continued)

'Densa': a dense conical form.

'Nana': dwarf and congested with short silver needles.

'Zebrina': graceful downward-hanging needles are banded with a yellow stripe, needs winter protection, sometimes labeled 'Oculus-draconis'.

Pinus wallichiana 'Zebrina'

*Podocarpus* typical foliage

*Podocarpus lawrencei* 'Blue Gem'

*Podocarpus lawrencei*

*Podocarpus macrophyllus* foliage and seed-bearing cone

## *Podocarpus*   yellowwood

*Podocarpus*, although a very large genus of conifers, is less well-known and not widely grown in Europe or the United States. It is a group of generally tropical plants found in mountain forests of the southern hemisphere, nearly all in New Zealand. Many can be grown as houseplants in more temperate climates. For the most part it has little economic importance for the timber industry, although some species are reportedly threatened by overcutting. Podocarps will grow in most types of soil. The leaves are variable but normally spirally arranged. The seed-bearing cone is a fleshy red receptacle.

*Podocarpus lawrencei* (syn. *P. alpinus*) is a hardier (zones 7 and 8) dwarf species that grows as a low densely branched mound or ground-hugging carpet. The foliage resembles yew. Its selection 'Blue Gem' is a vigorous spreading groundcover with blue-green foliage.

*Podocarpus macrophyllus* is another hardier species, native

*Podocarpus lawrencei* foliage

### Podocarpus (continued)

to Japan and China. It is a shrub or small tree with willowy leaves 3 to 8 in. (7.5 to 20 cm) long, bright green above, gray beneath, arranged in dense spirals. Used for hedging and screens in warmer areas. 'Aureus' is its yellow-variegated form. Zones 8 to 10.

*Podocarpus nivalis* is native to New Zealand and widely grown in Great Britain. It is a slow-spreading dense mound of narrow, fleshy, yellow-green foliage, spirally arranged on short branches. It reaches 2 to 3 ft. (0.6 to 0.9 m) tall and 6 to 10 ft. (1.8 to 3 m) wide and can be grown as bonsai. Its selection 'Bronze' offers bronze-tinged new growth. Hybrids between *P. lawrencei* and *P. nivalis* are widely available in England. Zone 7.

*Podocarpus totara* is a slow-growing shrub in cultivation but a tall tree in its native New Zealand. The yellow-green leaves are two-ranked, leathery and sharply pointed. 'Pendulus' (also listed as 'Pendula') is a pendulous form.

*Podocarpus macrophyllus* 'Aureus' foliage

*Podocarpus macrophyllus* 'Aureus'

*Podocarpus nivalis*

*Podocarpus nivalis* 'Bronze'

*Podocarpus totara* 'Pendulus'

***Pseudolarix amabilis*** golden-
   larch   Zones 4 to 7

This monotypic genus is native to the mountains of eastern China. The species is a deciduous conifer like the larch, *Larix*, but it is not a true larch, hence the hyphen in its common name. Some consider the foliage of the golden-larch the most eye-catching of any conifer. The mint-green leaves emerge in early spring and unfold into soft, feathery, flat needles. They are in whorls of 15 to 30, and the length of the individual needles varies from 1 to 2½ in. (2.5 to 6 cm). These clusters of needles are arranged spirally, widely spaced on spur shoots that are noticeably longer than those of *Larix*. There is a distinct constriction between the annual rings. The leaves turn a dazzling golden orange in the fall, appearing as if lighted from within. The pollen-bearing cones are catkin-like in clusters. The seed-bearing cones mature in one year on the upper side of the branch. They are in the form of rosettes with pointed triangular scales resembling artichokes up to 2½ in. (6 cm) long, blue-green maturing to golden brown. The ripe cones disintegrate and release the winged seeds, and the thick cone scales fall to the ground. The bark is charcoal-gray.

Golden-larch will reach 40 to 70 ft.

*Pseudolarix amabilis*

*Pseudolarix amabilis* spring foliage emerging

*Pseudolarix amabilis* foliage in summer (note spur growth)

*Pseudolarix amabilis* pollen-bearing cones

*Pseudolarix amabilis* seed-bearing cones

### *Pseudolarix amabilis* (continued)

(12 to 21 m) tall by 50 ft. (15 m) wide in the landscape, perhaps taller in the wild. It has a pyramidal habit with ascending limbs, and the open nature of the foliage makes some underplanting possible. It is very slow-growing. A six-year-old seedling will be only 9 ft. (2.7 m) tall. A 100-year-old specimen was reported to be 45 ft. (14 m) tall.

The golden-larch does best in full sun, although it will tolerate light shade. Give it fertile, well-drained moist soil. It is said to be tolerant of summer heat and humidity and will grow successfully in the southeastern United States, where most true larches and firs do poorly; however, one would be wise to protect it from harsh winter winds. It does not like limestone soil. It is difficult to propagate (it seldom produces viable seed unless growing in a grove, and cuttings do not root) and is therefore hard to find in nurseries; but this does not daunt collectors. It has also been called *Pseudolarix kaempferi*. The wood has been used for furniture, boat-building, and bridges.

*Amabilis* means "worthy of love." The glory of this plant is the burnt-orange fall color. Unfortunately, like many love affairs, this fall display is brief.

*Pseudolarix amabilis* fall color

*Pseudolarix amabilis* fall foliage

*Pseudolarix amabilis* bonsai

*Pseudotsuga menziesii*

### *Pseudotsuga menziesii*
Douglas-fir   Zones 4 to 7

The Douglas-fir is native from British Columbia south to Washington, Oregon, and California and eastward into Idaho, Montana, Wyoming, Utah, Colorado, Arizona, and New Mexico. In the wild with abundant rainfall and mild winters it can reach 225 ft. (68 m) with almost half that height free of branches. Specimens have been recorded at well over 300 ft. (90 m) in height, making the Douglas-fir the largest conifer in the world except for the coast redwoods of California. It can live up to 1,000 years. There are several geographic varieties. A pioneer species, it often colonizes areas that have been subjected to wildfires or logging and will develop best in full sun; however, it can do well in a wide range of climatic conditions. It grows best in deep, well-drained, sandy loams with plentiful moisture. It is tough and durable and will tolerate some shade, but it would be wise to avoid this species in the dry, windy sections of the midwestern United States. In the landscape it will grow 40 to 80 ft. (12 to 24 m). The habit is dense and conical; if crowded, it will be spire-like. The branches sweep downward. It has a strong and wide-spreading root system.

Through the years this species has been referred to as a spruce and a pine as well as a fir and hemlock. This is very understandable when one examines the foliage. The ¾ to 1¼ in. (2 to 3 cm) needles are held singly and are flat, with a row of white dots on the bottom. The needles are arranged spirally around the stem. The foliage is a dark blue-green with a brighter spring growth. The needles remain on the tree for four to eight years. Since the needles are confusing, one should look at the buds. The buds are an easy ID feature for this species: they are long, shiny, covered with chestnut-

*Pseudotsuga menziesii* buds

*Pseudotsuga menziesii* foliage showing lighter new growth

*Pseudotsuga menziesii* seed-bearing cone

### *Pseudotsuga menziesii* (continued)

brown overlapping scales, and pointed. The pollen-bearing cones are catkin-like, yellow to orange-red, and pendulous. The stalked 2 to 4 in. (5 to 10 cm) seed-bearing cones are egg-shaped and dark brown with long extruded, three-forked, pointed papery bracts between the scales of the cones. They mature in the first autumn. They will drop intact after the seeds are dispersed. The red-brown bark is deeply furrowed and thickens with age. In youth it is gray and smooth with resin blisters.

The entire northwest section of the United States was once a vast forest of Douglas-fir. This species became the world's most important timber tree source when the towering white pines of the eastern United States were exhausted by the end of the nineteenth century. With the Douglas-fir, coast redwood, and cedars, the Northwest became the lumber capital of the world. *Pseudotsuga* was used for telephone and telegraph poles and railroad ties, and is now used for all sorts of construction and for plywood manufacture. The wood is resistant to decay, does not warp, and is stronger for its weight than any other native tree. Since the trees are so large, it is possible to produce very large beams for use in building bridges, docks, and

*Pseudotsuga menziesii* bark

*Pseudotsuga menziesii* 'Astro Blue'

large structures. It is commonly grown as a holiday tree because the needles remain on the tree long after it is cut. The seeds are an important food source for wildlife, including squirrels, chipmunks, crossbills, nutcrackers, and juncos.

Mature specimens are appropriate for large estates, commercial areas, or arboretums. It is not suitable for a small residential garden. *Pseudotsuga menziesii* is the state tree of Oregon.

'Astro Blue': dense, broadly conical, tends to keep lower limbs, foliage light blue, reaches 40 × 20 ft. (12 × 6 m).

'Bílé Lhotě': slow-growing, an outstanding blue, grows 1 in. (2.5 cm) a year.

*Pseudotsuga menziesii* 'Bílé Lhotě'

*Pseudotsuga menziesii* 'Densa'

*Pseudotsuga menziesii* 'Emerald Twister'

*Pseudotsuga menziesii* 'Emerald Twister' foliage

*Pseudotsuga menziesii* 'Environmentals'

'Densa': irregular oval habit, flat-topped, short dark green needles on twiggy, horizontally held branches, grows only to 3 ft. (0.9 m) tall, suitable for rock garden.

'Emerald Twister': sculptural twisting branches, dark green foliage.

'Environmentals': upright, broadly conical to 15 ft. (4.5 m) tall and wide, tough.

*Pseudotsuga menziesii* 'Fastigiata'

*Pseudotsuga menziesii* var. *glauca*

## *Pseudotsuga menziesii* (continued)

'Fastigiata': narrow with short upright branches, reaches 40 ft. (12 m) tall with a 10 to 15 ft. (3 to 4.5 m) spread, dense, useful for screen planting.

'Fletcheri': slow-growing, low-spreading, congested blue-gray foliage, will not exceed 10 ft. (3 m) even with great age.

var. *glauca*: a regional variation, more compact than species, upward-branching.

'Glauca Pendula': graceful, columnar, weeping blue-gray foliage, slow-growing to 30 ft. (9 m).

*Pseudotsuga menziesii* 'Fletcheri'

'Graceful Grace': fast-growing with long blue-green needles, irregular upright leader, lateral branches drooping, does not need staking.

'Idaho Weeper': upright and variable, twisting leader and drooping branches, sometimes listed as 'Idaho Weeping'.

'Les Barres': dwarf, dense dark green foliage, grows under 2 in. (5 cm) a year.

'Little Jon': dense dark green cone, eventually upright, slow growth, 30 in. (75 cm) in ten years.

'Loggerhead': dense, low-spreading form.

'Marshall': densely pyramidal habit, blue-green foliage, reaches 12 to 15 ft. (3.6 to 4.5 m) in ten years.

'Panonia': irregular growth, under 2 in. (5 cm) a year, good for rock gardens.

*Pseudotsuga menziesii* 'Graceful Grace'

*Pseudotsuga menziesii* 'Les Barres'

*Pseudotsuga menziesii* 'Little Jon'

*Pseudotsuga menziesii* 'Marshall'

*Pseudotsuga menziesii* 'Loggerhead'

*Pseudotsuga menziesii* 'Panonia'

## *Pseudotsuga menziesii* (continued)

'Pendula': slow-growing, crown pendulous and irregular.

'Pumila': shrub form.

'Slg. Rijt': dark green, conical, grows ¾ in. (2 cm) a year.

'Wycoff's Big Blue': upright and pyramidal, one of the best for blue foliage, produces abundant cones, reaches 40 × 20 ft. (12 × 6 m).

'Wycoff's Dwarf': dense bright green needles, ½ in. (1.2 cm) annual growth, reaches 7 ft. (2 m) in 50 years.

*Pseudotsuga menziesii* 'Pendula'

*Pseudotsuga menziesii* 'Pumila'

*Pseudotsuga menziesii* 'Pendula' in a mixed border

*Pseudotsuga menziesii* 'Slg. Rijt'

*Pseudotsuga menziesii* 'Wycoff's Big Blue'

*Pseudotsuga menziesii* 'Wycoff's Dwarf'

### *Sciadopitys verticillata*   umbrella-pine   Zones 5 to 8

The umbrella-pine (not actually a pine) is native to southern Japan. It is the sole species in this genus and has a history dating back to the dinosaurs. In the wild it has been observed over 100 ft. (30 m) tall. In cultivation it is more likely to reach 30 ft. (9 m) by half as wide. *Sciadopitys verticillata* is usually grown as a feature plant by connoisseurs or in collections. It should be grown in rich, moist soils in full sun but in a site not exposed to high winds. It will grow in part shade but dislikes lime soils. It is very slow-growing in youth. It is often multistemmed and matures into a dense and conical tree with ascending upper branches. The stems are light brown. The foliage is luxuriant. The 3 to 5 in. (7.5 to 12 cm) long needles are displayed on orange-brown shoots in whorls of 10 to 30, like the spokes of an umbrella. They are fleshy and pliable. The upper surface is glossy dark green but paler beneath with a center groove on both surfaces (actually two needles fused in pairs). The foliage yellows in winter in cold climates. The pollen-bearing cones are in dense clusters spirally arranged at the tip of branches.

*Sciadopitys verticillata*

*Sciadopitys verticillata* foliage

*Sciadopitys verticillata* yellowed winter foliage

*Sciadopitys verticillata* pollen-bearing cones

*Sciadopitys verticillata* immature seed-bearing cones

*Sciadopitys verticillata* mature seed-bearing cone

*Sciadopitys verticillata* 'Golden Rush'

*Sciadopitys verticillata* 'Green Star'

### *Sciadopitys verticillata* (continued)

The solitary green seed-bearing cones are 2 to 4 in. (5 to 10 cm) long on a short stalk, maturing to brown in the second year. The handsome bark is red-brown and peels in long strips.

Hoofed browsers will select it over more common species. The spicy scented wood is water-resistant and used for boat-building.

'Aurea': gold splotches on the green needles, probably no different from 'Variegata'.

'Golden Rush': good golden color, also listed as 'Gold Rush'.

*Sciadopitys verticillata* 'Grüne Kugel'

'Green Star': slow-growing, thick, short needles.

'Grüne Kugel': multibranched dwarf.

'Jim Cross': slow-growing, dense, and compact with rich dark green foliage, reaches 10 ft. (3 m) in ten years.

'Joe Kozey': a columnar habit with dominant leader and rich green foliage, reaches 6 × 3 ft. (1.8 × 0.9 m) in ten years.

*Sciadopitys verticillata* 'Mecki'

*Sciadopitys verticillata* 'Ossorio Gold'

*Sciadopitys verticillata* 'Sternschnuppe'

*Sciadopitys verticillata* 'Wintergreen'

*Sciadopitys verticillata* 'Variegata'

'Mecki': small and round with dark foliage.

'Ossorio Gold': golden yellow needles, upright cones, 4 × 3 ft. (1.2 × 0.9 m) in ten years, rare and prized.

'Sternschnuppe': upright and narrow with short thick branches and needles, 4 × 2 ft. (1.2 × 0.6 m) in ten years.

'Variegata': green needles with yellow blotches.

'Wintergreen': narrow conical habit, deep green color that does not yellow in winter, grows 9 in. (23 cm) a year, better for colder climates.

## *Sequoia sempervirens* coast redwood Zones 7 to 9

This imposing tree is native to coastal mountain ranges in California and Oregon. A very large tree reaching more than 300 ft. (90 m) in its native habitat, it is the world's tallest living tree. It can live 2,000 years. It thrives in an area with lots of fog and consistent soil moisture, and mild winters. It is pyramidal in youth but with age will lose lower branches. The foliage is held in flat sprays and looks like yew with two-ranked needles ¼ to ¾ in. (0.6 to 2 cm) long, dark green above, with two white bands beneath. The seed-bearing cones are ¾ to 1¼ in. (2 to 3 cm) long and ripen in one season. The reddish brown bark is thick, 3 to 12 in. (7.5 to 30 cm), fibrous, soft, and spongy with deep furrows and ridges and a bright cinnamon underbark. Suckers often surround the base. This is obviously not a conifer for the home landscape although, as noted, some of the following cultivars could be grown as shrubs in warmer areas.

Redwoods were cut in the last cen-

Sequoia sempervirens

Sequoia sempervirens bark

*Sequoia sempervirens* 'Adpressa'

*Sequoia sempervirens* 'Glauca' foliage

*Sequoia sempervirens* 'Glauca'

*Sequoia sempervirens* 'Henderson Blue'

tury for timber for all possible construction uses and shipped all over the world. It is an extremely versatile wood, easily worked, knot-free, straight-grained, and smooth, and since it does not decay can even be used to make water tanks and wine casks. Today the cutting of these remarkable conifers is surrounded with controversy. The genus was named to honor Chief Sequoyah, a Cherokee who invented a Native American alphabet.

'Adpressa': dense, pyramidal tree, shoots more narrow than species, new growth creamy white, needles smaller and bluer and uniformly directed forward, slow-growing, usually grown as shrub.

'Glauca': foliage more blue-green and shorter than the species.

'Henderson Blue': very slow-growing, foliage strikingly pale blue, often grown as a shrub, cones profusely.

### *Sequoiadendron giganteum*
### giant sequoia    Zones 6 to 8

These large trees with massive fluted trunks and thick bark are found in groves on the western slopes of the Sierra Nevada in California. There they thrive in cool autumn mists and deep winter snows followed by dry summers. It is the world's largest tree in terms of mass (volume). Heights up to 350 ft. (106 m) have been claimed. In cultivation it is likely to reach 60 ft. (18 m). The younger trees have a pyramidal outline with branches that droop at the ends. When grown in the open as a garden specimen, the branches are retained to the ground. After a century of growth, the trees are tall and straight and clear of branches with a high crown. The tiny blue-green leaves, ⅛ to ¼ in. (0.3 to 0.6 cm), are awl-shaped and sharp and arranged spirally on the stem, overlapping and tightly appressed to it, lending a cord-like appearance. The needles persist for four years. The stalked cone is absurdly small, 1½ to 2 in. (3.5 to 5 cm), for so large a tree. It has thick woody scales that are swollen at

*Sequoiadendron giganteum* bark

*Sequoiadendron giganteum*

Sequoiadendron giganteum foliage

Sequoiadendron giganteum cone

Sequoiadendron giganteum in California

the edge. The cones mature from green to brown the second season and persist on the tree for several years. The spongy bark is a rich red-brown and is said to be up to 12 in. (30 cm) thick, or even thicker on mature specimens, with deep furrows and fibrous ridges. The sap is high in tannic acid, which is claimed to protect the tree from fire damage and aid in wound healing. The bark is soft and easily hollowed out by birds and squirrels. This tree does not sucker.

The giant sequoia is striking with its huge red trunk and neat pyramidal shape. Logged trees have been recorded at over 3,000 years old. It is widely planted through Europe and is especially popular in Great Britain and Germany. Redwood, which includes *Sequoiadendron giganteum* and *Sequoia sempervirens*, is the state tree of California.

Sequoiadendron giganteum in Germany

*Sequoiadendron giganteum* 'Albospica'

*Sequoiadendron giganteum* 'Blauer Eichzwerg'

*Sequoiadendron giganteum* 'Glaucum'

## *Sequoiadendron giganteum*
(continued)

'Albospica': compact irregular globe with white shoot tips, reaches 4 ft. (1.2 m) tall and wide in ten years.

'Blauer Eichzwerg': slow-growing pyramidal miniature, blue foliage, reaches 3 ft. (0.9 m) in ten years, ideal for garden railroad or rock garden.

'Glaucum': narrow habit, slower growing than species, bright blue foliage.

'Greenpeace': narrow with bright green needles.

'Hazel Smith': selected for hardiness to zone 6, uniformly pyramidal, blue-green compared to species, grows 18 in. (46 cm) a year.

*Sequoiadendron giganteum* 'Hazel Smith'

*Sequoiadendron giganteum* 'Hazel Smith' foliage

*Sequoiadendron giganteum* 'Moonie's Mini'

*Sequoiadendron giganteum* 'Pendulum'

*Sequoiadendron giganteum* 'Powder Blue'

*Sequoiadendron giganteum* 'Pygmaeum'

'Moonie's Mini': twisted main trunk and foliage.

'Pendulum': tall pillar with branches completely pendulous and parallel with trunk, sometimes leaning this way and that, with upward branches contorted, growing upright, then dipping and growing upright again, often multiple leaders. Freaky.

'Powder Blue': light blue needles, reaches 12 × 6 ft. (3.6 × 1.8 m) in ten years.

'Pygmaeum': dense conical dwarf with light green foliage.

### *Taiwania cryptomerioides*
Taiwan-cedar    Zone 8

This very large pyramidal tree, native to Taiwan (and also known as Formosan redwood), is rarely found in nurseries. In the wild it reaches 160 ft. (49 m) with scale-like leaves; in cultivation it is much smaller and often displays sickle-shaped foliage that resembles that of *Cryptomeria japonica*. These sharply pointed blue-green leaves become more scale-like with age. It has slender, drooping, whip-like branches. The bark is gray-red-brown and ridged, and exfoliates in narrow strips. *Taiwania cryptomerioides* prefers full sun and requires a moist but well-drained soil and protection. The timber is used to make coffins.

*Taiwania cryptomerioides*

*Taiwania cryptomerioides* bonsai

*Taiwania cryptomerioides* foliage

## *Taxodium*   bald-cypress, pond-cypress

The two species we are concerned with in this genus are now found naturally only in eastern North America; however, in the past they were much more widely distributed. Both plants have alternately arranged deciduous foliage that is a pale yellow-green. Both will grow in very wet conditions and produce large buttressed trunks, sometimes generating peculiar knee-like projections. The "knees" are roots that come above the surface of the soil and are thought to help anchor the tree; they form only in wet habitats.

## *Taxodium ascendens*   pond-cypress   Zones 5 to 10

Many authorities list this as *Taxodium distichum* var. *nutans*. The pond-cypress is found in swampy areas and pine barrens from southeastern Virginia to Florida and west to Louisiana. It has a slow to medium growth rate, commonly reaching 80 × 20 ft. (24 × 6 m), although ultimate heights of as much as 125 ft. (38 m) are possible. The habit is narrowly conical or columnar. The deciduous branchlets ascend rigidly from the twig rather than spreading out. The leaves are ⅛ to ⅝ in. (0.3 to 1.5 cm) long, narrow, and spirally arranged in a plane closely held against the twigs; they appear scale-like on the branchlets. The foliage is bright green in the summer and turns orange-brown in fall. The pollen-bearing cones are in drooping terminal panicles. The seed-bearing cones are ½ to 1¼ in. (1.2 to 3 cm) round on short stalks. The bark is ridged and deeply furrowed with long vertical plates. This species does not readily develop knees such as those found with *T. distichum*. It is adaptable and wind-tolerant.

*Taxodium ascendens*

*Taxodium ascendens* foliage

*Taxodium ascendens* pollen-bearing cones

### *Taxodium ascendens* (continued)

'Nutans': slow-growing, columnar, young foliage somewhat pendulous on the erect branchlets.

'Prairie Sentinel': tall narrow habit with shorter branches than the species, reaches 60 × 10 ft. (18 × 3 m).

*Taxodium ascendens* 'Nutans' foliage

*Taxodium ascendens* 'Nutans'

*Taxodium ascendens* 'Prairie Sentinel'

*Taxodium distichum* fall foliage

*Taxodium distichum* winter silhouette

### *Taxodium distichum*  bald-cypress   Zones 4 to 11

This large tree is found in swamps from the coastal plain of Delaware to Florida, west to Texas, and up the Mississippi Valley to Illinois and Indiana. It often reaches 100 ft. (30 m) in height in its native stands; in cultivation it is more likely to be 50 ft. (15 m) at maturity. It sometimes lives 1,000 years or more. It is pyramidal when young, becoming more rounded as it ages. Mature trees have flat-topped crowns; Spanish moss drapes from their branches in the south. Bald-cypress requires full sun and acidic soil to thrive. It does best in moist, deep soil with good drainage but will grow in standing water and is also tolerant of dry soil. Of all trees it has probably the greatest known

tolerance for flooding; some specimens are in standing water half of the growing season. It is a tough and adaptable species.

The buds are tiny, roundish, and alternately arranged. The sage-green deciduous leaves are ½ to ¾ in. (1.2 to 2 cm) long, in a flat, feather-like arrangement in two rows on narrow branchlets. The autumn color is russet or a soft brown. The leaves drop from the tree to form a carpet of soft needles. The pollen-bearing cones appear in winter; they are catkin-like, in 4 to 5 in. (10 to 12 cm) drooping terminal panicles in March and April. The seed-bearing cones are ¾ to 1 in. (2 to 2.5 cm) in diameter, globular, appearing singly or in pairs at the end of twigs. The trunk is straight and buttressed at the base. The bark is fibrous, reddish brown, and peels off in thin, narrow

### *Taxodium distichum* (continued)

strips. Its roots form natural crooks or knees that extend above ground when it is grown near water. This species has knees more sharply pointed than those of the pond-cypress.

This is an important timber species. The wood is very durable and is used for construction of objects that will be exposed to water: boats, docks, bridges, greenhouses, crates, railroad ties, livestock- and birdhouses. The number of mature bald-cypresses is declining because of the widespread draining of swamplands. It is the state tree of Louisiana.

*Taxodium distichum* seed-bearing cones

*Taxodium distichum* buttressed trunk and bark

*Taxodium distichum* bonsai

*Taxodium distichum* "knees"

*Taxodium distichum* in standing water

*Taxodium distichum* 'Cascade Falls'

'Cascade Falls': pendulous large shrub or small tree, doesn't exceed 20 ft. (6 m) in height, sage-green foliage, red-brown bark, russet fall color.

'Fastigiata': more upright and narrow than the species.

'Heritage': narrowly pyramidal, pendulous short-needled branches, red-brown bark, bronze fall color, reaches 50 ft. (15 m), also called 'Nelson'.

*Taxodium distichum* 'Heritage'

*Taxodium distichum* 'Mickelson' tailored

*Taxodium distichum* 'Peve Minaret'

### *Taxodium distichum* (continued)

'Mickelson': upright branching, narrowly pyramidal, fast-growing, adaptable for urban conditions, orange-bronze fall color, reaches 75 × 20 ft. (23 × 6 m), also called 'Shawnee Brave'.

'Monarch of Illinois': wider than the species, reaches 80 ft. (24 m) tall and 60 ft. (18 m) wide.

'Pendens': slender and cone-shaped with pendulous branch tips, reaches 50 ft. (15 m).

'Peve Minaret': spire-shaped, fine-textured overlapping needles, reaches 12 × 3 ft. (3.6 × 0.9 m) in ten years, bright green in summer turning rusty red in fall.

'Secrest': globose, flat-topped, grows 3 to 6 in. (7.5 to 15 cm) a year to 6 ft. (1.8 m).

*Taxodium distichum* 'Secrest'

*Taxus* grown as a tree

*Taxus* topiary

*Taxus* breaks growth on old wood

### *Taxus* yew

The nomenclature of *Taxus* is very confused: it is a small genus, with about ten species, but all are relatively similar. Three species are native to North America and one to England. Yews can be shrubs or trees to 70 ft. (21 m) tall and can live for hundreds of years. They usually display an irregular crown and are often broad-spreading. They will tolerate considerable shade but do best in full sun. They are tolerant of most soils provided they are well drained. Yews will not survive wet conditions or extreme heat. Many selections from these species are used in public landscaping and in both estate and home gardens. They tolerate trimming and shaping into hedges or topiaries and tolerate urban pollution. They are not salt-tolerant.

### *Taxus* (continued)

The flat evergreen needles of *Taxus* are single and arranged spirally or in a flat plane, often appearing to be two-ranked, with the edge of the leaf often slightly curled. The tips are sharp and pointed (whether abruptly or not is an ID feature among some yews). They remain on the tree for up to eight years. Growth is vigorous in the spring with side shoots on the new growth. Yews are dioecious, with the seed- and pollen-bearing cones on separate trees. The pollen-bearing cones are small and yellow on the underside of the previous year'sgrowth. The seed-bearing cones mature in autumn, with the single seed embedded in a bright red aril (a fleshy pulp that is open at the apex). The bark is reddish to dark chestnut-brown and exfoliates from the trunk and larger branches in long, thin strips. Available selections of *Taxus* vary from low and wide-spreading to tall and columnar. Many of the cultivars are similar and difficult to single out one from another.

Yew foliage, bark, and seeds are very poisonous to farm livestock, but not to moose, elk, or deer. Suburban gardeners are well aware of the special fondness of white-tailed deer for garden yews. The fleshy red aril that surrounds the seeds is not poisonous. Birds eat the arils and spread the seed. The wood of yews is very hard and heavy. It is a pale and very durable wood. It is even-grained and polishes beautifully. Yews are a symbol of immortality, and over the centuries have been widely planted in cemeteries.

*Taxus* seed-bearing cones

*Taxus* bark

### *Taxus baccata*   English yew   Zones 6 to 8

The English or common yew is native to Europe, northern Africa, and southwest Asia. It is one of Britain's three native conifers (many magnificent specimens can be seen there, some thousands of years old) and was planted in New Jersey as early as 1713. It is a dense, wide-spreading tree, growing 30 to 60 ft. (9 to 18 m) tall, with a thick trunk; however, it is often grown with multiple trunks. The very dark green to black-green needles are ½ to 1½ in. (1.2 to 3.5 cm) long; they gradually taper to a point. They are convex with a prominent midrib and are usually spirally arranged. The pollen-bearing cones are inconspicuous. The seed-bearing cones are ½ in. (1.2 cm) long and coral-red. It must have well-drained soils but is remarkably tolerant of shade and is easy to transplant. It will grow 8 in. (20 cm) a year. The bark is reddish brown and furrowed; older trunks become fluted.

The wood makes excellent firewood and can be used for furniture, tool handles, and bows; it is claimed that Robin

*Taxus baccata*

*Taxus baccata* 'Adpressa'

*Taxus baccata* 'Adpressa' foliage

*Taxus baccata* 'Adpressa Aurea'

*Taxus baccata* 'Aldenham Gold'

*Taxus baccata* 'Amersfoort'

Hood made his weapons from this wood and was married under a yew as well as buried beneath one. English yew is most often seen trimmed into dense hedges and screens or shaped into topiary and used on large estates. The species is not often found, but many narrow, upright cultivars are available as well as hardier crosses (*Taxus* ×*media*) with the Japanese yew (*T. cuspidata*).

'Adpressa': dense and wide-spreading with short ¼ to ½ in. (0.6 to 1.2 cm) needles, female.

'Adpressa Aurea': wide-spreading and dense, small yellow leaves are more golden in spring growth, brightest when grown in sun, eventually reaches 5 ft. (1.5 m), female.

'Aldenham Gold': a cushion-shaped dwarf, can be upright, gold new growth fades to variegated through the season.

'Amersfoort': slow-growing open shrub with rigid upright branches, needles arranged radially, flat oval leaves look a bit like boxwood, reaches 4 ft. (1.2 m) high and 2 ft. (0.6 m) wide in ten years, said to tolerate full shade and dry conditions, dislikes wet soil.

### *Taxus baccata* (continued)

'Aurea': dense, compact, new growth bright golden yellow, fading by autumn, erect pyramid in youth, broader with age.

'David': upright form with yellow needles.

'Dovastonii Aurea': slow-growing large bush to small tree with wide-spreading branches and golden yellow pendulous tips, retains color in shade, 20 in. (50 cm) high by 4 ft. (1.2 m) wide in ten years, male.

'Erecta Aurea': broadly fastigiate tree, gold leaves.

'Fastigiata': markedly upright, dense broad column, black-green needles whorled around the stem, fast-growing, can reach 30 ft. (9 m), will take hard pruning and always sprouts from old wood, female, also known as Irish yew.

'Fastigiata Aureovariegata': variegated form.

*Taxus baccata* 'David'

*Taxus baccata* 'Dovastonii Aurea'

*Taxus baccata* 'Erecta Aurea'

*Taxus baccata* 'Fastigiata'

*Taxus baccata* 'Fastigiata Aureovariegata'

*Taxus baccata* 'Fowle'

*Taxus baccata* 'Fastigiata Robusta'          *Taxus baccata* 'Green Column'          *Taxus baccata* 'Green Diamond'

*Taxus baccata* 'Nissens Corona'

'Fastigiata Robusta': vigorous and upright, leaves lighter green.

'Fowle': compact, dense, dark green leaves are short and thick, grows much wider than tall, sometimes grafted to a standard, female, also listed as 'Adpressa Fowle'.

'Green Column': very slow-growing upright form with dark green oval leaves, useful for rock and trough gardens.

'Green Diamond': slow-growing and rounded with a flat top, rich dark green.

'Nissens Corona': broad-spreading shrub with medium green needles.

## *Taxus baccata* (continued)

'Procumbens': low and wide-spreading, bright green.

'Repandens': prostrate and wide-spreading with pendulous branch tips, seldom exceeds 4 ft. (1.2 m) tall but can spread to 15 ft. (4.5 m) across in time, dense, glossy black-green foliage, tolerates shady conditions, can be shaped easily, female, hardy to zone 5.

'Rushmore': dwarf with upright, spreading habit, roundish rich green leaves.

'Semperaurea': slow-growing, wide-spreading, golden yellow color retained all seasons even in semi-shade, trims well, male.

'Standishii': slow-growing dense column of tightly packed branches, golden yellow foliage, female.

'Watnong Gold': low-growing selection with bright gold needles.

*Taxus baccata* 'Repandens'

*Taxus baccata* 'Semperaurea'

*Taxus baccata* 'Standishii'

*Taxus baccata* 'Rushmore'

*Taxus baccata* 'Watnong Gold'

### *Taxus brevifolia*   Pacific yew
Zone 4

The Pacific or western yew is native in moist forests from the southern tip of Alaska south along the coast through British Columbia, Washington, and Oregon to California. It is the only *Taxus* species within its range. In its native stands it can reach 50 ft. (15 m). It is known to live for 500 years. These slow-growing, shade-tolerant trees grow on deep moist soils surrounded by other natives of the area: Douglas-fir, redwoods, and western hemlock. The trees usually have a broad crown with horizontal branches. The foliage is often scant in appearance, but the weeping branches are maintained to the ground. The leaves are curved, ½ to ¾ in. (1.2 to 2 cm) long, dark olive-green, keeled, and lying in one plane with an abruptly pointed or rounded tip. The upper surface is deep green with a raised rib along the midrib; the lower surface, a pale green. The new twigs remain green. The seed, ⅓ in. (0.8 cm) long, is contained within a succulent green (maturing to coral-red) aril. The sweet arils are devoured by birds, which deposit the seeds within far and wide, although seedlings are never abundant; arils are also eaten and cached by rodents. The bark is thin with papery scales that peel constantly to reveal a rosy-colored underbark; it is one of this plant's most appealing characteristics. The trunk is often fluted and twisted and not symmetrical. Pacific yews will sprout from cut stumps and replace felled trees. This species is rare in cultivation.

Like the English yew, this yew was used by the First Nations peoples for the making of bows (their preferred bow wood was osage orange) and was exceptional for the making of canoe paddles. Coastal peoples used it for making harpoons and fish spears. Pacific yew was also used for fashioning wedges for splitting cedars. Its name in various native languages meant "wedge plant" or "bow plant." It is best known in more recent times from the discovery that an extract from its bark, diterpene taxol, can be used in the treatment of ovarian and breast cancer.

### *Taxus canadensis*   Canadian yew
Zones 2 to 6

A multistemmed shrub commonly found growing in colonies in the understory of rich forests in eastern Canada. It is wide-spreading, prostrate, and monoecious. It is the hardiest of yews, but its ragged habit reduces its appeal for landscape and garden uses.

### *Taxus cuspidata*   Japanese yew
Zones 4 to 7

The Japanese yew is a small tree native to Japan, Korea, and China. The tree has an irregular habit and can reach 40 ft. (12 m), but most garden selections are shrub-sized. It prefers moist, well-drained, sandy, slightly acidic soil in sun or shade. The ½ to 1 in. (1.2 to 2.5 cm) foliage is irregularly arranged, a dark lustrous green with yellow-green bands on the underside. The apex is abruptly sharp-pointed. The seed-bearing cone is a red aril. It is perhaps the hardiest and fastest-growing yew, and the easiest of the yews to cultivate. It is a common ornamental in Japan, and the wood has been used for construction, carving, bathtubs, chopsticks, clogs, and bows. In the West it is useful for groundcovers, foundation planting, and hedging.

*Taxus cuspidata* is hardier than *T. baccata* and is often crossed with that species producing *T.* ×*media*. This makes the correct naming of some cultivars difficult.

'Aurescens': low-growing, compact, can be wide-spreading, small needles with yellow new growth, shade-tolerant, seldom exceeds 3 ft. (0.9 m) tall and wide, avoid wet sites.

*Taxus cuspidata* 'Aurescens'

### *Taxus cuspidata* (continued)

'Capitata': vigorous, broadly pyramidal, dark green, bronzes in winter, common in commerce, useful for topiary, otherwise can reach 50 ft. (15 m).

'Columnaris': upright and narrow, stays full at base, quickly produces a dense hedge, reaches 10 to 12 ft. (3 to 3.6 m).

'Fastigiata': pyramidal, good green winter color, uniform, reaches 10 to 12 ft. (3 to 3.6 m) by 3 to 5 ft. (0.9 to 1.5 m).

'Luteobaccata': shrub-sized and informal, dark green, yellow seed-bearing cones.

'Nana': spreading form with dense, dark green needles all seasons, grows slowly, eventually reaching 10 × 20 ft. (3 × 6 m), male.

'Tvurdy': slow-growing, pyramidal, dark foliage all seasons, retains shape with minimal pruning, reaches 6 to 8 ft. (1.8 to 2.5 m).

*Taxus cuspidata* 'Capitata'

*Taxus cuspidata* 'Tvurdy'

### *Taxus ×media*    hybrid yew
Zones 4 to 7(8)

This very common hybrid (*Taxus baccata* × *T. cuspidata*) has many similar cultivars. It is valued for its hardiness and vigor, and its shade tolerance, which it inherits from its parent Japanese yew. The growth characteristics of these hybrids can vary widely; most selections are shrubby, from 2 to 20 ft. (0.6 to 6 m). The pointed needles are usually two-ranked; they are dark green with a lighter underside. The fleshy red aril encloses a single seed. The bark is brown and scaly. These yews are indispensable for use in foundation and mass plantings and as screens and hedges.

*Taxus ×media* foliage and seed-bearing cones

*Taxus ×media* 'Beanpole'

*Taxus ×media* 'Bright Gold'

*Taxus ×media* 'Fastigiata'

'Beanpole': very narrow, 8 in. (20 cm), and dense fastigiate female, slow-growing.

'Bright Gold': low-growing spreading mound, 1 to 3 ft. (0.3 to 0.9 m) tall, new growth very bright golden yellow turning green in summer.

'Brownii': upright vase-shaped, reaches 9 ft. (2.7 m), wider than tall, waxy dark green foliage, needs only minimal pruning, good for low hedges, male.

'Densiformis': dense, compact, and spreading shrub, reaches 4 × 8 ft. (1.2 × 2.5 m), bright green, accepts shearing, variable in trade.

'Fastigiata': slow-growing column, dark green needles, also listed as 'Green Candle'.

'Flushing': upright, narrow, columnar, glossy dark green foliage with bright red cones, reaches 12 to 15 ft. (3.6 to 4.5 m) tall but only 3 ft. (0.9 m) wide.

'Grandifolia': narrow columnar habit, dark green needles with yellow bands beneath, tolerates deep shade, must have good drainage.

*Taxus ×media* 'Flushing'

*Taxus ×media* 'Grandifolia'

## *Taxus ×media* (continued)

'Helleri': a fast-growing erect male.

'Hicksii': fast-growing and erect with shiny rich green needles, can reach 20 ft. (6 m) after many years but usually pruned, excellent for hedging, usually female.

'Maureen': dense, slow-growing column, dark green, reaches 6 to 8 ft. (1.8 to 2.5 m).

'Moon': upright, compact, columnar, reaches 10 ft. (3 m).

'Newport': slow-growing, irregular rounded, dense, reaching 4 ft. (1.2 m) in 30 years, male.

'Pilaris': narrow column, medium green, reaches 9 × 3 ft. (2.7 × 0.9 m) in ten years, male.

'Stovekenii': vigorous, fastigiate, broadly columnar, dense deep green foliage, male, reaches 20 ft. (6 m) in 30 years, one of the best narrow yews.

*Taxus ×media* 'Helleri'

*Taxus ×media* 'Moon'

*Taxus ×media* 'Maureen'

*Taxus ×media* 'Newport'

*Taxus ×media* 'Pilaris'

*Taxus ×media* 'Stovekenii'

## *Thuja*  arborvitae

*Thuja* is a small genus, with four species from Asia and two from North America: *Thuja plicata* on the west coast and *T. occidentalis* from the east. Arborvitaes are trees of moist forests and stream banks. They are valued as ornamental plants in landscapes of every size. Generally speaking, arborvitaes do best in fertile, moist, well-drained soils; some species tolerate wet conditions. They prefer full sun but will grow in part shade. They are usually shapely trees and are excellent choices for hedging because they continue to grow all season and produce new shoots after trimming. The foliage is usually scale-like and in flattened sprays; it is aromatic and somewhat resinous. Many arborvitaes tend to discolor in the winter. They can live to great age and develop massive buttressed trunks. The pollen- and seed-bearing cones occur on different branches of the same tree. The few-scaled cones are leathery and erect and mature the first season. The scores of cultivars offer every possible size, shape, and growth rate, in a wide range of colors, from green to yellow and bronze.

This genus is an important source of food for wildlife and provides shelter. The wood is durable and useful. Representatives of it are widely used (elitists would say they are overused) in public spaces and private gardens for screening and foundation plantings or as specimens. They grow without much attention and are among the most versatile and easy-to-grow conifers that adapt to colder northern landscapes. And the splendor of the western native *Thuja plicata* has not been fully appreciated in the east.

Although the foliage of *Thuja* looks similar to that of *Chamaecyparis* on first glance, the two genera can be differentiated by their dissimilar cones, the prominent white markings on most falsecypresses, and the pleasant aroma of arborvitaes.

*Thuja*, along with *Juniperus* and many other genera of conifers, is subject to infestation with bagworms, especially in warmer growing zones. These dark brown caterpillars (*Thyridopteryx ephemeraeformis*) are ⅛ to ¼ in. (0.3 to 0.6 cm) long when they hatch but will grow to 1 in. (2.5 cm). As they feed on the foliage over several months, they bind leaves together with silken thread and make a bag enclosure in which to overwinter up to 1,000 eggs. These 2 in. (5 cm) long cocoon-like cases can appear to be cones to the untrained eye; a bagworm infestation often goes unnoticed until the damage becomes extensive. A severe infestation can defoliate plants, eventually killing them. The egg-filled bags should be handpicked and destroyed from fall to spring. Insecticides can be effective if applied just after the bagworms begin to hatch. *Bacillus thuringiensis* (Bt) is effective against the larvae.

Scale can also be troublesome. These insects are pinhead-sized in their juvenile crawling stage, but with maturity they become immobile and are covered with a protective shell that can be up to ⅜ in. (0.9 cm) in size. They pierce plant tissue and feed on plant sap, which reduces plant vigor and causes twig dieback.

Bagworm infestation on a juniper

### *Thuja occidentalis* northern white-cedar Zones 3 to 7

Generally available, popular, and very widely used for ornamental purposes, this conifer is the one most commonly meant when people speak of arborvitaes. The name arborvitae ("tree of life") is a reference to the high vitamin C content in the foliage, which was used by the early explorers of the New World to prevent or treat scurvy. True to its common names (swamp-cedar is another), this species is found in the northern areas in swampy locations and along the banks of streams, where the soil is deep and humusy. It is also found at higher elevations, notably on limestone outcroppings, along the Appalachian Mountains of Virginia. It is native from Labrador and Nova Scotia west to Manitoba and south to Massachusetts, New York, Ohio, Indiana, Illinois, and Minnesota. It can live 200 to 300 years. In the wild, it can reach a height of 30 to 60 ft. (9 to 18 m), often with a forked trunk, but is usually below 30 ft. (9 m) in cultivation. It is a dense tree with a pyramidal shape. The branches are arranged in flat, fan-shaped sprays, more or less in one plane, and are commonly maintained to the ground. The aromatic scale-like leaves have resin glands and no white markings. They are yellow-green and turn

*Thuja occidentalis*

*Thuja occidentalis* foliage and immature seed-bearing cones

*Thuja occidentalis* mature seed-bearing cones

*Thuja occidentalis* forked trunks

*Thuja occidentalis* trimmed as a hedge

*Thuja occidentalis* in a mixed border

*Thuja occidentalis* bonsai 95 years old

slightly bronze in the winter; therefore, cultivars that stay green all seasons are particularly valued. The pollen-bearing cones are small, yellow, and terminal. The seed-bearing cones are ¼ to ½ in. (0.6 to 1.2 cm), upright, and oblong in clusters. They mature to a cinnamon-brown and open in the first autumn but persist through the winter. The cone scales are rounded at the tips. The fibrous bark is light red-brown (on older trees gray-brown) and shreds in long strips.

*Thuja occidentalis* was one of the earliest plants introduced from the New World to Europe and was growing in France before 1550. It is moderately fast-growing and very hardy; it does not do well in the southern United States. It does best in full sun in moist, well-drained soil; in shade, the plants will open up and look shabby. It is tolerant of limestone soil. It is frequently used as a hedge plant and tolerates shearing on a regular basis, though it does not sprout from old wood. This species is usually multistemmed and therefore easily damaged by wet snow and ice storms. The wood is soft and light but durable in contact with soil, making it useful for posts, shingles, and boxes. Eastern First Nations peoples used it to make canoes.

Thuja occidentalis 'Asplenifolia'

Thuja occidentalis 'Aurea'

## Thuja occidentalis (continued)

Gardeners in suburban areas are well aware of the fondness of deer for this species. It is also grazed by snowshoe hares, porcupines, and red squirrels.

There are loads of cultivars, some nearly indistinguishable from each other. Since so many turn an unattractive brown-green in the winter, one should select cultivars that retain their rich green color in colder climates.

'Asplenifolia': open-growing and broadly conical, dark green in summer, more purple-green in winter, appreciates some shade, best to prune to a single trunk.

'Aurea': globose, golden yellow foliage, does not require shearing, reaches 30 in. (75 cm) tall and wide.

'Aureovariegata': a good variegated selection, will tolerate wet soil and some shade, reaches 10 to 20 ft. (3 to 6 m).

'Bail John': compact, conical, broadly based, dark green, also known as 'Dense Techny'.

'Berkmanii': conical, yellow foliage, reaches 3 ft. (0.9 m), sometimes listed as *Thuja orientalis*.

Thuja occidentalis 'Aurea' foliage

Thuja occidentalis 'Bail John'

Thuja occidentalis 'Aureovariegata'

Thuja occidentalis 'Berkmanii'

*Thuja occidentalis* 'Betler'

*Thuja occidentalis* 'Boothii'

*Thuja occidentalis* 'Bodmeri'

*Thuja occidentalis* 'Brandon'

'Betler': broad conical shape, grows less than 6 in. (15 cm) a year, appreciates deep well-drained soil.

'Bodmeri': weird form with thick congested foliage.

'Boothii': dwarf, rounded and dense, rich green foliage, becomes flat-topped with age, reaches 6 to 10 ft. (1.8 to 3 m).

'Brandon': fast-growing, narrow and upright, does not brown, reaches 12 to 15 ft. (3.6 to 4.5 m) by 6 to 8 ft. (1.8 to 2.5 m).

'Cloth of Gold': slow-growing, round becoming conical, golden yellow leaves during warm season, reaches 12 ft. (3.6 m) in 40 years.

'Compacta': broadly oval, dark green in summer, yellows in winter, compact, useful for hedging, reaches 15 × 8 ft. (4.5 × 2.5 m).

*Thuja occidentalis* 'Cloth of Gold'

*Thuja occidentalis* 'Compacta'

### *Thuja occidentalis* (continued)

'Conica Densa': dense and rounded with upright branching.

'Danica': slow-growing, dense, dwarf and bushy, compact foliage held vertically in flat sprays, rich emerald-green, browns slightly in winter, to 18 in. (46 cm) high and wider than that.

'Degroot's Spire': slow-growing, rich green, very nice narrow, tightly branched, upright form but requires attention to be sure it develops a central leader, bronzes slightly in winter.

'Ellwangeriana Aurea': conical, golden-needled, adult and juvenile foliage, slow-growing, reaches 9 ft. (2.7 m).

'Emerald Green': see 'Smaragd'.

'Emerald Variegated': a variegated form splashed with gold.

*Thuja occidentalis* 'Conica Densa'

*Thuja occidentalis* 'Danica'

*Thuja occidentalis* 'Emerald Variegated'

*Thuja occidentalis* 'Degroot's Spire'

*Thuja occidentalis* 'Ellwangeriana Aurea'

Thuja occidentalis 'Europa Gold'

Thuja occidentalis 'Fastigiata'

Thuja occidentalis 'Filiformis'

Thuja occidentalis 'Franky'

Thuja occidentalis 'Froebelii'

'Europa Gold': slender, conical, with light yellow foliage, reaches 8 ft. (2.5 m) in 15 years, winter foliage is bright orange-copper.

'Fastigiata': tall and conical, dense and compact, light green, formal-looking.

'Filiformis': very slow-growing, compact, globose to conical, long-stranded foliage, eventually reaches 6 ft. (1.8 m), sometimes listed as *Thuja orientalis*.

'Franky': slow-growing with twisted branches.

'Froebelii': dwarf, globose, wide-spreading, slow-growing, light green.

*Thuja occidentalis* 'George Washington'

*Thuja occidentalis* 'Globosa'

### *Thuja occidentalis* (continued)

'George Washington': compact cone, bright golden all seasons.

'Globosa': slow-growing, dense and rounded, deep green foliage, reaches 6 ft. (1.8 m).

'Globosa Rheindiana': dense spherical form with medium green tufted foliage.

'Gold Cargo': gold foliage that does not tend to scorch in winter, reaches 25 × 6 ft. (8 × 1.8 m).

'Gold Cone': markedly upright habit, yellow foliage in summer.

'Gold Drop': dense bright yellow foliage, 2 ft. (0.6 m) tall and wide.

*Thuja occidentalis* 'Globosa Rheindiana'

*Thuja occidentalis* 'Gold Cargo'

*Thuja occidentalis* 'Gold Cone'

*Thuja occidentalis* 'Gold Drop'

*Thuja occidentalis* 'Golden Globe'

*Thuja occidentalis* 'Green Midget'

*Thuja occidentalis* 'Golden Tuffet'

*Thuja occidentalis* 'Hetz Midget'

*Thuja occidentalis* 'Gracilis'

*Thuja occidentalis* 'Hetz Wintergreen'

'Golden Globe': slow-growing, globose, wide-spreading, soft yellow foliage, said not to scorch, reaches 4 ft. (1.2 m).

'Golden Tuffet': pillow-shaped, golden orange foliage looks braided.

'Gracilis': tall, develops an open, pendulous, graceful habit.

'Green Midget': very slow-growing, globose, dark green, ultimately 3 ft. (0.9 m) tall and wide.

'Hetz Midget': extremely slow-growing, broad, rounded, dense dark green foliage turns bronze-purple in winter, reaches 3 to 4 ft. (0.9 to 1.2 m).

'Hetz Wintergreen': vigorous, dark green all year, grows ramrod straight with no snow load or ice problems if trained to a central leader, one of the best upright forms, reaches 35 × 8 ft. (10.5 × 2.5 m) in 35 years.

**Thuja occidentalis** (continued)

'Hollandica': compact, dense, broad, dark green in summer, yellow-green in winter, usually multistemmed, 25 × 16 ft. (8 × 5 m) in 50 years.

'Holmstrup': slow-growing, medium-sized, dense and conical, vertical sprays of foliage deep green all year, eventually reaches 5 to 10 ft. (1.5 to 3 m), ideal for making a low hedge.

'Hoseri': dwarf, upright, shrubby, globose, dense dark green foliage.

'Hoveyi': slow-growing, rounded, flat and regular fanning branches, reaches height and width of 9 ft. (2.7 m).

'Indomitable': vigorous spreading form, dark green in summer turning red-brown in winter, likely to reach 20 ft. (6 m) tall and wide.

'Little Champion': dark green dwarf becoming a 2 ft. (0.6 m) globe.

*Thuja occidentalis* 'Hoseri'

*Thuja occidentalis* 'Hollandica'

*Thuja occidentalis* 'Holmstrup'

*Thuja occidentalis* 'Indomitable'

*Thuja occidentalis* 'Hoveyi'

*Thuja occidentalis* 'Little Champion'

*Thuja occidentalis* 'Little Elfie'

*Thuja occidentalis* 'Little Gem'

*Thuja occidentalis* 'Lutea'

*Thuja occidentalis* 'Malonyana'

'Little Elfie': rounded dwarf, bright green, tips turn red-brown in winter, reaches 4 ft. (1.2 m).

'Little Gem': dwarf and rounded, reaches 3 ft. (0.9 m) in height but will be wider, dark green but discolors in winter.

'Lutea': a narrow cone, golden yellow foliage with green interior, reaches 30 ft. (9 m).

'Lutea Nana': a dwarf form of 'Lutea'.

'Malonyana': vigorous, narrow and columnar, uniform dense deep green foliage, grows to 60 ft. (18 m).

*Thuja occidentalis* 'Miky'

*Thuja occidentalis* 'Milleri'

*Thuja occidentalis* 'Minima'

*Thuja occidentalis* 'Nana'

*Thuja occidentalis* 'Nigra' in March

### *Thuja occidentalis* (continued)

'Miky': compact narrow cone, pale green foliage.

'Milleri': round, multistemmed, emerald-colored foliage held in erect flat sprays, tends to brown in winter, reaches 4 ft. (1.2 m) in height and often wider.

'Minima': similar to 'Hetz Midget'.

'Nana': compact, irregular mound, dense branches in vertical planes, blue-green foliage, reaches 3 to 6 ft. (0.9 to 1.8 m).

'Nigra': narrow and pyramidal, said to remain dark green through all seasons, reaches 30 ft. (9 m) tall.

'Ohlendorfii': round cushion with juvenile foliage with whips of adult foliage, 3 ft. (0.9 m) high.

*Thuja occidentalis* 'Pendula'

*Thuja occidentalis* 'Piccolo'

*Thuja occidentalis* 'Pumila'

*Thuja occidentalis* 'Pumila Sudworthii'

*Thuja occidentalis* 'Recurva Nana'

'Pendula': a small tree with ascending branches and pendulous branchlets, becomes broad if not trained, pale green, reaches 6 ft. (1.8 m) in eight years.

'Piccolo': dwarf cone with tight dark green foliage, 5 × 2 ft. (1.5 × 0.6 m).

'Pulcherrima': similar to 'Lutea' but brighter.

'Pumila': cushion-shaped, compact, dark green.

'Pumila Sudworthii': upright, pyramidal, gold to orange-gold through the seasons, reaches 8 ft. (2.5 m) in ten years.

'Recurva Nana': low-growing, flat-topped dome with curving branch tips.

**Thuja occidentalis** (continued)

'Reevesii': slow-growing, rounded and dense, reaches height and width of 9 ft. (2.7 m).

'Rheingold': slow-growing, oval or cone-shaped, golden yellow in summer, deep coppery gold in winter, soft juvenile type foliage, can be sheared, can be up to 10 ft. (3 m) but usually expect to be 2 ft. (0.6 m), will split open with snow, various forms sold under this name.

'Rockwood Gold': globose, dense foliage is lacy, light green tipped in gold, reaches 8 ft. (2.5 m) tall and wide.

'Rosenthalii': dwarf compact column, very slow-growing, dark green, takes a long time to reach 10 ft. (3 m).

'Sherwood Column': columnar with soft, dense foliage, green all seasons.

'Sherwood Frost': vigorous, dense, tall, cone-shaped, light green with creamy white edges in summer, olive-green with honey-colored edges in winter, to 10 ft. (3 m), will split open with snow.

*Thuja occidentalis* 'Reevesii'

*Thuja occidentalis* 'Rheingold'

*Thuja occidentalis* 'Rockwood Gold'

*Thuja occidentalis* 'Rosenthalii'

*Thuja occidentalis* 'Sherwood Column'

*Thuja occidentalis* 'Sherwood Frost'

*Thuja occidentalis* 'Sherwood Moss'

'Sherwood Moss': conical, medium green, bronzes in winter, prickly but feathery texture, reaches 4 × 2 ft. (1.2 × 0.6 m).

'Smaragd': German for "emerald" (the color of its vertical foliage sprays), grows rapidly, reaching 15 × 4 ft. (4.5 × 1.2 m) in 15 years, stays compact, narrow, and upright, unaffected by snow or ice loads if trained to a single leader, considered by many to be the best green among the arborvitaes, maintains color all seasons, good for hedging, heat- and cold-tolerant, also listed as 'Emerald Green'.

'Smithiana': low and compact, slow-growing, dark green turning purple in winter.

'Snowtip': upright with creamy white variegation.

'Spiralis': narrow, compact, conical, twisted upright branching.

*Thuja occidentalis* 'Smaragd'

*Thuja occidentalis* 'Smithiana'

*Thuja occidentalis* 'Snowtip'

*Thuja occidentalis* 'Spiralis'

### *Thuja occidentalis* (continued)

'St. John's Mini': dwarf, spreading to 6 ft. (1.8 m).

'Sudworth': broad and upright, yellow foliage turns orangish in winter.

'Sudworth Gold': slow-growing, conical, gold foliage.

'Sunkist': dense, small, slow-growing, round-topped cone, gold yellow color in summer, burnished gold in winter, 5 to 8 ft. (1.5 to 2.5 m) high.

'Techny': globose, fast-growing with strong tendency to form multiple stems and trunks, stays dark green all year, reaches 10 to 25 ft. (3 to 8 m) tall, also called 'Mission'.

'Teddy': globose with soft new growth, reaches 15 in. (38 cm) tall and wide.

'Tiny Tim': slow-growing ball, reaches 16 × 12 in. (40 × 30 cm) in eight to ten years, nice for knot gardens.

*Thuja occidentalis* 'St. John's Mini'

*Thuja occidentalis* 'Sudworth'

*Thuja occidentalis* 'Sunkist'

*Thuja occidentalis* 'Sudworth Gold'

*Thuja occidentalis* 'Teddy'

*Thuja occidentalis* 'Tiny Tim'

*Thuja occidentalis* 'Trompenburg'

*Thuja occidentalis* 'Umbraculifera'

*Thuja occidentalis* 'Unicorn'

*Thuja occidentalis* 'Wagneri'

*Thuja occidentalis* 'Wansdyke Silver'

'Trompenburg': upright dwarf, irregular habit, light yellow.

'Umbraculifera': dwarf, irregularly rounded, compact, foliage blue-green, 2 × 4 ft. (0.6 × 1.2 m).

'Unicorn': upright narrow cone, fine-textured dark green foliage.

'Wagneri': compact cone, dark green turning olive in winter, 15 × 11 ft. (4.5 × 3.4 m) in 20 years.

'Wansdyke Silver': densely branched slow-growing cone, variegated creamy white all seasons, reaches 4 ft. (1.2 m).

'Wareana': slow-growing, low and dense with thick rich green foliage, great upright form if trained to a central leader, yellow-green in winter, takes 20 years to reach 10 ft. (3 m).

### *Thuja occidentalis* (continued)

'Wareana Lutescens': similar but more compact and pale yellow foliage.

'Watnong Gold': narrow compact column, stays gold in winter.

'Wintergreen': same as 'Hetz Wintergreen'.

'Woodwardii': dense and egg-shaped without trimming, green all year, reaches 4 to 5 ft. (1.2 to 1.5 m) by 3 to 4 ft. (0.9 to 1.2 m).

'Yellow Ribbon': narrow and upright, reaching 10 ft. (3 m) tall and only 3 ft. (0.9 m) wide, bright yellow in summer, bronze in winter.

*Thuja occidentalis* 'Watnong Gold'

*Thuja occidentalis* 'Wareana Lutescens'

*Thuja occidentalis* 'Woodwardii'

*Thuja occidentalis* 'Yellow Ribbon'

*Thuja orientalis*

## *Thuja orientalis*　oriental arborvitae　Zones 6 to 11

This conifer, a good one for the south, is included in *Thuja* or listed as *Platycladus orientalis*, of the monotypic genus *Platy-cladus*, depending on which authority one encounters; it has also been labeled *Biota orientalis*. It is distinct among the thujas for its formal habit as a large shrub or small tree, up to 25 ft. (8 m) high, and its foliage, which is held nearly vertical on erect branches; these parallel foliage sprays have earned it the common name bookleaf cypress. The leaves are in ferny sprays and have a faint scent. The pale blue-green cones are larger than the other species, ¾ in. (2 cm), and the cone scales are thick and fleshy with stout points (recurved hooks) on their outer surface. It is native to northern China, Manchuria, and Korea. The species is said to be very adaptable, tolerant of heat and dryness as well as of cold. It should not be placed in a wet situation. Its numerous cultivars are becoming more widely appreciated, especially for containers and small gardens.

'Aurea': golden foliage, sometimes considered a group name since various forms exist, as those following.

*Thuja orientalis* foliage and cones

*Thuja orientalis* 'Aurea'

*Thuja orientalis* 'Aurea Nana'

*Thuja orientalis* 'Berckman'

*Thuja orientalis* 'Beverleyensis' in February

### *Thuja orientalis* (continued)

'Aurea Densa': the name says it.

'Aurea Nana': compact, dense, oval bush, deep yellow, reaches 5 ft. (1.5 m).

'Berckman': columnar, dense, shrub-sized, light yellow foliage, also called 'Conspicua'.

'Beverleyensis': compact, narrow, and pyramidal, bright gold on new growth becoming green as the season progresses, bronze in winter, fern-like leaf sprays, grows rapidly to 15 to 20 ft. (4.5 to 6 m).

'Elegantissima': pyramidal, compact in youth opening with age, gold-tipped in spring, turning green and then bronze by winter, reaches 20 ft. (6 m).

'Franky Boy': dwarf, weeping, thread-like golden yellow foliage fading to yellow-green, reaches 30 × 24 in. (75 × 60 cm) in ten years.

*Thuja orientalis* 'Franky Boy'

roses. The mature cone scales often have a small sharp point near the tip. The bark is thin, red-brown to gray-brown, fibrous, and shredding, forming narrow flat ridges with age.

First Nations peoples used this species for making their celebrated totem poles (these were not religious symbols but heraldic and a record of genealogy). As a matter of fact, all parts of this and another native conifer of that area, *Chamaecyparis nootkatensis*, were the main resources for their material needs. Not only the wood but the roots, bark, and branchlets were used in the construction of household necessities and textiles. Today the wood is widely used for roof shingles or any situation where durability and resistance to water decay is important. It is a very handsome tree for the home landscape with its luxuriant wide-sweeping boughs. One wonders why it is not more widely used. It makes a wonderful background plant or screen. It responds well to pruning and can be trained into a lush hedge. It will even tolerate some shade. And it has been observed that deer do not rush to browse on it the way they do toward *Thuja occidentalis*.

'Atrovirens': narrow and pyramidal, glossy dark green foliage all year, useful for hedging because it is said to produce new growth on old wood, tolerates wet soil and takes considerable shade, reaches 30 to 45 ft. (9 to 14 m).

'Aurea': yellow-green with areas of rich old-gold tint.

'Canadian Gold': pyramidal, dense yellow foliage all seasons, reaches 65 × 20 ft. (19.5 × 6 m), possibly same as 'Sunshine'.

'Clemson Select': slow-growing with splashes of cream.

*Thuja plicata* 'Atrovirens'

*Thuja plicata* 'Aurea'

*Thuja plicata* 'Canadian Gold' hedge

*Thuja plicata* 'Clemson Select'

### *Thuja plicata* (continued)

'Collyer's Gold': slow-growing and upright, green with golden yellow tips, similar to 'Stoneham Gold' but brighter.

'Copper Kettle': slow-growing, upright, golden-bronze foliage during cold seasons.

'Cuprea': low-spreading without a leader, rich green tipped with light yellow foliage turns copper-yellow in winter, reaches 3 ft. (0.9 m), good choice for rock gardens.

'Emerald Cone': dense and compact, rich emerald-green foliage, reaches 25 to 40 ft. (8 to 12 m) with a 12 ft. (3.6 m) spread.

'Excelsa': fast-growing, tall open column, strongly ascending branches, dark glossy green all seasons, useful for hedging, similar to 'Atrovirens'.

'Extra Gold': same as 'Zebrina Extra Gold'.

'Fastigiata': dense and compact, to 40 ft. (12 m) with only a 10 ft. (3 m) spread, slender ascending branches, obviously useful for hedging.

*Thuja plicata* 'Collyer's Gold'

*Thuja plicata* 'Copper Kettle'

*Thuja plicata* 'Cuprea'

*Thuja plicata* 'Fastigiata'

*Thuja plicata* 'Green Giant'

*Thuja plicata* 'Grovepli'

*Thuja plicata* 'Hogan'

*Thuja plicata* 'Rogersii'

'Green Giant': tall, narrow, and densely conical, vigorous, grows 3 to 5 ft. (0.9 to 1.5 m) a year, reaching 60 × 20 ft. (18 × 6 m), glossy dark green foliage all seasons is claimed, often listed as *Thuja* 'Green Giant', thought to be a hybrid between *T. standishii* and *T. plicata*.

'Grovepli': fast-growing pyramidal, rich green foliage all seasons, excellent for hedges or screening, reaches 18 to 25 ft. (5.5 to 8 m) by 3 to 6 ft. (0.9 to 1.8 m).

'Hogan': dense and compact, narrowly upright, rich green foliage, browns in winter.

'Holly Turner': wide-spreading with a definite leader.

'Rogersii': dense, oval, pillow-shaped, golden yellow in summer, bronze-yellow in winter, reaches 4 to 6 ft. (1.2 to 1.8 m) in 20 years.

### *Thuja plicata* (continued)

'Stoneham Gold': slow-growing, broad upright conical form, green in center, new growth is a bright yellow in full sun, reaches 6 × 2 ft. (1.8 × 0.6 m) in 15 years, popular in England.

'Sunshine': broadly conical, often multistemmed with pendulous tips, bright gold summer foliage, turns definite bronze in winter, reaches 60 to 70 ft. (18 to 21 m) with a 15 to 20 ft. (4.5 to 6 m) spread.

'Virescens': upright with ascending branches, shiny dark green foliage.

'Whipcord': many-branched mounding bush with long yarn-like foliage, looks like a glossy green rag mop, bronzes in winter, reaches 5 × 4 ft. (1.5 × 1.2 m) in 20 years.

*Thuja plicata* 'Sunshine'

*Thuja plicata* 'Stoneham Gold'

*Thuja plicata* 'Whipcord'

*Thuja plicata* 'Winter Pink'

*Thuja plicata* 'Zebrina'

*Thuja plicata* 'Zebrina' foliage

'Winter Pink': compact and dwarf, with a pink-tinged variegation in the winter.

'Zebrina': fast-growing tree for the open landscape, pale green foliage with creamy yellow zebra-stripe variegation all year. Stunning.

'Zebrina Extra Gold': similar but slower growing with even more gold variegation.

*Thuja standishii*

### *Thuja standishii*    Japanese arborvitae    Zones 5 and 6

This arborvitae is native to subalpine forests in Japan. A small to medium-sized tree with a conical habit, upcurved branches, and pendulous branchlets, it is seldom found in cultivation. The yellowish green foliage is displayed loosely in large sprays. The foliage smells like lemon verbena. The bark is deep red and fibrous.

### *Thujopsis dolabrata*    hiba arborvitae    Zones 5 to 7

The lone species in its monotypic genus, the hiba arborvitae is native to Japan. Slow-growing, dense, and pyramidal, it ranges in size from a shrub to a 30 to 50 ft. (9 to 15 m) tall and 10 to 20 ft. (3 to 6 m) wide tree. *Thujopsis dolabrata* has many ornamental features. Its foliage is similar to that of *Thuja* but larger and broader with flat branchlets. The glossy scale-like leaves are bright green above with distinctive white markings (*dolabra* means "hatchet") underneath. The twigs branch in a staghorn-like pattern. The open seed-bearing cones, ½ to ¾ in. (1.2

*Thujopsis dolabrata*

*Thujopsis dolabrata* foliage underside (note white "hatchets") and seed-bearing cone

*Thujopsis dolabrata* immature seed-bearing cone

*Thujopsis dolabrata* 'Aurea'

*Thujopsis dolabrata* 'Aurea' foliage

*Thujopsis dolabrata* 'Nana'

*Thujopsis dolabrata* 'Variegata'

to 2 cm) long, resemble tiny woody flowers. The bark is reddish brown, furrowed into thin strips.

*Thujopsis dolabrata* tolerates cold winters and a wide range of soils but requires adequate moisture. It will grow in full sun, though it grows best in an area of partial shade, shelter, and cool dampness. It has been used for hedging. This has been a plant for the collector but deserves much wider use. In Japan it provides lumber for general construction and railroad ties.

'Aurea': yellow-gold foliage.

var. *hondai*: wide-spreading dense tree, reaches 100 ft. (30 m) in the wild.

'Nana': dwarf, compact, mounded plant slowly reaching 3 ft. (7.5 m), bright green foliage turns olive-green in winter.

'Variegata': scattered patches of creamy white, variable.

### *Torreya nucifera*   Japanese torreya   Zones 6 to 8

*Torreya nucifera* is native to Japan. In the wild it reaches 75 ft. (23 m) but will grow slowly to 15 to 30 ft. (4.5 to 9 m) tall and wide in the garden. The genus is allied to *Taxus* and its members prefer growing in a shaded area in well-drained soil. This species needs sufficient summer moisture and will not tolerate dry, exposed locations. Torreyas need protection from harsh winter winds. It has graceful branches and glossy dark green 1¼ in. (3 cm) needles in a flat plane. The foliage is pungent when crushed. The fleshy seed-bearing cones are plum-like, 1 in. (2.5 cm) long, green maturing to pale purple, and contain a single seed. The wood is used to make the playing surface for Go, as the Japanese call it, a traditional board game enjoyed by millions of Asians.

  'Gold Strike': scattered, bright yellow variegation.

  'Variegata': yellow and green variegation.

*Torreya nucifera* foliage and seed-bearing cones

*Torreya nucifera* 'Gold Strike'

*Torreya nucifera*

*Torreya nucifera* 'Variegata' foliage and seed-bearing cone

## *Tsuga*   hemlock

Four species of hemlock are native to the eastern and western forests of North America; a half-dozen other species grow in the Himalayas and the Far East. Representatives of this genus are typically found in relatively moist areas. One can identify a hemlock from a distance by its delicate texture, pyramidal habit, and the fact that the terminal leader always droops a bit. Hemlocks are widely planted as specimens in gardens and are very important in the timber industry, especially for pulp production. This is not the poison hemlock of classical times; that deadly brew was made from *Conium maculatum*, an herbaceous species of the family Apiaceae (carrots and parsley). *Tsuga* is not poisonous.

## *Tsuga canadensis*   eastern hemlock   Zones 3 to 7

The eastern hemlock is native from Nova Scotia to eastern Minnesota, and south to Maryland and Illinois. It follows the Appalachian Mountains to Georgia and northern Alabama. It is a large tree and can reach a height of 80 ft. (24 m) or more. In the open it presents a very graceful appearance, dense and branched to the ground, but in crowded stands, where it is commonly seen, it will be free of lower branches. Hemlocks like to grow in cool, moist, woodland conditions, where they are rather slow-growing. Seedlings are able to establish under the canopy of mature trees. They thrive streamside and are often discovered on steep north-facing rocky slopes. They take 200 to 300 years to reach maturity and can live 600 years or more. This species will not tolerate air pollution and is damaged by salt. The soft ½ in. (1.2 cm) needles are arranged spirally on the stem but often appear two-ranked. They are flat, lustrous dark green, and have two white lines on the lower surface. They remain on the tree for up to ten years. A row of smaller leaves along the upper surface of the twigs appears to be flipped over—

*Tsuga canadensis*

*Tsuga canadensis* foliage and seed-bearing cones

## *Tsuga canadensis* (continued)

flat on the stem, with the silver bands showing. This is a useful ID feature.

The ½ to ¾ in. (1.2 to 2 cm) cones hang down on short stalks. They are among the smallest of all cones. They mature in one season but remain until the following year. Eastern hemlocks don't start producing seeds until they are several decades old. The bark is red-brown to gray-brown at maturity with long fissures and scaly ridges. The eastern hemlock will take 15 to 20 years to reach 30 to 40 ft. (9 to 12 m) in height.

Vast native stands were harvested for the tannin-rich bark, which is used for tanning leather. The brittle wood is not durable and is used primarily for making boxes and as pulpwood. The foliage provides food, nesting, and cover for wildlife, and numerous birds, especially warblers, seek out the seeds. It is the state tree of Pennsylvania.

*Tsuga canadensis* makes a very desirable ornamental plant for the landscape. It is shade-tolerant and fine-textured, has good foliage color, and can be shaped into an elegant hedge. This species lends a graceful touch among stiffer-looking conifers. It is somewhat shallow-rooted and can be felled by strong winds. Protect it from hot, dry situations. In sun it will need moist soil. There are dozens of named cultivars in the trade. It is not widely planted in Europe.

This hemlock was included with the pines (as *Pinus canadensis*) by Linnaeus in 1763. Michaux later grouped it (as *Abies canadensis*) with the firs. *Tsuga* (Japanese for "yew-leaved") was applied in 1847 by Austrian botanist Stephen Endlicher. Thus a plant native to North America has a Japanese name specified by an Austrian and established by a Swede and a Frenchman.

This beautiful conifer is threatened by an insect pest, *Adelges tsugae*, the hem-

*Tsuga canadensis* bark

Hemlock woolly adelgid on *Tsuga canadensis*

*Tsuga canadensis* sheared into a hedge

lock woolly adelgid, which has since the mid 20th century spread relentlessly throughout the eastern United States. Recent climate changes with warmer winters have accelerated the problem. This sap-sucking adelgid infests eastern hemlocks of all ages, causing reduction in new shoot development, thinning of foliage, branch dieback, and the eventual death of the tree. An infestation is easy to recognize: the egg sacs of these insects look like bits of cotton clinging to the undersides of the needles. Horticultural oil and insecticidal soap give some control of this pest, but there is no known effective way to prevent its spread. The fear is that *Tsuga canadensis* mortality could reach 100 percent, affecting forest composition and the ecology of wildlife habitats. *Tsuga caroliniana, T. diversifolia,* and *T. sieboldii* are also susceptible to hemlock woolly adelgid damage; *T. heterophylla* and *T. mertensiana* are not.

*Tsuga canadensis* 'Aurea'

*Tsuga canadensis* 'Brandley'

*Tsuga canadensis* 'Beaujean'

*Tsuga canadensis* 'Bennett'

Potential substitutes for eastern hemlock include *Chamae-cyparis nootkatensis*, *C. obtusa*, *Cryptomeria japonica*, *Picea orientalis*, *Thuja plicata*, *T. p.* 'Green Giant', and *Tsuga chinensis*.

'Aurea': pyramidal, young foliage golden yellow.

'Beaujean': compact, nest-like dwarf, good for rock gardens, 3 × 4 ft. (0.9 × 1.2 m) in ten years.

'Bennett': slow-growing dwarf, spreading mound with pendulous branch tips, dark green foliage, 2 × 4 ft. (0.6 × 1.2 m) in ten years.

'Boulevard': dense and compact, irregular habit, dark green foliage.

'Brandley': slow-growing, dense and rounded with ascending branches, dark green.

*Tsuga canadensis* 'Burkett's White Tip'

*Tsuga canadensis* 'Cole's Prostrate'

## *Tsuga canadensis* (continued)

'Burkett's White Tip': compact large shrub or small tree, white branch tips in summer.

'Cole's Prostrate': slow-growing, mat-forming with branches extending flat along the ground, silver-gray center branches become exposed with maturity, useful for shady rock garden or vest-pocket garden, grows 3 ft. (0.9 m) in 20 years.

'Creamey': upright narrow dwarf, white variegation, 4 × 2 ft. (1.2 × 0.6 m) in ten years.

'Curley': contorted form, new growth dense and curled around the stem, strong grower.

'Devil's Fork': vase-shaped with upright forked branches and drooping branch tips, glossy dark green in summer, lighter in winter, reaches 5 ft. (1.5 m).

'Everitt's Golden': slow-growing stiff small tree with ascending branches, tight needles, golden yellow early in season, green to bronze by fall, needs afternoon shade, also called 'Everitt Golden'.

'Frosty': slow-growing, globe-shaped, white new shoots in shade, will burn in sun.

*Tsuga canadensis* 'Curley'

*Tsuga canadensis* 'Everitt's Golden'

*Tsuga canadensis* 'Devil's Fork'

*Tsuga canadensis* 'Frosty'

*Tsuga canadensis* 'Geneva'

*Tsuga canadensis* 'Greenwood Lake'

*Tsuga canadensis* 'Hussii'

*Tsuga canadensis* 'Gentsch White'

*Tsuga canadensis* 'Guldemond's Dwarf'

'Geneva': compact, slow-growing small tree, upright to oval shape, tolerates full sun.

'Gentsch White': slow-growing shrub form, white-tipped or variegated foliage, benefits from occasional shearing, reaches 2 × 3 ft. (0.6 × 0.9 m).

'Gracilis': mounded shape with glossy foliage and drooping branch tips.

'Greenwood Lake': slow-growing, develops into a large shrub with dense irregular branches, good winter color.

'Guldemond's Dwarf': slow-growing, compact, irregular pyramid, dense short needles.

'Humphrey Welch': short gray-green curved needles on arching branches, lacy appearance, 4 × 2 ft. (1.2 × 0.6 m) in ten years.

'Hussii': compact, dense, upright, grows 2 in. (5 cm) a year.

**Tsuga canadensis** (continued)

'Jacqueline Verkade': dwarf, conical with vertical branches, tiny dark green needles.

'Jeddeloh': low-spreading bush, nest-like form with pendulous branch tips, medium green, reaches 4 to 5 ft. (1.2 to 1.5 m), similar to 'Bennett', popular in Europe.

'Kelsey's Weeping': fast-growing, irregular weeper, 2 × 5 ft. (0.6 × 1.5 m) in ten years.

'LaBar White Tip': irregularly shaped small tree, white new growth turns dark green.

*Tsuga canadensis* 'Jeddeloh'

*Tsuga canadensis* 'Jacqueline Verkade'

*Tsuga canadensis* 'Kelsey's Weeping'

*Tsuga canadensis* 'LaBar White Tip'

*Tsuga canadensis* 'Lewis'

*Tsuga canadensis* 'Little Joe'

'Lewis': irregular dwarf upright, deep green needles are short and thick.

'Little Joe': dwarf and rounded, dark green needles, ideal for shady trough garden or bonsai.

'Minima': very slow-growing, short dense branches, gray-green, eventually reaches 5 × 9 ft. (1.5 × 2.7 m).

'Nana': slow-growing, flat spreading form, rich green all year, reaches 3 ft. (0.9 m) tall with 9 ft. (2.7 m) spread, useful for trough or rock gardens, collective name but often superior plant.

'Palomino': dwarf and slow-growing, compact round bun, seldom reaches 3 ft. (0.9 m).

*Tsuga canadensis* 'Minima'

*Tsuga canadensis* 'Palomino'

*Tsuga canadensis* 'Nana'

### *Tsuga canadensis* (continued)

'Pendula': overlapping, pendulous branches, a magnificent spreading lawn specimen after several decades, also known as Sargent's hemlock.

'Sherwood Compact': compact globular dwarf, twisted branch structure with dark green foliage, 4 × 5 ft. (1.2 × 1.5 m) in ten years.

'Snowflake': whitish foliage, reaches 10 ft. (3 m), less variegated in dense shade.

'Stewart's Gem': dwarf dense globe, dark green with russet tips, reaches 2 ft. (0.6 m) wide and tall.

*Tsuga canadensis* 'Pendula'

*Tsuga canadensis* 'Pendula' young specimen in mixed border

*Tsuga canadensis* 'Sherwood Compact'

*Tsuga canadensis* 'Snowflake'

*Tsuga canadensis* 'Stewart's Gem'

*Tsuga canadensis* 'Stockman's Dwarf'

'Stockman's Dwarf': slow-growing, upright conical form, densely needled.

'Summer Snow': fast-growing, upright and conical, green foliage with white tips.

'Thurlow': fast-growing, dense, upright.

'Verkade Recurved': upright, irregular with twisted dark green needles and branchlets, 3 × 4 ft. (0.9 × 1.2 m) in ten years.

'Vermeulen's Wintergold': upright cone with yellow needles, grows 6 to 8 in. (15 to 20 cm) a year.

'Von Helms': dwarf irregular cone, dense ascending branches with drooping tips, dark green.

'Warner's Globe': irregular upright bush, tufted dark green foliage.

'Watnong Star': slow-growing globe, pale green with white tips, reaches 4 ft. (1.2 m) tall and wide, less variegation in dense shade.

'Wind's Way': dense branching with drooping tips, grows 6 in. (15 cm) a year, reaches 10 to 15 ft. (3 to 4.5 m).

*Tsuga canadensis* 'Summer Snow'

*Tsuga canadensis* 'Verkade Recurved'

*Tsuga canadensis* 'Vermeulen's Wintergold'

*Tsuga canadensis* 'Watnong Star'

### *Tsuga caroliniana*   Carolina hemlock
Zones 4 to 7

This beautiful native hemlock is not as widely distributed as *Tsuga canadensis*, but their ranges overlap. It is found in scattered stands from southern Virginia to northern Georgia. It prefers growing on the southeastern faces of mountains on rocky slopes. It is smaller than eastern hemlock, reaching 40 to 60 ft. (12 to 18 m) tall by 25 ft. (8 m) wide, and is considered more difficult to grow in cultivation. It is not tolerant of heat and drought, nor does it transplant well. In youth it is symmetrical, but with advanced age it develops a more irregular outline. The branches are somewhat pendulous. The bright green needles are up to ¾ in. (2 cm) long with two white lines beneath. They are arranged in all directions off the stem, giving a bristly appearance. The cones are larger than the eastern hemlock's, from 1 to 1½ in. (2.5 to 3.5 cm) long; they have a short stalk or are stalkless. It is occasionally grown as an ornamental, but given the relative rarity of this species in nature, its wood is of little commercial importance.

The bristly foliage of *Tsuga caroliniana*

### *Tsuga diversifolia*   Japanese hemlock
Zones (4)5 and 6

This hemlock is found near the timberline in Japan. In the wild it can reach 30 to 90 ft. (9 to 27 m), a graceful pyramidal tree with a narrow conical crown; but in cultivation it is more often shrubby. It grows in sun or shade and is the most wind-tolerant of the hemlocks, notable for its orange bark and twisty orange shoots with short fine hairs. The needles are a glossy dark green. This species is used for bonsai.

'Gotelli': dense irregular dwarf.

*Tsuga diversifolia*

*Tsuga diversifolia* foliage and cones

*Tsuga diversifolia* 'Gotelli'

## *Tsuga heterophylla* western hemlock Zone 6

This North American native is found from southeastern Alaska south through British Columbia, Washington, and Oregon into California. It is the dominant species in parts of its range, thriving in areas of high rainfall and cool summers; despite being slow-growing, in that environment it can reach up to 150 ft. (46 m), much taller than its eastern cousins. In youth it is pyramidal, but with age its branches develop a weeping habit. It can live 500 years. This species is capable of establishing in the forest understory and surviving for centuries before reaching the canopy.

Like the other hemlocks, the leading shoot will dip over at the tip, away from the prevailing wind. The variable leaves (hence the epithet) are ¼ to ¾ in. (0.6 to 2 cm) long, shiny dark green with white rows beneath. They are arranged in a flat spray in two ranks, with short needles pressing against the twig on the upper side ("flipped"). The cones are ¾ to 1 in. (2 to 2.5 cm) long and hang downward from the ends of small branches. The red-brown bark is up to 1½ in. (3.5 cm) thick with deep scaly ridges.

*Tsuga heterophylla* will grow well in full sun or in shade. The tree provides dense shade. It is rarely found in gardens except around its native range. The bark is even higher in tannin than the eastern species. The wood is considered of a higher grade and is used for general construction, flooring, and paneling; however, it is principally valued as a pulpwood and in the manufacture of cellulose products. It is the state tree of Washington.

'Iron Springs': slow-growing, rigid and upright, dark green foliage, grows 4 to 6 in. (10 to 15 cm) a year.

'Thorsen's Weeping': prostrate groundcover (can be staked into a mounding habit, as shown), emerald-green, excellent for rock gardens, 4 in. (10 cm) high and 5 ft. (1.5 m) across in ten years.

*Tsuga heterophylla* 'Iron Springs'

*Tsuga heterophylla* 'Thorsen's Weeping'

*Tsuga heterophylla*

### *Tsuga mertensiana*  mountain hemlock  Zone 5

The mountain hemlock is found in California, Oregon, Washington, Idaho, and Montana, and north through British Columbia into Alaska, in subalpine areas that have a deep snow cover early in the fall. It grows slowly and ranges from 30 to 100 ft. (9 to 30 m) in height. Like other hemlocks, it is shade-tolerant and can live 800 years. It is much admired in its native stands for its graceful pendulous form. The glossy ¼ to 1 in. (0.6 to 2.5 cm) blue-green needles cover the branches densely on all sides. The 1 to 3 in. (2.5 to 7.5 cm) cones are purple-green and hang on the ends of small branches. The bark is a dark red-brown with deep narrow ridges. This hemlock has been used in designed landscapes in the Pacific Northwest and throughout Great Britain; its attractive compact foliage and slow growth rate are appealing.

*Tsuga mertensiana* foliage

*Tsuga mertensiana*

*Tsuga mertensiana* cones

*Tsuga mertensiana* 'Elizabeth'

*Tsuga mertensiana* 'Bump's Blue'

*Tsuga mertensiana* 'Glauca'

It should be protected from wind. It provides habitat for many wildlife species. The wood is unimportant as commercial timber but is used in pulp production.

'Bump's Blue': slow-growing, excellent silver-blue foliage.

'Elizabeth': dwarf, flat and spreading, excellent blue needles, good for container or rockery, 4 × 1 ft. (1.2 × 0.3 m) in 15 years.

'Glauca': slow-growing, blue needles, eventually 50 ft. (15 m) high.

### *Tsuga sieboldii* southern Japanese hemlock
Zones 5 and 6

The southern Japanese hemlock is native to the moist mountains of South Japan. It is an irregular, conical tree that can reach 90 ft. (27 m) in its native habitat; in cultivation it will be 15 to 45 ft. (4.5 to 14 m). It is often slow-growing and shrubby. The branches are rather horizontal with pendulous tips. The needles are glossy green above, marked with white bands below. The seed-bearing cone is ¾ to 1 in. (2 to 2.5 cm) with cone scales that appear cupped, even at maturity. It will grow in sun or light shade but is seldom found in gardens.

*Tsuga sieboldii*

*Tsuga sieboldii* foliage and seed-bearing cones

### *Wollemia nobilis* Wollemi-pine
Zone 10

This recently described conifer (not a pine, of course) was found in 1994 by an observant Park Service officer and explorer, David Noble, growing in a wet and sheltered gorge in the Wollemi National Park, a mountainous area northwest of Sydney in New South Wales, Australia. The specific epithet, *nobilis*, honors both the tree's majestic qualities and its discoverer. It is reported that the wild population consists of about three dozen plants and hundreds of seedlings. The tree is pyramidal and grows about 12 in. (30 cm) a year. It will reach more than 100 ft. (30 m) at maturity. The dark green leaves are distinctive; they are arranged in four ranks. It tends to shed whole branches rather than individual leaves. New growth will appear from the base of trees that have been cut or damaged by nature. The pollen- and seed-bearing cones appear on the same tree. The seed-bearing cones are at the very top of the trees. The bark has been described as resembling bubbling chocolate.

There seems to be no genetic variation within the Wollemi-pine populations; this monotypic genus is related to *Araucaria*, an ancient genus (monkey puzzle tree, Norfolk Island pine) with fossil records that date from more than 200 million years ago. It is believed that Wollemi-pines grew in vast forests in Australia at one time. Efforts are underway to propagate the plant and initiate worldwide distribution, with royalties from sales going to support conservation of this and other rare and endangered plant species. The Wollemi-pine will be a conservatory plant for much of North America and northern Europe. In 1999, yet another previously unknown conifer, *Xanthocyparis vietnamensis* (golden cypress), was discovered in Vietnam. Perhaps the next edition of this encyclopedia will include pictures of these intriguing conifers.

# Appendix

## Genera listed by plant family

Araucariaceae
- *Araucaria*
- *Wollemia*

Cephalotaxaceae (plum-yew family)
- *Cephalotaxus*

Cupressaceae (cypress family)
- *Calocedrus*
- *Chamaecyparis*
- *Cryptomeria*
- *Cunninghamia*
- ×*Cupressocyparis*
- *Cupressus*
- *Juniperus*
- *Metasequoia*
- *Microbiota*
- *Sequoia*
- *Sequoiadendron*
- *Taiwania*
- *Taxodium*
- *Thuja*
- *Thujopsis*

Ginkgoaceae
- *Ginkgo*

Pinaceae (pine family)
- *Abies*
- *Cedrus*
- *Larix*
- *Picea*
- *Pinus*
- *Pseudolarix*
- *Pseudotsuga*
- *Tsuga*

Podocarpaceae (podocarpus family)
- *Podocarpus*

Sciadopityaceae (sciadopitys family)
- *Sciadopitys*

Taxaceae (yew family)
- *Taxus*
- *Torreya*

## Selecting plants for specific characteristics or purposes

### Gray to silver-gray or blue-gray foliage

Cultivars labeled 'Glauca', 'Glabra', or 'Argenteo', or with "blue" or "silver" in their name.

*Abies concolor*
*Chamaecyparis lawsoniana* 'Oregon Blue'
*Chamaecyparis pisifera* 'Boulevard'
*Juniperus squamata* 'Blue Star'
*Juniperus virginiana* 'Grey Owl'
*Picea pungens*

### Yellow or gold foliage

Cultivars labeled 'Aurea' or 'Lutea', or with "gold" in their name.

*Chamaecyparis obtusa* 'Crippsii'
*Cryptomeria japonica* 'Sekkan-sugi'
×*Cupressocyparis leylandii* 'Castlewellan'
*Taxus baccata* 'Standishii'

*Thuja plicata* 'Rogersii'
*Thuja plicata* 'Zebrina'

### Upright, narrow habit

Cultivars labeled 'Columnaris' or 'Fastigiata'.

*Calocedrus decurrens*
*Cephalotaxus harringtonia* 'Fastigiata'
*Ginkgo biloba* 'Princeton Sentry'
*Picea omorika*
*Pinus cembra*
*Taxodium ascendens*
*Taxus baccata* 'Standishii'
*Taxus* ×*media* 'Hicksii'
*Thuja occidentalis* 'Smaragd'

### Weeping habit

Cultivars labeled 'Pendula', or with "weeping" in their name.

### Ornamental bark

*Pinus bungeana*
*Pinus densiflora*
*Pinus resinosa*
*Pinus sylvestris*
*Sequoiadendron giganteum*

### Rapid growers

*Cryptomeria japonica*
×*Cupressocyparis leylandii*
*Larix decidua*
*Larix kaempferi*

## Rapid growers (continued)

*Metasequoia glyptostroboides*
*Picea abies*
*Pinus strobus*
*Pseudotsuga menziesii*
*Taxus baccata*
*Thuja occidentalis*
*Thuja plicata*
*Tsuga canadensis*

## Tolerant of somewhat moist soils

*Abies*
*Chamaecyparis pisifera*
*Juniperus communis*
*Larix laricina*
*Metasequoia glyptostroboides*
*Picea abies*
*Picea glauca*
*Picea mariana*
*Picea sitchensis*
*Taxodium*
*Thuja occidentalis*

## Tolerant of moist to wet soils

*Larix laricina*
*Metasequoia glyptostroboides*
*Taxodium*

## Tolerant of sandy, dry to poor soil

*Abies concolor*
*Cupressus arizonica*
*Juniperus*
*Picea omorika*
*Picea pungens*
*Pinus banksiana*
*Pinus mugo*
*Pinus nigra*
*Pinus sylvestris*
*Pinus virginiana*

## Tolerant of compacted soils, drought, and heat

*Ginkgo biloba*

## Tolerant of alkaline soil

*Cedrus atlantica*
*Cephalotaxus harringtonia*
*Chamaecyparis lawsoniana*
*Chamaecyparis nootkatensis*
*×Cupressocyparis leylandii*
*Ginkgo biloba*
*Juniperus*
*Picea omorika*
*Pinus leucodermis*
*Pinus mugo*
*Pinus nigra*
*Taxus baccata*
*Thuja*
*Thujopsis*

## Tolerant of clay soil

*Abies*
*Chamaecyparis*
*Juniperus*
*Larix*
*Picea pungens*
*Pinus nigra*
*Taxodium*
*Taxus*
*Thuja*

## Tolerant of acid soil

*Cupressus arizonica*
*Juniperus*
*Picea pungens*
*Pinus aristata*
*Pinus cembra*
*Pinus leucodermis*
*Pinus mugo*
*Pinus parviflora*

## Tolerant of seacoast conditions

*Araucaria*
*Cedrus deodara*
*Chamaecyparis thyoides*
*Cryptomeria japonica*
*×Cupressocyparis leylandii*
*Cupressus macrocarpa*
*Juniperus chinensis*
*Juniperus conferta*

*Juniperus horizontalis*
*Juniperus virginiana*
*Picea glauca*
*Picea pungens*
*Picea sitchensis*
*Pinus cembra*
*Pinus leucodermis*
*Pinus mugo*
*Pinus nigra*
*Pinus parviflora*
*Pinus sylvestris*
*Pinus thunbergii*
*Podocarpus*

## Tolerant of light shade

*Cephalotaxus*
*Chamaecyparis obtusa*
*Cryptomeria japonica*
*×Cupressocyparis leylandii*
*Microbiota decussata*
*Picea abies*
*Picea orientalis*
*Podocarpus*
*Sciadopitys*
*Taxus*
*Thuja*
*Thujopsis dolabrata*
*Tsuga*

## Tolerant of urban pollution

*Araucaria*
*Cedrus atlantica*
*Cephalotaxus*
*Chamaecyparis*
*Cryptomeria*
*Ginkgo biloba*
*Juniperus*
*Larix kaempferi*
*Metasequoia glyptostroboides*
*Picea abies*
*Picea omorika*
*Picea orientalis*
*Picea pungens*
*Pinus cembra*
*Pinus densiflora*
*Pinus mugo*
*Pinus nigra*

*Pseudotsuga menziesii*
*Sciadopitys*
*Sequoiadendron giganteum*
*Taxodium distichum*
*Taxus baccata*
*Taxus cuspidata*
*Thuja*
*Thujopsis dolabrata*
*Torreya*
*Tsuga canadensis*

## Tolerant of cold, to zone 3

*Abies veitchii*
*Juniperus communis*
*Juniperus sabina*
*Juniperus scopulorum*
*Microbiota decussata*
*Picea engelmannii*
*Picea pungens*
*Pinus aristata*
*Pinus cembra*
*Pinus flexilis*
*Pinus koraiensis*
*Pinus mugo*
*Pinus resinosa*
*Pinus strobus*

## Tolerant of cold, to zone 4

*Abies alba*
*Abies concolor*
*Abies fraseri*
*Abies homolepsis*
*Abies nordmanniana*
*Ginkgo biloba*
*Juniperus chinensis*
*Juniperus horizontalis*
*Juniperus virginiana*
*Larix decidua*
*Larix kaempferi*
*Picea abies*
*Picea glehnii*
*Picea pungens*
*Pinus longaeva*
*Pinus ponderosa*
*Pinus rigida*
*Thuja*

*Tsuga canadensis*
*Tsuga mertensiana*

## Tolerant of heat, to zone 9

*Cedrus libani*
*Cephalotaxus harringtonia*
*Juniperus virginiana*
*Taxodium distichum*

## Suitable for hedging

*Calocedrus*
*Chamaecyparis lawsoniana*
×*Cupressocyparis leylandii*
*Juniperus*
*Taxus*
*Thuja*
*Thujopsis*
*Tsuga*

# Favorite species for holiday trees

Holiday greens are a tradition going back to the ancient Egyptians and Romans; not exclusive to any one religion, the customs are usually associated with the winter solstice.

Production and sale of holiday trees is a multimillion-dollar industry. In the United States alone, over 35 million trees are harvested from natural forests or grown in plantations established especially for holiday tree production. Sometimes customers can select and cut their own tree. The conifers preferred will vary with region and local climatic conditions.

## Characteristics of a good holiday tree species

growth rate: rapid enough to produce a salable tree in seven to ten years
habit: conical in form with sufficient foliage and branch density
needles: rich dark green or blue-green remain on the tree for a long time after it is cut
soft and easy to handle
pleasant fragrance and free from pungent odors
branches: capable of supporting ornaments but not so thick that they cause difficulty
durable to tolerate shipment

## Most popular holiday tree species

*Abies balsamea* (balsam fir)
*Abies concolor* (concolor fir)
*Abies fraseri* (Fraser fir)
*Abies grandis* (grand fir)
*Abies procera* (noble fir)
×*Cupressocyparis leylandii* (Leyland cypress)
*Cupressus arizonica* (Arizona cypress)
*Juniperus virginiana* (eastern red-cedar)
*Picea abies* (Norway spruce)
*Picea glauca* (white spruce)
*Picea pungens* (Colorado spruce)
*Pinus strobus* (eastern white pine)
*Pinus sylvestris* (Scots pine)
*Pinus virginiana* (scrub pine)
*Pseudotsuga menziesii* (Douglas-fir)

## Where to see conifers

### United States

**Arnold Arboretum of Harvard University**
125 Arborway
Jamaica Plain, MA 02130
617 524 1718
www.arboretum.harvard.edu/

**Bartlett Arboretum and Gardens**
151 Brookdale Road
Stamford, CT 06903
203 322 6971
bartlett.arboretum.uconn.edu/

**Bellevue Botanical Garden**
12001 Main Street
Bellevue, WA 98005
425 452 2750
www.bellevuebotanical.org

**Bernheim Arboretum and Research Forest**
State Highway 245
P.O. Box 130
Clermont, KY 40110
502 955 8512
www.bernheim.org/

**Bickelhaupt Arboretum**
The Heartland Collection
340 S. 14th Street
Clinton, IA 52732
563 242 4771
www.bickarb.org/

**The Bloedel Reserve**
7571 NE Dolphin Drive
Bainbridge Island, WA 98110
206 842 7631
www.bloedelreserve.org

**Brooklyn Botanic Garden**
1000 Washington Avenue
Brooklyn, NY 11225
718 623 7200
www.bbg.org

**Brookside Gardens**
1800 Glenallan Avenue
Wheaton, MD 20902
301 962 1400
www.mc-mncppc.org/parks/brookside/

**Chanticleer**
786 Church Road
Wayne, PA 19087
610 687 4163
www.chanticleergarden.org/

**Chicago Botanic Garden**
1000 Lake Cook Road
Glencoe, IL 60022
847 835 5440
www.chicago-botanic.org

**Dawes Arboretum**
7770 Jacksontown Road SE
Newark, OH 43056
740 323 2355
800 44 DAWES
www.dawesarab.org

**Denver Botanic Gardens**
1005 York Street
Denver, CO 80206
720 865 3500
www.botanicgardens.org/pageinpage/
    home.cfm

**Hidden Lake Gardens**
Michigan State University
The Harper Collection
RT M-50
6280 W. Munger Road
Tipton, MI 49287
517 431 2060
http://hiddenlakegardens.msu.edu/

**Holden Arboretum**
9500 Sperry Road
Kirtland, OH 44060
440 946 4400
www.holdenarb.org/

**Hoyt Arboretum**
4000 SW Fairview Blvd.
Portland, OR 97221
503 865 8733
www.hoytarboretum.org/

**Japanese Garden**
611 Kingston Avenue
P.O. Box 3847
Portland, OR 97208
503 223 1321
www.japanesegarden.com

**Japanese Garden**
1502 Lake Washington Blvd. E
Seattle, WA 98109
206 684 4725
www.ci.seattle.wa.us/parks/parkspaces/
    japanesegarden.htm

**JC Raulston Arboretum at North Carolina State University**
4415 Beryl Road
P.O. Box 7522
Raleigh, NC 27695
919 515 3132
www.ncsu.edu/jcraulstonarboretum/

**Longwood Gardens**
Route 1
P.O. Box 501
Kennett Square, PA 19348
610 388 1000
www.longwoodgardens.org/

**Minnesota Landscape Arboretum**
3675 Arboretum Drive
Chaska, MN 55318
952 443 1400
www.arboretum.umn.edu/

**Missouri Botanical Garden**
4344 Shaw Blvd.
St. Louis, MO 63110
314 577 9400
www.mobot.org/

**Morris Arboretum of the University of Pennsylvania**
100 E. Northwestern Avenue
Philadelphia, PA 19118
215 247 5777
www.business-services.upenn.edu/
arboretum/

**Morton Arboretum**
4100 Illinois Route 53
Lisle, IL 60532
630 968 0074
www.mortonarb.org/

**Mount Auburn Cemetery**
580 Mount Auburn Street
Cambridge, MA 02138
617 547 7105
www.mountauburn.org/

**New York Botanical Garden**
200th Street and Kazimiroff Blvd.
Bronx, NY 10458
718 817 8700
www.nybg.org

**The Oregon Garden**
879 W. Main Street
Silverton, OR 97381
503 874 8100
www.oregongarden.org/

**Pacific Rim Bonsai Collection**
Weyerhaeuser Company
33663 Weyerhaeuser Way S.
Federal Way, WA 98003
253 924 5206
www.weyerhaeuser.com/bonsai

**Planting Fields Arboretum State Historic Park**
1395 Planting Fields Road
Oyster Bay, NY 11771
516 922 9206
www.plantingfields.org/

**San Francisco Botanical Garden at Strybing Arboretum**
Noble Collection
9th Avenue at Lincoln Way
San Francisco, CA 94122
415 564 3239 ext. 303
www.sfbotanicalgarden.org/

**Scott Arboretum of Swarthmore College**
500 College Avenue
Swarthmore, PA 19081
610 328 8025
www.scottarboretum.org/

**Secrest Arboretum**
1680 Madison Avenue
Wooster, OH 44691
330 263 3761
secrest.osu.edu/

**Tower Hill Botanic Garden**
11 French Drive
P.O. Box 598
Boylston, MA 01505
508 869 6111
www.towerhillbg.org/

**Tyler Arboretum**
515 Painter Road
Media, PA 19064
610 566 9134
www.tylerarboretum.org/

**U.S. National Arboretum**
Gotelli Dwarf Conifer Collection
3501 New York Avenue NE
Washington, DC 20002
202 245 2726
www.usna.usda.gov/

**University of California Botanical Garden**
200 Centennial Drive, #5045
Berkeley, CA 94729
510 643 2755
botanicalgarden.berkeley.edu/

**University of California, Davis Arboretum**
One Shields Avenue
Davis, CA 95616
530 752 4880
arboretum.ucdavis.edu/

**University of California, Santa Cruz Arboretum**
1156 High Street
Santa Cruz, CA 95064
831 427 2998
www2.ucsc.edu/arboretum/

**University of Wisconsin-Madison Arboretum**
1207 Seminole Highway
Madison, WI 53711
608 263 7888
uwarboretum.org/

**Washington Park Arboretum**
University of Washington
Seattle, WA 98195
206 543 8800
depts.washington.edu/wpa/

Canada

**Devonian Botanic Garden**
University of Alberta
Edmonton, AB T6G 2E1
780 987 3054

**Domaine de Maizerets**
2000, Boulevard Montmorency
Québec, QC G1J 5E7
418 641 6117
418 641 6335
www.capitale.gouv.qc.ca
societedudomainemaizerets.org

**Jardin Daniel A. Séguin**
3215, rue Sicotte
Saint-Hyacinthe, QC J2S 7B3
450 778 6504 poste 215
450 778 0372

## Where to see conifers

Canada (continued)

**Montreal Botanical Garden**
4101 Sherbrooke East
Montreal, QC H1X 2B2
514 872 1400
www2.ville.montreal.qc.ca/jardin/
    jardin.htm

**New Brunswick Botanical Garden**
P.O. Box 1629
33, Principale Street
Saint-Jacques, NB E7B 1A3
506 737 5383
www.umce.ca/jardin

**Nitobe Memorial Garden**
UBC Botanical Garden and Centre for
Plant Research
6804 SW Marine Drive
Vancouver, BC V6T 1Z4
604 822 6038
www.nitobe.org/

**Quarry Garden at Queen Elizabeth**
    **Park**
2099 Beach Avenue
Vancouver, BC V6G 1Z4
604 257 8584
www.city.vancouver.bc.ca/Parks/parks/
    queenelizabeth

**Roger-Van den Hende Garden**
Université Laval
Pavillon de l'Envirotron
Sainte-Foy, QC G1K 7P4
418 656 3410
www.jardin.ulaval.ca

**Royal Botanical Gardens**
680 Plains Road
Burlington, ON L7T 4H4
www.rbg.ca/

**University of British Columbia**
    **Botanical Garden**
6804 SW Marine Drive
Vancouver, BC V6T 1Z4
604 822 9666
www.ubcbotanicalgarden.org/

**University of Guelph Arboretum**
University of Guelph
Guelph, ON N1G 2W1
519 824 4120
www.uoguelph.ca/arboretum/

**Van Dusen Botanical Gardens**
5251 Oak Street
Vancouver, BC V6M 4H1
604 878 9274
www.city.vancouver.bc.ca/parks/parks/
    vandusen/website/


## Europe

**Baumpark Arboretum**
Thiensen 17
Ellerhoop 25373
Germany
www.ellerhoop.de/html/arboretum.
    html

**Bedgebury National Pinetum**
Goudhurst Cranbrook
Kent TN17 2SL
England
www.bedgeburypinetum.org.uk/

**Benmore Botanic Garden**
Dunoon, Argyll
Edinburgh PA23 8QU
Scotland
www.rbge.org.uk/rbge/web/visiting/
    bbg.jsp

**Berlin Botanic Garden**
Königin-Luise-Strasse 6-8
Berlin 14195
Germany
www.bgbm.org/

**Bicton Park Botanical Gardens**
East Budleigh
Devon EX9 7JT
England
www.bictongardens.co.uk

**Bokrijk Arboretum**
Bokrijk (Genk) 3600
Belgium
www.plantcol.be/web-content/
    arboretumbokrijk.html

**Bressingham Gardens**
Thetford Road
Bressingham Diss
Norfolk IP22 2AB
England
www.bressinghamgardens.com

**Castlewellan Forest Park**
Upper Newtownards Road
Belfast BT4 3SB
Ireland
www.forestserviceni.gov.uk/our_forests/
    castlewellan/castle_wellan.htm

**Dawyck Botanic Garden**
Stobo
Peeblesshire EH45 9JU
Scotland
www.rbge.org.uk/rbge/web/visiting/
    dbg.jsp

**Greifswald Botanic Garden**
Ernst-Moritz-Arndt-Universität
Greifswald 17487
Germany
www.uni-greifswald.de/~botanik/
    botgar.htm

**Hamburg Botanic Garden**
Hesten 10
Hamburg 22609
Germany
www.biologie.uni-hamburg.de/bzf/
    garten/garten.htm

**Munich Botanic Garden**
Menzinger Strasse 65
Munich 80638
Germany
www.botanik.biologie.uni-muenchen.
de/botgart

**Pinetum Blijdenstein**
Van der Lindenlaan 125
Hilversum 1217 PJ
Netherlands
www.pinetum.nl/

**Planten un Blomen**
Klosterwall 8
Hamburg 20095
Germany
www.plantenunblomen.hamburg.de/

**Royal Botanic Garden Edinburgh**
20A Inverleith Row
Edinburgh EH3 5LR
Scotland
www.rbge.org.uk/

**Royal Botanic Gardens, Kew**
Richmond
Surrey TW9 3AB
England
www.rbgkew.org.uk/

**Royal Botanic Gardens, Wakehurst
   Place**
Ardingly
Nr Haywards Heath
West Sussex RH17 6TN
England
www.rbgkew.org.uk/visitor/visitwp.
   html

**Royal Horticultural Society Garden,
   Wisley**
Woking
Surrey GU23 6QB
England
www.rhs.org.uk/whatson/gardens/
   wisley/index.asp

**Savill Garden**
Crown Estate Office
The Great Park
Windsor, Berks SL4 2HT
England
www.theroyallandscape.co.uk/savill_
   garden.asp

**Sheffield Park Garden**
East Sussex TN22 3QX
England
www.nationaltrust.org.uk/main/w-vh/
   w-visits/w-findaplace/
   w-sheffieldparkgarden

**Trompenburg Arboretum**
Honingerdijk 86
Rotterdam 3062
Netherlands
www.trompenburg.nl

**University of Dundee**
Riverside Drive
Dundee DD2 1QH
Scotland
www.dundee.ac.uk/botanic

**Von Gimborn Arboretum**
Vossensteinsesteeg 8
Doorn 3941 BL
Netherlands
www.bio.uu.nl/bottuinen/

**Westonbirt Arboretum**
Silvan House
231 Corstorphine Road
Edinburgh EH12 7AT
Scotland
www.forestry.gov.uk/westonbirt

## Specialty nurseries

### United States

**Bethlehem Nursery**
66 Jackson Lane
Bethlehem, CT 06751
203 266 7783
www.bethlehemnursery.com

**Buchholz & Buchholz Nursery**
41840 SW Vandehey Road
Gaston, OR 97119
503 985 3253

**Coenosium Gardens**
4412 354th Street E.
Eatonville, WA 98328
360 832 8655
www.coenosium.com

**Collector's Nursery**
16804 NE 102nd Avenue
Battle Ground, WA 98604
360 574 3832
www.collectorsnursery.com

**Gee Farms**
14928 Bunkerhill Road
Stockbridge, MI 49285
517 769 6772
www.geefarms.com

**Girard Nurseries**
P.O. Box 428
Geneva, OH 44041
440 466 2881
www.girardnurseries.com

**Iseli Nursery**
30590 SE Kelso Road
Boring, OR 97009
800 777 6202
www.iselinursery.com

## Specialty nurseries

### United States (continued)

**Porterhowse Farms**
41370 SE Thomas Road
Sandy, OR 97055
503 668 5834
www.porterhowse.com

**Rich's Foxwillow Pines Nursery**
11618 McConnell Road
Woodstock, IL 60098
815 338 7442
www.richsfoxwillowpines.com

**Roslyn Nursery**
211 Burrs Lane
Dix Hills, NY 11746
631 643 9347
www.roslynnursery.com

**Stanley & Sons Nursery, Inc.**
11740 SE Orient Drive
Boring, OR 97009
503 663 4391
www.stanleyandsons.com

**Suncrest Gardens**
816 Holly Pike
Mt. Holly Springs, PA 17065
717 486 5142
www.suncrest-gardens.com

**Twombley Nursery**
163 Barn Hill Road
Monroe, CT 06468
203 261 2133
www.twombleynursery.com

**Wolf-Run Nursery**
29 Klapperthal Road
Reading, PA 19606
610 779 5717
www.wolfrunnursery.com

## International

**Cedar Lodge Nursery**
63 Egmont Road, RD 2
New Plymouth
New Zealand
www.conifers.co.nz

**Hachmann Baumschule**
Brunnenstrasse 68
25355 Barmstedt
Germany
www.hachmann.de

**zu Jeddeloh Pflanzenhandels**
Wischenstrasse 7
26188 Edewecht
Germany
www.jeddeloh.de

**Kenwith Nursery**
Beaford Winkleigh
Devon EX19 8NT
England
www.kenwithnursery.co.uk

**Kilworth Conifers**
South Kilworth
Leicestershire LE17 6DX
England
www.kilworth-conifers.co.uk

**Lime Cross Nursery**
Hailsham
East Sussex BN27 4RS
England
www.limecross.co.uk

**Uwe Horstmann Baumschulen**
Rotenburger Strasse 80
29640 Schneverdingen
Germany
www.tsuga-shop.de

## Societies

**American Conifer Society**
P.O. Box 3422
Crofton, MD 21114
410 721 6611
www.conifersociety.org

**British Conifer Society**
Bedgebury Pinetum
Goudhurst
Kent TN17 2SL
England
www.britishconifersociety.org.uk

# References

Arno, Stephen F. 1977. *Northwest Trees*. The Mountaineers: Seattle, Wash.

Bloom, Adrian. 2002. *Gardening with Conifers*. Firefly Books: Buffalo, N.Y.

Blouin, Glen. 2001. *An Eclectic Guide to Trees East of the Rockies*. Boston Mills Press: Erin, Ontario.

Cope, Edward A. 1986. *Native and Cultivated Conifers of Northeastern North America*. Cornell University: Ithaca, N.Y.

Cutler, Sandra McLean. 1997. *Dwarf and Unusual Conifers Coming of Age*. Barton-Bradley Crossroads: North Olmsted, Ohio.

Dirr, Michael A. 1998. *Manual of Woody Landscape Plants*. Stipes: Champaign, Ill.

Farjon, Aljos. 1998. *World Checklist and Bibliography of Conifers*. Royal Botanic Gardens, Kew.

Farrar, John Laird. 1995. *Trees in Canada*. Fitzhenry & Whiteside and Canadian Forest Service.

Grimm, William Carey. 2002. *The Illustrated Book of Trees*, rev. ed. by John Kartesz. Stackpole Books: Mechanicsburg, Pa.

Hillier, John, and Allen Coombes, consultant eds. 2002. *The Hillier Manual of Trees and Shrubs*. David & Charles: Devon, England.

Jacobson, Arthur Lee. 1996. *North American Landscape Trees*. Ten Speed Press: Berkeley, Calif.

Lanner, Ronald M. 2002. *Conifers of California*. Cachuma Press: Los Olivos, Calif.

Leopold, Donald J. 2003. *Trees of New York State Native and Naturalized*. Syracuse University Press, N.Y.

Lewis, John. 1987–98. *International Conifer Register*. 4 parts. The Royal Horticultural Society: London.

Lord, Tony, ed. 2005. *RHS Plant Finder 2005–2006*. Dorling Kindersley, Ltd.: London.

Peattie, Donald Culross. 1953. *A Natural History of Western Trees*. Houghton Mifflin: Boston.

———. 1966. *A Natural History of Trees of Eastern and Central North America*. Houghton Mifflin: Boston.

Thomas, R. William, Susan F. Martin, and Kim Tripp, eds. 1997. *Growing Conifers: Four-Season Plants*. Brooklyn Botanic Garden Handbook.

Welch, Humphrey J. 1979. *Manual of Dwarf Conifers*. Theophrastus: Little Compton, R.I.

Welch, Humphrey, and Gordon Haddow. 1993. *The World Checklist of Conifers*. The World Conifer Data Pool, Landsman's Bookshop Ltd, Herefordshire.

Woodward, James. 2002. *The Wollemi Pine*. Text Publishing: Melbourne.

# Hardiness Zone Map

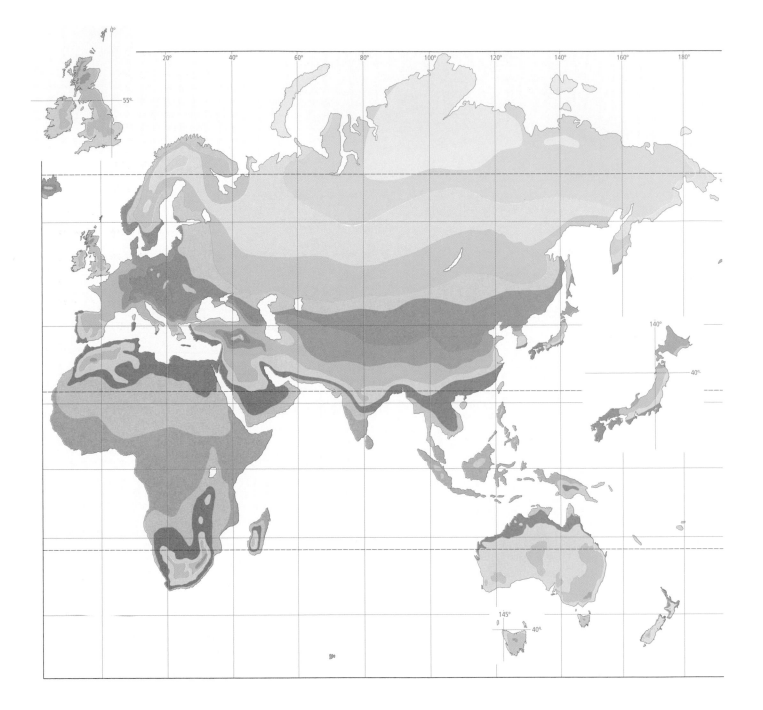

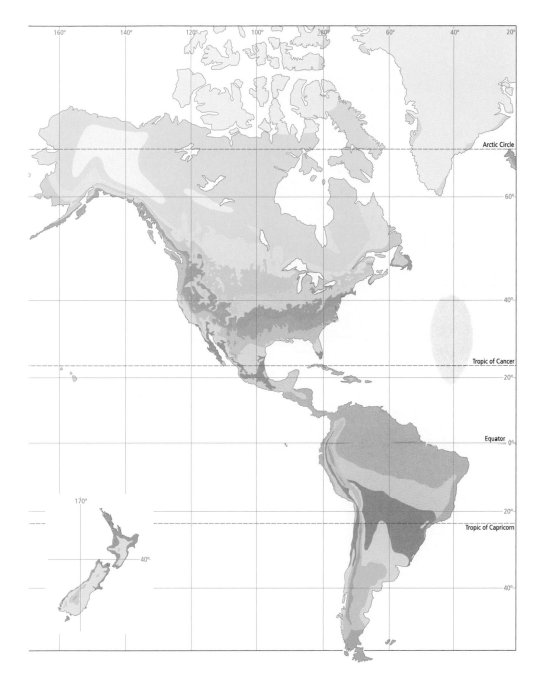

| Zone | °Farenheit | °Celsius |
|------|-----------|----------|
| 12 | 50 to 60 | 10 to 16 |
| 11 | 40 to 50 | 4 to 10 |
| 10 | 30 to 40 | -1 to 4 |
| 9 | 20 to 30 | -7 to -1 |
| 8 | 10 to 20 | -12 to -7 |
| 7 | 0 to 10 | -18 to -12 |
| 6 | -10 to 0 | -23 to -18 |
| 5 | -20 to -10 | -29 to -23 |
| 4 | -30 to -20 | -34 to -29 |
| 3 | -40 to -30 | -40 to -34 |
| 2 | -50 to -40 | -46 to -40 |
| 1 | -60 to -50 | -51 to -46 |

# Index